The handbook of international trade finance

The handbook of international trade finance

EDITED BY

CAMPBELL DUNFORD

WOODHEAD-FAULKNER

NEW YORK LONDON TORONTO SYDNEY
TOKYO SINGAPORE

Published by Woodhead-Faulkner (Publishers) Limited,
Simon & Schuster International Group,
Fitzwilliam House, 32 Trumpington Street,
Cambridge CB2 1QY, England

First published 1991

British Library Cataloguing in Publication Data

The handbook of international trade finance.
1. Foreign trade
I. Dunford Campbell
382

ISBN 0–85941–696–8

Designed by Geoff Green
Typeset by Vision Typesetting, Manchester
Printed in Great Britain by BPCC Wheatons Ltd, Exeter

Contents

Preface

The dependency of manufacturing and agricultural nations on their ability to trade internationally has grown year by year for decades and the trend shows no sign of slowing down. In the 1990s the world order is changing. The countries of Eastern Europe are trying to open up to foreign trade, the Single European Market is creating greater trading opportunities for Western countries, and markets generally are becoming more international as the result of increased competition and improved communications.

It is against this background that *The Handbook of International Trade Finance* is written. As the trade flows around the globe change and as international trade impacts more and more upon not only businesses but also the life and well-being of every man, woman and child on the planet, it is a matter of deep importance that the decision-makers in countries and companies have clear and ready reference to the tools available.

It redounds to the credit of business people, bankers and statesmen world-wide that major initiatives have been launched at the start of the final decade of this century – debt forgiveness in Africa and Latin America, rapid moves to a single currency in Europe and an increase in world aid percentages. This is welcome but it means that the seas in which we sail are increasingly uncharted. This handbook is intended to provide guidance to exporters and their bankers world-wide on how to handle trade and protect themselves from loss. The contributions are state of the art in each case from current, deeply experienced practitioners, and from the outset the goals have been simple:

1. To provide a readable work for both the beginner and the expert.
2. To enable any reader to progress from the relatively routine through to the more demanding areas painlessly.
3. To provide chapters in such a way that specialists can focus upon them without reference to the rest.

4. To provide reference and contact points that will enable the trader or banker to access additional help at need.
5. Above all to make the information current and applicable in many markets. It is also a work for ready reference.

Taking up the last point, while it is realistically impossible to develop, in a readable form, one work to cover the interests of all countries that trade world-wide, it is, however, possible to create the medium which will apply to the vast majority of those concerned. The fundamental rules of, for example, export credits are adhered to by all the signatories of the Berne Union (whose President is one of the contributors). The use and application of aid and trade finance equally fall within the international ambit and, except where countries decide upon a unique and bilateral approach for special reasons, the rules and regulations for donor and recipient are fairly well established world-wide. Even more is this true in the complex but critical field of currency and interest rate management where no single national regime could or can apply.

The bedrock of the chapters offered here represents best industry practice, much of which was originally developed in the United Kingdom, as, for example, the following:

1. The UK export credit agency (ECGD) was the first founded in the world – in 1919 – and more than half the world's agencies use its skills and documentation.
2. Standard letter of credit documentation and all the ensuing banking conventions derived under UK law.
3. Shipping conventions were developed in the London market, and Lloyd's of London is the doyen of insurers. More vessels and aircraft are insured in the London market than in the rest of the world put together.

To state that is merely to define the foundations, however, and what we have tried to do is attempt a world-wide context as applicable to a North American manufacturer as to a member of the European Community. The enormous changes in Eastern Europe and their pace have to some extent overshadowed the rapid integration of the European Community, the recovery of Latin America (relatively) and an improved performance from Africa.

Thus what this handbook offers to the beginner and expert alike is a quick but informed insight into trade finance, either overall or subject by subject, and the ability to focus an approach towards a particular market-place. The volume moves from the earliest stages of becoming involved in international trade and how to do it, to choosing markets and the tools needed. From that point it progresses step by step through all of the principal techniques available for the provision of finance, and protection from loss.

Topics covered include basic documentation, banking support, basic credit insurance, the private insurance market, other financial techniques, as well as aid and specialist forms of finance.

Despite the great range of topics addressed, certain strands emerge again and again. Among these, the following are worthy of further consideration:

1. Official export credits; the old order is changing and only the poorer countries can realistically look to supported credits in future, yet the official agencies are trying to reduce their exposure in this very arena in which they can be most useful. The Single European Market now has the official agencies within each sovereign state competing against each other and there is a proposal to establish a pan-European credit agency to compete with the United States and ASEAN countries. If created it could dwarf the others and have a major impact on world markets.
2. More and more as governments of all persuasions seek to de-link themselves from currency and interest rate support, the exporter is left to cope alone, although dealing in one of the most sophisticated and dangerous markets where only the truly skilled or powerful may safely venture.
3. The burden of protection world-wide by banks and business alike is increasingly being passed to the private sector, which may not yet (or ever) have the tools or capacity to cope.
4. Traditional banking relationships are changing with the turbulent times the banking sector now endures. Around the world, albeit for different reasons, the banks in the United States, Japan, Australia and Europe are cutting back on their activity or, at the very least, requiring a higher degree of security to satisfy central regulators. This trend will surely continue. It is no longer a buyer's market, and long-standing banking relationships in the old-fashioned manner are perhaps becoming more relevant than the simple ethic of the bazaar employed by so many corporate treasurers in the 1980s.

So the handbook is here to provide both a guide and a working tool. It progresses through the various necessary steps, but each chapter is a discrete entity and can be read as such. There are also appendices of terms, techniques and contact points which we hope will prove helpful.

Campbell Dunford

The contributors

CLIVE BATESON is Director of the Examinations Board of the London Chamber of Commerce and Industry. He is also General Manager of the Training Department at the London Chamber of Commerce and Industry. His career has embraced both business and education. In business he has held major posts at senior levels in general management with a number of companies including Ford, Black and Decker, Massey Ferguson and Transworld Oil. Professor Bateson holds a first class honours degree in Politics and Economics from the LSE and his academic record includes six years as Senior Visiting Fellow at the Management Centre, Bradford University. Currently Visiting Professor in Business Studies at Middlesex Polytechnic, he was also appointed a Governor in 1988. He sits on the Management Advisory Committee of the Management Centre, Bradford University. Professor Bateson is also a member of the Executive Committee of the Council for Education in the Commonwealth. He has lectured widely in Europe, Asia and the United States on business topics.

JOHN BEANEY is Manager of the International Department of Griffin Factors. PETER ROFF is Griffin's Marketing Manager. Griffin is a member of the Midland Group and was established in 1963. As such, it was one of the first factoring companies established in the United Kingdom and today it is one of the largest and most successful. Griffin is also a founder member of Factors Chain International, whose members currently handle 50 per cent of world-wide international factoring. John Beaney has worked for the Midland Group since graduating in 1979, becoming Manager of Griffin's international activities in September 1987. John holds diplomas in factoring from the United Kingdom's Association of British Factors and Discounters and Factors Chain International. He is a member of the Communication Committee of FCI, whose responsibilities include the development of international factoring communication. Griffin's international team handle sales of £150m, covering thirty-five countries across the globe.

ROSAMUND BLOMFIELD-SMITH joined the Project Finance Department of J. Henry Schroder Wagg & Co. in 1979, after a three-year period in the export finance department of Morgan Grenfell and a short time with the Financial Times Group. For many years, she was responsible for the bank's project financing activities in the Middle East and during that time acquired considerable experience of financing major projects in developing countries. For the past two years she has been responsible for the bank's project financing business in Europe where the emphasis is on build–own–transfer (BOT) arrangements and where she has led teams responsible for advising both European governments and companies bidding to secure concessions. Rosamund Blomfield-Smith has published numerous articles about project finance and is a frequent speaker at conferences.

TERRY BRIDGMAN first became involved with export finance in 1962, after an early career start in law, both in the private sector and government service. Financing the export of textile machinery and factory installations gave him an early user's view of export credit insurance and the place it occupies in the successful negotiation of overseas contracts. That experience was a good foundation for his next twenty-five years as a specialist insurance broker, negotiating export credit cover on behalf of many of the world's major companies. He travelled extensively, particularly in the Far East, and became Managing Director of the credit insurance and political risk broking activities of the Hogg Robinson Group in 1985. Shortly before the demerging of that Group in 1988, he joined Trade Indemnity Group where, as Director of Reinsurance, he is in the vanguard of the development of credit and political risk reinsurance capacity, the essential feature for export credit schemes as 'privatisation' occurs around the world.

TOM BUDGETT graduated in law from Pembroke College, Cambridge University in England in 1969 and qualified as an English solicitor two years later. He is a partner in the law firm of Clifford Chance. He has specialised in ship and aircraft financing and spent a number of years abroad working in the foreign offices of Clifford Chance, including over five years in their Tokyo office. He is now based in London and is one of the senior members of the aerospace team at Clifford Chance.

TONY CANNELL graduated in law at Hull University in England in 1973 and qualified as an English solicitor two years later. He is also a solicitor of The Supreme Court of Hong Kong and, from 1987, was licensed to practise English and Hong Kong law in Tokyo (as a Gaikokuho Jimu Bengoshi) by the Japanese Ministry of Justice. He is a partner in the law firm of Clifford Chance and he has specialised in asset-based financing, secured lending, trade finance and associated areas of banking law. He has also worked in the Tokyo office of Clifford Chance and has just returned after three years stationed there. He is now based in London and is principally engaged in ship financing.

CAMPBELL DUNFORD is a graduate of Oxford University and has for two decades been involved in international trade finance at every level. He is currently Chairman of the London Chamber of Commerce & Industry Export Committee and a Council Member. He is also Chairman of the British Exporters Association and holds several public offices. He has worked with companies and governments around the world and has spent considerable time in the United States, Japan, the Middle East and Africa. He was for many years Trade Finance Director of Midland Bank PLC and latterly General Manager of the Moscow Narodny Bank in London. He is now Chairman of Trade-Aide Financial Services Ltd and is involved in promoting trade world-wide.

BOB GILLESPIE is a Scot, now residing in Norfolk, who has for the last twenty-five years worked in the fields of export finance, credit insurance, export documentation and credit control. He has been employed in the steel, automotive and electronic industries and spent several years in the Far East with a subsidiary of a major UK manufacturing company. Until now Bob has always worked for companies who manufacture and export, and in his new role of Managing Director, Operations with Trade-Aide Financial Services Ltd, will use his experience in continuing to assist exporters in the ever-changing world of international trade.

D. IAN GUILD started his banking career in 1958 when he joined the Chartered Bank in London. He first became involved in forfaiting when he joined the Swiss company UFITEC SA in 1968. In 1973 he became the first chairman of Gerrard International, a specialist forfaiting company set up by Gerrard and National Discount Company Ltd in London. In 1980 Guinness Peat Group purchased Gerrard International and Ian Guild became Chief Executive of Guinness Peat Aval. In 1983 Midland Bank purchased the management and assets to form Midland Bank Aval and Ian Guild was appointed Vice Chairman and Chief Executive. In November 1990 Ian Guild resigned from MidAval to become Chief Executive of Banque Indosuez Sogem Aval ('Indosuez Aval'), a new company formed by Group Indosuez. He is co-author of *Forfaiting: An alternative approach to export trade finance*, published by Woodhead-Faulkner.

JOHN HOLLOWS joined Barclays in 1978 from Cambridge University, where he read law and economics. After initial training he was appointed in 1982 to the Bank's Profit Improvement Unit. There he was involved in a variety of projects designed to enhance profitability in UK branches of Barclays. In 1984 he was appointed as a Corporate Manager to the Watford Business Centre, where he was responsible for 200 corporate customers of the Bank. In 1986 he was appointed Head of International Trade Services at Barclays Bank PLC with responsibility for the management of a range of short-term trade finance products made available to support UK exporters and importers. He is also Deputy Chairman of the British Exporters Association.

KEITH JOHNSON qualified in business studies and spent his formative business years in Rolls Royce Aero Engine Group taking on a variety of commercial assignments culminating in taking responsibility for negotiating overseas sales and support contracts. He then joined Bell & Howell Ltd, heading up their credit management activity, before joining The Plessey Co. PLC, where he rose to head up the export finance activity for the defence group. The Plessey takeover by GEC Siemens has positioned him in Siemens Plessey Radar Ltd, where he manages the Export Finance and Commercial Services Department.

GRAHAM MCBAIN is an open scholar and graduate of Peterhouse, Cambridge University in England and Fulbright scholar of Harvard Law School, Boston, United States. He has specialised in banking and, in particular, aircraft financing. He is co-author of the work *Aircraft Finance: Registration, security and enforcement* and consultant editor of Butterworth's *Banking Law Handbook.* He is based in London and is a member of the aerospace team at Clifford Chance.

ANDREW NEILL is the International Director of The Credit Insurance Association Ltd, the leading broker of credit and political risk insurances. Following a time in London he moved to the newly formed Leeds office in 1975 and returned to London in 1978. He then became Deputy Managing Director of the subsidiary Commercial and Political Risk Consultants in 1982, Director of CIA London Branches in 1983, and Director of Hogg Robinson (Credit & Political) in 1985. He went to Australia in 1986 following his appointment as Managing Director of The Credit Insurance Association (Brokers) Ltd. He returned to the United Kingdom in 1988 and assumed his current position shortly afterwards.

VICTORIA PARRY is a law graduate of the University College, Cardiff and is a solicitor in the Banking Department of Clifford Chance in London. She has a general banking law practice with particular emphasis on securities and ship finance.

ROBIN ROACH is 44 years old and has a degree in mathematics. However, after a brief period as a mathematician with Plessey, the rest of his career has focused on business planning and international market development. His special area of interest has been developing countries and following further experience in these disciplines for Plessey and later British Airways, STC and British Telecom, he left in 1985 to found Trade Through Aid Ltd, the United Kingdom's first Export Marketing Consultancy specialising in aid-funded business. Mr Roach is well known in his field and has spoken frequently at seminars organised by chambers of commerce, trade associations, export clubs and other export marketing functions, as well as contributing to numerous specialised publications. He is a passionate believer in the value of a properly organised international development effort which encourages self-help and free market forces.

DAVID SENIOR is a member of the Board and General Manager Policy Studies of the London Chamber of Commerce and Industry, one of the United Kingdom's most active business organisations in the field of international trade promotion. During his time at the Chamber Mr Senior has been involved in many aspects of trade promotion and in dealing with the problems of member companies in their activities at home and overseas. He serves as a member of European chamber of commerce committees dealing with international trade and transport and has contributed to various publications dealing with these issues.

MALCOLM STEPHENS joined ECGD in 1965, after twelve years in the diplomatic service, and held various positions including Principal Finance Officer from 1979–82. He left ECGD to become International Finance Director of Barclays Bank International in 1982, and from 1983–7 was Export Finance Director of Barclays Bank and Director of Barclays Export Services. He was appointed Chief Executive of ECGD (Export Credits Guarantee Department) in 1987.

FRANCESCA TAYLOR is currently an Associate Director at Mayflower Brokers Ltd, based in the City of London. She specialises in interest rate and currency risk management and numbers amongst her clients some major international household names. Before joining the Mayflower Group, Francesca was at Midland Bank PLC (latterly Midland Montagu) in the Group Treasury and ran the Treasury Financial Engineering Group. She gained her corporate experience working for three years within the Treasury department at BICC plc which she joined straight after leaving Imperial College London where she graduated with an MSc in Management Science. She is an Associate Member of the Association of Corporate Treasurers.

PAUL TURNER is a William Butler prize holder, scholar and graduate of Peterhouse, Cambridge University in England. He became a barrister in London, England in 1981 and, subsequently, he was admitted as a solicitor in England and in Hong Kong. He has specialised in all aspects of shipping work, including the handling of major international disputes, ship financing and other non-contentious shipping projects. He has spent three years working in the Hong Kong office of Clifford Chance. He is now based in London and is a member of the shipping and banking teams at Clifford Chance.

DAVID WATSON is a Glaswegian and his first sortie into the world of trade was via the Clydeside shipyards. Then, with time in the textile industry and local government behind him, he joined Albion Motors as the Export Finance Manager and was eventually moved south to join BL International. After several years seconded to Switzerland and Australia he returned to join Leyland Special Products as their Treasury Manager. In 1979, David joined Philips Electronics as their new Group Export Finance Manager, and along with Bob Gillespie was instrumental in putting together the finance for major projects world-wide. As of July 1990, David and Bob joined forces with Campbell Dunford to create Trade-Aide Financial Services Ltd. David is a member of the CG Group (which looks after the interests of export insurance policy holders), the CBI Export Finance Committee and BEAMA.

1

Exporting: choosing your market and method

DAVID SENIOR
Director, and General Manager Policy Studies, London Chamber of Commerce and Industry

This chapter first gives introductory general considerations, to set the scene, and then more specific comment is given.

Introduction

Any business that is considering exporting its goods or services for the first time needs to answer certain questions on the basis of its own knowledge of its products, resources and experience and the information it can obtain on the markets in which it proposes to sell. This chapter aims to clarify some of the issues that a potential exporter needs to resolve.

The first issue is quite simply whether it is desirable to export at all. The initial benefits of exporting should be looked at primarily in economic terms: whether selling abroad will enable the company to strengthen its market position by increasing sales and, crucially, profits. Selling in more than one market can also have the advantage of providing a more balanced demand and thus reducing the risk of being totally dependent on the fluctuations arising from the economic conditions in the home market.

However, a potential international operator should also realise that exporting frequently involves longer lines of communication; the practical hazards of crossing frontiers; and, in the case of certain types of goods, the need to maintain supplies of spare parts close to the customer. There are no benefits to be gained by an individual business – nor indeed does it do any good to the reputation of the exporting country as a whole – if deliveries are late, service is inadequate or overseas customers are neglected in favour of those at home. An enterprise which cannot offer long-term reliability to its foreign customers does much better to concentrate on doing a good job in the home market, competing effectively with foreign firms exporting into the home market.

Once it has been ascertained that there are no fundamental objections to developing an export business, then the question of the choice of markets and the methods of operation need to be resolved.

The decision as to which non-domestic markets to explore should be based on two aspects: the knowledge of the demand for the product (or service) and the knowledge of the market in which it is proposed to sell.

Knowledge of the demand for the product should come largely from the company itself. Any successful business will already have a good idea of the types of customer likely to purchase its products, their requirements in terms of availability and cost, and the strength of the competition that is likely to be encountered.

The potential exporter will first need to know whether there are any fundamental restrictions on the sale of the product. These may be based on national legislation, health or safety requirements, on the acceptance of technical standards or on local prejudices and habits. In any event, the restrictions must be investigated thoroughly.

Assuming that there are no fundamental objections of this kind, the exporter will then need to take into account the additional costs likely to be incurred, and their effect on consumer prices and hence on the prospects of profitable sales.

In examining the costs which arise from supplying another market, the potential exporter will need to take into account the direct costs which arise from selling goods in a foreign country – transport, distribution, local taxes – as well as the secondary charges which these in turn demand. These may, for example, include not only the basic freight costs, but insurance to cover a number of different methods of transportation and trans-shipment. While most of Western mainland Europe is accessible to road delivery, any goods delivered to more remote regions of Europe, or to other continents, are likely to require more effective packaging. This is also a service and a cost that has to be taken into account in looking at the export potential of particular products.

The cost of currency fluctuations and possible precautions against loss and the overall cost of providing credit, which may be higher and more complex than those needed for operating within the home market, also need to be taken into account. In the United States particularly, but to an increasing extent in Europe, the demands of product liability and the availability and cost of insurance against relevant claims are assuming increased importance in international trade.

Experience at the London Chamber of Commerce and Industry suggests that most businesses contemplating entering the export market already have a good idea of the kind of market in which their products would sell. Initial informal research is a matter of putting together this knowledge from the business with the knowledge of relevant overseas markets provided by company experience and an appropriate advisory body.

Any business which is familiar with the regional variations in taste and demand which occur within the home market will readily recognise that, despite the advent of the Single European Market, the twelve member countries of the Community will still represent a diversity of taste and consumer demand which administrative decisions from Brussels cannot possibly extinguish overnight – if indeed at all. Nevertheless, the Single European Market is a factor to be taken into account by potential exporters. Administrative procedures within the Community are being considerably simplified and the Community as a whole will offer an area for close examination as a potential launch pad for the new exporter.

One of the facts of commercial life within the Community, however, is the diversity of languages and to the exporter for whom languages present a barrier to communication, the prospects of an English-speaking market may be more attractive. In this case, the United States and Canada, Australia and New Zealand may be worthy of further study, while within Europe, the United Kingdom and the Republic of Ireland have the advantage of being Community members, English-speaking and easily accessible.

The boundaries of the European Community, comprehension of language, or the limits of distance are, however, only quoted as possible guides to the choice of export markets. The nature of the product or the service which is being sold may itself determine the choice of markets whatever practical barriers may be involved. However, within the general area of business there are specialists who can help to overcome every kind of barrier and it is essential to underline that exporting does not automatically require the actual manufacturer to engage directly in selling and delivering the goods overseas. There are a whole range of choices open to the potential exporter which may be appropriate to help facilitate the export of goods overseas.

Let us now look in more detail at some specific areas. As a strategy, a business contemplating exporting must accept four cardinal guidelines:

1. Concentrate on key markets.
2. Adapt the product for the market.
3. Allocate resources for a long-term commitment.
4. Do some serious market research.

Key markets

It is not possible to conquer the world in six months, or even to grab a sizeable share of the chosen export market in that time. A modest start has to be made by new exporters on no more than one market at first. The reason is that mistakes will be made and these mistakes should be the basis for learning. The aim is to try to make some sales in that chosen export market at the same time as gaining a toehold and testing the market reaction without losing much in time, effort or money.

In due course, with self-confidence polished by this encouraging experience, a second market can be entered with more confidence and with the prospect of early success. A business should be wary of being deflected from this precise strategy by offers emerging out of other markets, however attractive they may seem.

The criteria for choosing a market generally include these points:

1. Growth and continuity. Is the market static or expanding? Is it likely to repay the sales effort over the next few years?
2. Is the competition on price or on other considerations?
3. Would the products find a good reception and perhaps command a premium price?
4. Is there any problem with currency or the transfer of funds?
5. Are there good agents or distributors and efficient outlets for the products?
6. Are there technical, legal or cultural considerations which may affect the prospects for the success of the product?

New exporters are advised to concentrate on one or two markets until they have established themselves and gained in experience and confidence, while more established exporters must also make a positive decision about how many markets they can handle profitably.

By having more markets a business may feel that it has more customers. But it is possible that it will also have smaller sales to each, thus incurring higher unit costs and lower margins.

The benefits of selling, even in quantity, to fewer markets are these.

Market knowledge

By restricting itself to a smaller number of markets, a business has a better chance of understanding the problems and possibilities in each, including the fluctuating tastes and needs of the customers. A close understanding of agents' and distributors' practices and capabilities and more frequent personal contact with them leads to better results. This degree of knowledge of the market enables a business to judge more accurately the particular price bracket in which its product will best fit – whether competition is on price, whether the credit terms and discounts really have to be as generous as is generally believed, and so on. It is this depth of knowledge which is so important to success. But the more countries a business attempts to deal with, the more diluted its knowledge is likely to become.

Marketing and administrative organisation

A reduced span of contacts may provide a company with the opportunity to reduce its overheads or to improve the quality of its administrative services further still. A smaller marketing team will be sufficient to achieve the same results as before. This is a direct contribution to profitability.

Management efficiency

It is said that the 'complete export manager' has to have several qualities: engineer, diplomat, salesman, linguist, lawyer, accountant *and* be well versed in all documentation, transport and international regulations and standards. The export manager has to cope on a daily basis with an amazing variety of problems, queries, telephone calls from all parts of the world, changes in international regulations, variations in exchange rates and so on, all demanding his constant attention. As a result, he or she will deal with the most urgent matters first. The more markets there are, the more distractions there will be to prevent him or her from attending to the really vital matters. Therefore, by reducing the markets, distractions are reduced. Management efficiency will benefit from a reduced span of control, for example in a crucial process such as monitoring. The export manager should be able to review systematically the progress of the business in each market and to decide what action is required to redress or to improve matters.

Products

There is the thought that, for example, the United Kingdom's and United States' high labour costs and high exchange rates make their products uncompetitive in export markets. If only their labour rates were less and their exchange rate lower. Yet this is a fallacy. In West Germany before unification labour rates were much higher than most others and the exchange rate kept getting stronger. German exports of manufactured goods were about two and a half times those of the United Kingdom, by value. Export prices were higher, but the Germans seemed to have no difficulty in selling their products. They had such a reputation for quality and reliability that their customers seemed happy to pay more. The reason was that customers believed they were getting excellent value. And, in general, they were right.

A business should look at its present customers in its home market. Who are they (if selling retail direct to the end-user), or what sort of companies are they (if selling an industrial product)? What is the competition? Above all, what is so 'special' about the product? Why do customers buy it at all? What is the *unique selling point* (USP)? Could the product be made better or made to perform better? Just as important, are there local regulations or standards in potential export markets which must be met? There are many instances of companies that have shipped their product to an export market, and paid all the expenses, only to find that it cannot be put on sale because it fails to meet some local regulation.

There are also instances of companies who complain about the lack of support (from their governments and other agencies) and the high costs of taxes or of power or of something. All these complaints may well have some measure of justification, but a business cannot sit waiting patiently and passively for all these hurdles to be removed. The only practical solution is to accept these inhibitions and use them instead as a motivation to look for other solutions over which the business can have some control.

Look, then, at the product. Make sure it is as improved as possible, is of as high a quality as possible, is as attractive and acceptable as possible and that it conforms to local standards in the export market.

The rule is: design, test, measure and re-design until there is the highest quality at the lowest cost.

Resources

Selling

It will be necessary to have specialist export staff. This covers not only the actual export sales staff, but also the support staff in the export office. The number can grow as the exports grow. They can be recruited or trained, but it is unrealistic to expect some of the 'home' sales team to be able to divert occasional spare time to the affairs of exporting.

The export sales staff would be best organised by territory, rather than by product: the key to success is knowledge of the market. It is assumed that the staff would have knowledge of the product. If a business has such a wide, and incompatible, range of products then everything said here about exporting should apply to each of those product ranges.

Representation

A business cannot have its own office and staff in every country to which it is exporting; at least, not at first. With some products it is possible to sell direct to the one or two large users. In such cases a business will deal with those large users direct and it does not need any intermediary.

With most products, however, there will be several likely customers with differing demands for quantities, deliveries and mixture of model types. So a business will have to rely, locally, on someone else, a stranger, to make the arrangements for ordering and selling its product.

This is one of the most important, and most often neglected, areas of exporting: how does a business motivate and control someone else, at a distance, to do a good job for it? That 'someone' will be either an 'agent' or a 'distributor'. This is the keystone to the success of the business. The agent or distributor needs to know the product and its benefits from different angles:

1. Pure technical specification.
2. Standard features, functions and benefits.

3. From the representative's point of view.
4. From the end-user's point of view.
5. How it fits into their specific market.

Before appointing someone to act for you, it is also essential to get good advice about the law governing agency contracts in the export market – it is invariably easier to appoint an agent than to get rid of one.

Product performance has to be of value to the customer. It is rarely any good asking a customer what is needed: most customers are not even aware of what is possible until they see it and even then they may not be aware of the full implications or possibilities.

Promotion

It is a truism to say that customers will not buy the products of a business unless they know about them, so promotion is crucial. Promotion mainly means: brochures, advertising, exhibitions and point of sale. The emphasis and proportion spent on each of these will be governed by the type of product.

BROCHURES

These must be in the local language and the final draft should be checked by a native speaker of that language. A small mistake in the local language may not always cause confusion or misunderstanding, but it will show up the inefficiency of a business and thus raise doubts about its commitment to quality. This is a wholly avoidable problem. Anyone who has read the manual of instructions for operating a consumer product imported into an English-speaking country, which has obviously been translated by a non-native speaker of English, will have enjoyed a good laugh. It is precisely that reaction which the business should avoid in its own translations.

ADVERTISING

A business will almost certainly need to advertise in the local press or in appropriate trade journals. But it should take advice from its own agent or distributor, and from a local advertising agency, about the most relevant outlets, and about the content and style of the advertisements. The message should be readable, but not offend the culture.

EXHIBITIONS

Overseas exhibitions are a great opportunity for a business to display its product to all those visitors who are most interested. It also gives the business the opportunity to see (at least some of) the competitors' products.

But the business needs to be properly organised in order to take full advantage of an exhibition.

It is an expensive investment to equip a stand so that it looks attractive, and to staff it with enough people who can talk pleasantly and knowledgeably about the product. It is also advisable to have appointed the agent or distributor before the exhibition, because one of the first questions visitors will ask is 'who is your local agent?'

A system must be used to collect and record the details of all visitors, so that a comprehensive follow-up can be pursued after the event. The whole investment is a waste of time and money if actual leads are not followed and real opportunities not seized.

A personal technique to be developed is one often neglected by most exhibitors. How do you engage a prospective visitor to your stand in conversation? Most exhibitors ask the question, admittedly in a pleasant tone of voice, 'Can I help you?' If you have ever been asked that question yourself at an exhibition, you may remember muttering something like 'No thanks. I'm just looking round'. And that was the end of that encounter.

The key is to get a conversation going. This is best done by asking a question of alternatives, such as 'Do you prefer the red one or the blue one?'; 'Is it for your own use or for your business?' And so on. People love to be given the chance to air their own views and prejudices. You may have to listen to some boring comments, but you will get some real feedback from potential customers.

Good or bad, these comments should be treated as prime market research, recorded and discussed seriously with your colleagues later. This is one of the best ways of getting ideas about how to improve the quality and acceptability of your product.

POINT OF SALE

A business needs to visualise the actual face-to-face encounter between whoever is doing the selling (export salesperson, agent or distributor) and the potential customer who will be placing an order. What assistance should be immediately to hand, in the form of examples, working models, brochures, technical drawings, technical staff, financial arrangements or whatever is most appropriate to the product? It is difficult enough to compete without a business shooting itself in the foot by neglecting all such support. The whole purpose of the business is geared to this encounter. Make sure the representative team is well equipped and trained to extract the maximum benefit from the occasion.

Export office

The support given by this office is another factor in success. It is important to give quotations speedily, to check the order process easily, to know the profitability of exports and to build up a file of export statistics. A business starting to export would be well advised to use a personal computer with the appropriate software to handle this management support. This investment would be modest in cost, but valuable in information and control.

Market research

A business must get into the habit of thinking of Manchester, Munich and Madrid in the same way or it will miss the opportunities and dangers of the Single European Market quite apart from other export markets outside Europe.

Having decided who its customers are most likely to be, as retail end-users or as industrial companies, then some serious market research should be undertaken, preferably by a specialist organisation.

A checklist of key questions should be studied carefully. This should cover such vitally important matters as the following:

1. Market intelligence: what sort, how it is received and how it is evaluated.
2. Market size, structure, users, trends, share.
3. Methods of marketing, distribution, selling, transport, packaging.
4. Competition: share, pricing, methods.
5. User attitudes, behaviour and decision-making.

Apart from the initial research, a proper annual market research budget should be allocated. This will cover general reconnaissance visits by the management, sales visits by the sales staff and the market research activities, whether this is done by an in-house researcher or an outside specialist organisation.

The aim of this research is to identify the best market, the key sectors and customers in the market, the adaptations necessary to the product, the promotion, the timings and the price levels. The general advice is that the price should be set at 'what the market will bear'. This is one of those sayings that is true, but not as helpful as it sounds. Nevertheless, the business must find out what value a customer will place on the product. This will be governed by competition, quality, availability and several other factors.

This 'price' should not be confused with 'cost'. Cost is what the business needs to receive in order to cover its manufacturing cost and its gross margin. Cost also includes moving the product from the factory to the customer. Regardless of whoever *actually* pays for that movement, it must *eventually* come out of the price for the product. If the exporter pays, then he or she wants a higher price from the customer. If the customer pays, then the exporter will receive less.

Ideally, the price should cover the cost, with a little over for contingencies. In practice, the price may be negotiated down. The business must then look critically at its costs, the methods of manufacture and the movement of goods. This is back to the 'design, test, measure, re-design' practice mentioned earlier. A further point to be aware of is the currency of the invoice. Every export sale involves at least one currency transaction, by the exporter or the importer. Chapter 12 discusses the financial methods for dealing with this. Here we are concerned only with the marketing aspects.

The key point is to make it easier for the customer to buy from you rather than from your competitor. It is to your benefit that the buyer should be concerned only with what he has to pay, in his own currency, rather than what you, the exporter, want to receive in your currency. Pricing in the customer's currency also has the merit of concentrating your mind on what people will pay for your product, with their own money in their own market (which is all that interests them), and away from what it is costing you to produce, in your own currency (which is of little concern to them).

Furthermore, by pricing in your customer's currency, you remove the customer's risk, make the precise cost easier to understand and so give yourself the chance to increase your sales. You negotiate a better deal for yourself by saying: 'In return for my removing your risk and hassle, it is not unreasonable for you to give me bigger, and more frequent, orders'. It is a valid argument which has many times produced profitable results from several markets.

Conclusion

As a summary one might say that the three key factors in the success of choosing your market and method of exporting are as follows:

1. *Quality of the product*, with all that implies for design, acceptability and price.
2. *Knowledge of the market*, with all that implies for research, customer contact and anticipation of change.
3. *Relationship with the distribution channel*, with all that implies for managing and motivating agents and distributors.

Having got the marketing right, the next step is finance. The following chapters set out all the considerations of what is possible and what is available.

2

Basic export finance documentation

DAVID WATSON AND BOB GILLESPIE

Managing Director, Sales and Marketing, Trade-Aide Financial Services Ltd, and Managing Director, Operations, Trade-Aide Financial Services Ltd

Introduction

The exporter has now decided upon targeted markets and the strategy to be employed for maximum penetration. This chapter deals in some detail with the documents required to obtain payment for exported goods. The vast bulk of the information contained in these chapters is applicable to all major trading nations, which observe the prime protocols agreed over many decades. This is a handbook, and as such is not meant to be a definitive statement on all aspects of financial documentation for exports. It does, however, give guidance as to where professional assistance can be obtained and points out some of the more obvious hazards in the minefield.

You will note that one point is stressed on numerous occasions in this chapter, and that is that coordination of effort is vital! In the export 'paper-chase', documents, of necessity, percolate through the organisation and thence to third parties. It takes little imagination to realise what can happen without proper control. The progress of the documents must be kept in tune with the progress of the order.

If the company is serious about exports there must be trained personnel to operate the system. This expertise can be bought in; trained up; or devolved to a third party. It is not appropriate to suggest that one method is better than the other since each organisation will have differing criteria. What is cost-effective for a 'one-off' export transaction will not be the same for a company which depends on overseas markets for 50 per cent of sales.

Your banker will be able to provide a plethora of booklets designed to cover documentation and procedures with excellent illustrations as to what each document looks like and its purpose in the chain. As exporters we do well to study these carefully but also remember: these will be 'perfect' examples. Unfortunately we live in an imperfect world. Take, for instance, the 'perfect' letter of credit format described in Figure 2.1 and compare it with what can actually be received in Figure 2.2. This is not a particularly

THE PERFECT BANK PLC 22 Wool Street, Cottonville, England

Date 7 July 19 . .

(subject to Uniform Customs and Practice for Documentary Credits (19 . . Revision) ICC Publication No. . . .)

DOCUMENTARY CREDITS DEPARTMENT

IRREVOCABLE CREDIT No.: TPB/17/98765

To be quoted on all drafts and correspondence.

Beneficiary(ies) Silk and Tweed Ltd Nylon Road London W1	*Advised through*
Accreditor Flannel Ltd Old Road Nuzab Bazun	*To be completed only if applicable* Our Cable of *Advised through* *Refers*

Dear Sir(s)

In accordance with instructions received from The Correct Bank Trust Co. *we hereby issue in your favour a Documentary Credit for* £110,003 *(say)* One hundred and ten thousand and three pounds sterling . . . *available by your drafts drawn on us*

at sight

for the 100% c.i.p. invoice value, *accompanied by the following documents*:

1. Signed Invoice in quadruplicate.
2. Full set of clean Bills of Lading made out to order and blank endorsed, marked 'Freight Paid' and 'Notify Flannel Ltd, Old Road, Nuzab, Bazun'.
3. Insurance Policy or Certificate in duplicate, covering Marine and War Risks up to buyer's warehouse, for invoice value of the goods plus 10%.

Covering the following goods:
250,000 Rag Dolls
To be shipped from: London *to*: Bazun c.i.p.
not later than: 10 August 19 . .
Partshipment: not permitted *Transhipment*: not permitted
This credit is available for presentation to us until: 31 August 19 . .
Documents to be presented within 21 days of shipment but within credit validity.
Drafts drawn hereunder must be marked 'Drawn under The Perfect Bank Plc, 22 Wool Street, Cottonville, England.
Credit No: TPB/17/98765

We undertake that drafts and documents drawn under and in strict conformity with the terms of this credit will be honoured upon presentation.

Yours faithfully,

Co-signed ____________________ Signed ____________________

Figure 2.1 The 'perfect' letter of credit

Date: 6.11.90

SIMPLE BANK
LONDON ENGLAND

IN CONFIRMATION OF CABLE

AND DEFERRED PAYMENT
WE OPEN AN IRREVOCABLE DOCUMENTARY CREDIT NO 6/66166/9 IN FAVOUR
OF SILK AND TWEED LTD, NYLON ROAD, LONDON W1, ENGLAND
BY ORDER AND FOR ACCOUNT OF FLANNEL LTD, OLD ROAD, NUZAB, BAZUN
FOR AMOUNT OF £:20104/74 SAY P.STERLING: TWENTY THOUSAND ONE HUNDRED
FOUR AND 74/100
VALID UNTIL 6.7.XX91 IN ENGLAND AVAILABLE AGAINST THE FOLLOWING
DOCUMENTS THE ORIGINAL AND DUPLICATE OF WHICHPLEASE FORWARD TO US
SEPARATELY BY REGISTERED AIRMAIL OR COURIER: AIR WAYBILL CONSIGNED TO
OUR NUZAB BR.
XXXXXXXXXXXXXXXXXMARKED FREIGHT PAYABLE AT DESTINATION BY OPENER

DATED NOT LATER THAN 21.6.XX91NOR PRIOR TO THE DATE OF THIS CREDIT STOP
SIGNED INVOICES IN 5 6 COPIES OF WHICH 3 COPIES CERTIFIED BY THE CHAMBER
OF COMMERCE AND 3 COPIES LEGALIZED BY THE BAZUN CONSULATE STOP
BAZUN CUSTOMS TARIFF NO 12/93LL/10 SHOULD BE INDICATED IN THE INVOICES
STOP CERTIFICATE OF ORIGIN CERTIFIED BY THE CHAMBER OF COMMERCE
CONFIRMING THAT GOODS ORIGINATED IN XX ENGLAND AND LEGALIZED BY THE
BAZUN CONSULATE
IN 4 COPIES/STOP PACKING LIST IN 4 COPIES STOP EVIDENTING SHIPMENT OF THE
GOODS:
50,000 RAG DOLLS
TOTAL FOB VALUE £17515.56 PLUS INT. FOR 360 DYAS £: 2470/09
PHOTO COPIES OF WHICH ENCLOSED WITH CNF. OF THIS TLX IN 6 PAGES FOR
YOUR CHECKING AND FORMS AN INTEGRAL PART OF L/C
AS PER BENEFICIARIES' PROFORMA NO 61166 DATED 1955/89ON FOB BASIS
FROM ENGLAND TO NUZAB AIRPORT BY FOUR WAYS AIRLINE CO
PARTIAL SHIPMENT NOT ALLOWED TRANSHIPMENT NOT ALLOWED STOP
INSURANCE EFFECTED HERE STOP KINLY NOTIFY BENEFICIARY WITHOUT ADDING
YOUR CONFIRMATION STOP XXXXXXXXXXXX
PLEASE DEBIT OUR H.O. NUZAB ACC WITH YOURSELVES FOR PAYMENTS MADE
UNDER THIS CREDIT UNDER AIRMAIL ADVICE TO US STOP
XXXXXXXXXXXX KINDLY ACKNOWLEDGE RECEIPT
STOP CREDIT NUMBER FULL NAME AND ADDRESS OF OPENERS AS NOTIFY PARTY
HAVE TO BE MENTIONED ON ALL SHIPPING DOCUMENTS STOP THIS CREDIT IS
SUBJECT TO I.C.C. UNIFORM CUSTOMS AND PRACTICE (XXXX REVISION) IF NOT
TERMED OTHERWISE STOP 1983 PUBLICATION 400

R
ALL BANKING CHARGES OUTSIDE INCLUDING REIMBUSEMENT CHANGES ARE FOR
ACC OF THE BENE. L/C AVAILABLE DEFERRED PAYMENT 360 DAYS AFTER FINDING
DOCS FULLY COMPLIED WITH CREDIT TERMS STOP
COORDINATION AND CHARGES COLLECT AUTHORITY MADE THROUGH ANYONE
OF THE FOURWAYS AIRLINE OFFICE STOP

Figure 2.2 The actual letter of credit

onerous example by any means, nor is it designed for spotting mistakes, as they are deliberately not equal in detail or specification. It is simply an illustration of reality. Perhaps this is why the author, when commencing his career in export finance, was given a hard eraser, razor blade and black pen as the 'start-up' stationery requisites!

When describing the various documents which make up the bulk of export paperwork, no apology is made for the obvious bias towards the exporter. It is a commonly stated fact that over half of all sets of documents delivered to any bank for payment have to be rejected on first presentation because of error. If we add to that the documents which have already been corrected before approaching the bank, we realise the enormity of the problem.

Bonds and guarantees have also been given a fair airing since the ultimate onus is on the seller to ensure their return on expiry or validity. Banks and insurers will give much assistance but are disinclined to take action against their correspondents. In document collation, expertise and coordination are the key.

Documentary letters of credit

It is prudent to begin this section with an opinion, wrought from experience, which should be taken as a warning to all: the security afforded to the exporter in utilising a documentary letter of credit to obtain payment is diluted by its own simplicity, its reputation as a secure vehicle and the fact that, within *any* company, not all contributors to the success of a documentary letter of credit transaction appreciate that individual actions on their part may negate the security they *thought* the documentary letter of credit provided.

What is a documentary letter of credit?

A common definition is 'a written undertaking, by a bank to a seller, to pay a certain amount, within a certain time, against specified documents presented to the bank, in accordance with the terms and conditions contained in the letter of credit.'

Types of documentary letters of credit

The following types of documentary letters of credit are the most common.

IRREVOCABLE

All letters of credit must be irrevocable if they are to provide the exporter with a level of security better than, say, 'open account' or a 'documentary collection', and letters of credit which are revocable should, in the normal course of events, be rejected in that form.

CONFIRMED

A bank, which is normally the advising bank, may add its own irrevocable undertaking in addition to that given by the issuing bank. The undertaking may be to 'pay', accept or negotiate without recourse documents presented in accordance with the terms of the letter of credit.

UNCONFIRMED

'Unconfirmed letters of credit' is a term often used by exporters, but which in itself does not convey the real type of letter of credit, revocable, irrevocable, etc., other than to signify that the advising bank has not added its confirmation. The term is, in effect, a shortened version of an unconfirmed irrevocable letter of credit, and is used mainly to *stress* that a letter of credit is not confirmed.

REVOLVING

This is a word used to describe the manner under which the credit will operate. It may be revocable, irrevocable, confirmed, etc. A revolving credit is one in which the value and/or validity may revolve, usually by a specified action or event but, in a few cases, automatically. A credit which revolves automatically as to its value is a very rare bird indeed, since in the hands of an unscrupulous exporter any number of collections could be made within the life of the credit. The situation would be similar to issuing a 'top-up' bond (see later section on bonds and guarantees). To issue a credit in which the value and expiry date automatically revolved would be the equivalent of handing out a series of undated blank cheques.

Normally, the credit would stipulate the following:

1. A maximum total value.
2. Maximum individual collections.
3. Points 1 and 2 linked to set dates.
4. A final expiry date.

The exporter must ensure that the timetable for shipments and collection contained in the credit allows time for the credit to 'revolve' after each collection. This 'revolving' may in some cases be dependent on instructions/notices from both the buyer and the issuing bank, and when relevant, the confirming bank. It is not unknown for shipments to be frustrated whilst waiting for the credit to be reinstated (revolve).

TRANSFERABLE

This is the 'trader' or middleman credit, although it is possible for a supplier to use it to pay a sub-supplier to the contract. The beneficiary of a transferable credit has the right, within any restrictions contained in the credit, to transfer the credit via the advising bank to suppliers anywhere, including other countries. The credit will usually be a value equal to the trader's selling price to the buyer. The amount transferred will be an amount at which the supplier has agreed to sell. When the supplier presents his documents to the advising bank, his invoice is replaced with the trader's or beneficiary's invoice for the full value of the original credit. The advising bank pays the supplier the value of his invoice and will pay the difference to the trader. Transferable credits can become extremely complex, and beneficiaries and suppliers are advised to seek expert advice whenever clarification is needed.

Finally, if you think a transferable credit is what you need for a particular transaction, try to determine who the advising bank will be, and discuss with the bank what you are seeking to accomplish. This is important, since it must be remembered that the advising bank has the right to refuse to transfer any credit should it so decide.

ACCEPTANCE CREDIT

Acceptance credit is sometimes called a 'term credit' or 'usance credit'. It includes a draft for acceptance and denotes that payment is to be made at a specified date in the future, e.g. ninety days from date of bill of lading or air waybill. The seller will have his draft returned to him, endorsed on the face with the bank's acceptance, guaranteeing payment to the seller on the due date. It is usually the case that the advising bank will be prepared to discount its own acceptances, if asked to do so, allowing the seller to obtain earlier payment, albeit less the bank's interest costs for the appropriate period. This is thus a much-used method of giving credit to your customer at little cost and with minimal risk. It is often applicable where an exporter has a reliable regular customer but who might need regular working capital.

NEGOTIABLE CREDITS

Negotiable credits are probably one of the most confusing and misunderstood types of credit, particularly for the inexperienced exporter. The simplest way to identify a 'negotiable credit' is to establish on whom the drafts are to be drawn. It will be either the issuing bank or the buyer. Also, the credit will state that it is the issuing bank which will make payment at its counter overseas, on receipt of correct documentation. The advising bank may be asked to advise *without* adding its confirmation, and negotiation may be limited to the advising bank or freely negotiable with any bank. Whichever bank 'negotiates' the credit, payments (advances) will be 'with recourse' and the seller will incur interest until the negotiating bank is repaid by the issuing bank. Obviously, if the issuing bank fails to reimburse the negotiating bank, it is the seller who foots the bill by having to repay the issuing bank the amount 'advanced' plus any outstanding interest and bank charges. There are, as can be seen, certain risks in 'negotiable credits' when the advising bank is instructed *not* to add its confirmation. You should also be aware that a bank is not obligated to negotiate this type of credit. It is therefore *not* the type of credit a seller should request from his buyer, and it is most likely to arise when the supply contract has not been specific in the type of credit that is required. The adding of the advising bank's confirmation to a negotiable credit changes things dramatically. The advising bank is then obliged to negotiate or pay without recourse to the seller, on presentation of correct documentation, and from the seller's point of view this is the same as having a normal confirmed irrevocable letter of credit (l/c).

Some negotiable credits contain the instruction to the advising bank to 'honour correct documentation presented to them and to pay the seller'. This 'authority to purchase' is peculiar to the credit itself, which may therefore conflict with the terms of payment in the supply contract, e.g. the credit may call for drafts to be drawn by the buyer at 'sixty days from sight' whilst the contract says 'at sight'. The credit will also expire 'for negotiation' not 'for payment'.

Finally, you may be even more confused by what appear to be conflicting phrases or conditions contained in the credit, e.g. 'although requested to pay you the face amount of your drafts upon presentation, this credit is advised without engagement on our part'. This could leave the seller rather worried, particularly as the advising bank has added its confirmation. The answer is, regardless of the 'without engagement' condition, the advising bank, having added its confirmation, will pay the seller at sight, without recourse, against presentation of correct documentation.

Seven golden rules

We now move on to highlight the 'seven golden rules' a seller should attempt to abide by, and then to clear up some common misconceptions. It is not the intention to go through all the 'rules' contained in the *Uniform Customs and Practice for Documentary Credits 1983* (brochure 400), to which *virtually* all countries conform, and to which reference should be found somewhere in the body of the credit. The word 'rules' was mentioned earlier, but it is important to note the *Uniform Customs and Practice* is in effect a guide which attempts to establish uniformity in the interpretation of documentary credits.

One other point to watch for is the credit which states that, 'the credit is subject to the *Uniform Customs and Practice, if not termed otherwise*', but is no more specific than that. Advice should be sought from your bank, or the advising bank. The brochure mentioned is available from the London Chamber of Commerce International and other international chambers of commerce around the world.

The seven golden rules are as follows:

1. Remember that the confirming, advising or negotiating bank knows nothing of your business or products, and, unless they are in possession of a copy of your pro forma invoice which forms part of your sales contract and the documentary credit, they will know nothing of your contract.

   The l/c should be looked on as a contract which you must also be able to fulfil. It may not agree with your sales contract and you may have to decide whether to *accept* it in the form presented, to *reject* it because you cannot comply with the terms and conditions or, more likely, to request the opener to issue an amendment or amendments to bring the credit into line with the contract. You do not have to accept a credit which does not meet your requirements.
2. Prepare documents for presentation under the credit exactly as called for, and beware giving too much additional information since this increases the likelihood of error and contradiction, e.g. the contract describes the goods as one facsimile machine and includes the fact that it comes with two free rolls of paper. The credit describes the goods as 'one facsimile machine' no more, no less. Should the exporter's invoice, presented to the bank under the credit, also include a description of 'two paper rolls, free of charge' you will not have complied strictly with the credit, i.e. you have supplied goods not included in the credit (in the bank's eyes). It will not matter that you are giving them away free, it is still an error. Again, remember, state no more and no less than is required, and this, needless to say, applies to all documents called for in the credit. Banks are *only* concerned with documents, *not* goods.
3. A common error made by exporters familiar with having to provide a 'Marine Insurance Certificate' as part of the documentation is to overlook the maverick credit which calls for a 'Marine Insurance *Policy*'. You may be able to rectify the situation, but have you the time?
4. Always ensure you present the documents well within the twenty-one day rule, i.e. banks will refuse to accept them if presented later than twenty-one days after the date of issuance of the transport documents. It goes without saying, of course, that the documents must still be presented not later than the expiry date of the credit.
5. All corrections to documents *must* be authenticated by an official of the issuing company, shippers, insurers, etc.
6. Check that your company is correctly described in the credit as being

the beneficiary. You will have a problem if there are any doubts in the bank's mind when you present your invoices and bills of exchange, etc.; there should be no room for doubt that you are the intended beneficiary. *Get it amended* at the beginning is good advice.

7. The final rule should help avoid the foregoing problems and many more. Ensure that someone in your company has *total responsibility for controlling all credits.* This should include the coordination, collation and checking of all documentation, but most important, progressing each credit transaction from receipt of the credit to receipt of payment. Regular reviews of credits and the underlying contract can ensure the active participation of all personnel involved in the performance of the sales contract and the credit, and will help avoid pitfalls along the way.

Common misconceptions

Exporters can often be meticulous in agreeing contract details with a buyer, but careless to some degree when referring to a letter of credit in the payment terms contained in the contract. How many times have you seen something similar to the following contained in a contract: 'Payment: 100 per cent by letter of credit'? It leaves a few questions 'hanging in the air', and the likelihood is that when the credit is received there will be cries of 'But that's not what we asked for'. The 'misconception' in this case was your assumption that the buyer will apply for a 'credit' that suits you. What the buyer will apply for is a credit that, whilst providing him or her with maximum protection, gives you as little as possible, and costs the buyer the least.

What should the exporter have done? It is important to incorporate the basic terms and conditions of the credit into the contract using a checklist such as the following:

1. *Type of credit*: irrevocable/confirmed?
2. *Where payable/available for acceptance.* For example, in the United Kingdom it would state: UK clearing bank/UK bank registered with the Bank of England/an acceptable bank in the UK/the exporter's bank.
3. *Amount and basis of sale*: figures and currency, e.g. US$ 20,000 United States dollars (CIF/C&F/FOB/FAS, etc.)
4. *Confirmation*: yes/no – if yes, at whose cost?
5. *Beneficiary*: be precise – full name and address.
6. *Description of goods*: agree with the buyer a brief, but unambiguous, description.
7. *Latest shipment date*: should agree with the contract. Note that the contract should always state delivery periods in 'months from date of effective contract'. Effective contract should be the date of establishment of an acceptable l/c.

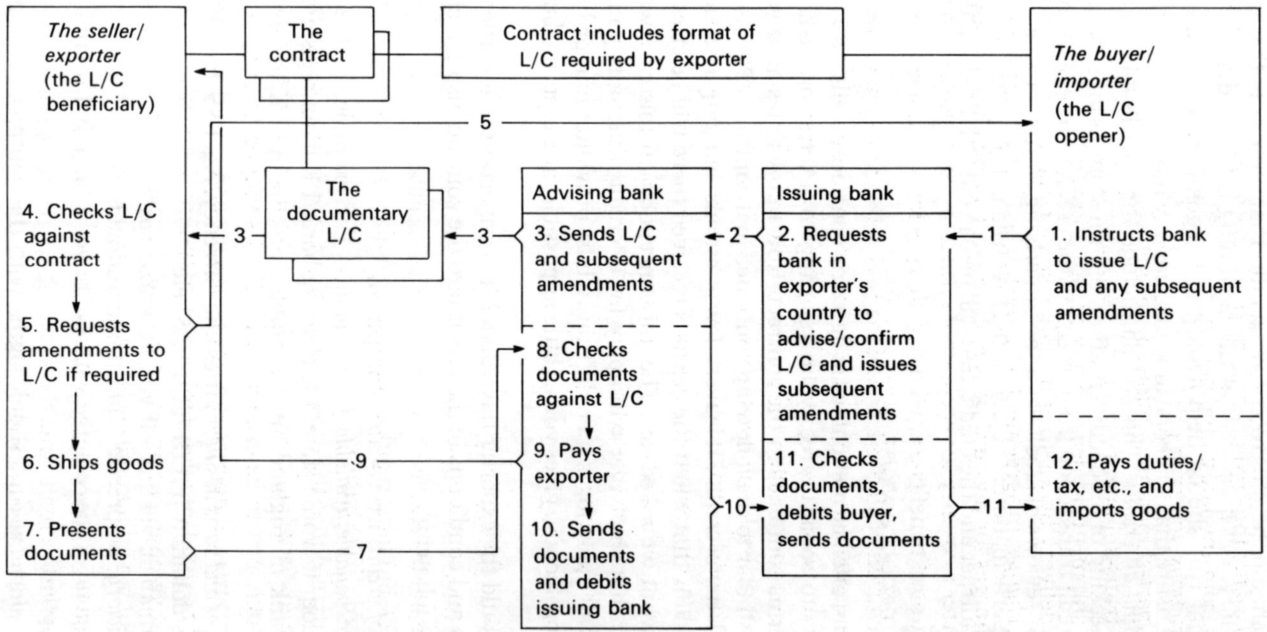

Figure 2.3 An export transaction with payment secured by documentary letter of credit

8. *Shipping/despatch route*: state clearly from which point in the exporter's country to which point in the buyer's country (see point 10 below).
9. *Expiry date*: the credit should be made valid until at least twenty-one days from the latest shipment date.
10. *Restrictions*, for example:
    (a) part-shipments – allowed/not allowed;
    (b) trans-shipment – allowed/not allowed;
    (c) shipment on deck – allowed/not allowed;
    (d) delivery by air freight – allowed/not allowed.
11. *Bank charges*: in agreement with the buyer, clarify who pays what, e.g. all charges for account of opener (buyer), *or* all charges outside the exporter's country for account of opener, *or* confirmation charges for account of beneficiary, all other charges for account of opener, etc.!

The conclusion of all this is that if the *basic* terms and conditions forming part of the credit can be agreed and incorporated into the contract, the chances of an unacceptable credit being received are greatly reduced.

Having put the problem of getting an acceptable credit to bed, the exporter can sit back and await its receipt, knowing that the troubles are over – or so he or she thinks! What the exporter often forgets is that so far, all negotiations/arrangements have been on a one-to-one basis. Now the third parties enter into the frame, i.e. the buyer's banker (the issuing bank) and the exporter's banker (the advising bank). So what can go wrong now? Consider the following:

1. The issuing bank does not follow the opener's instructions at some point.
2. Local regulations of which you and the buyer were unaware (but should have been!) make the opener's instructions to the issuing bank unacceptable, e.g. you have a cost of insurance and freight (CIF) contract, but local regulations state that all contracts must be on a free on board (FOB) basis.
3. It was agreed that the credit would be confirmed by the advising bank, but the advising bank refuses to do so, as do several other banks you try. The conclusion to be drawn is that the issuing bank or your buyer's country are no longer creditworthy, the lesson learnt that the exporter should have taken advice prior to negotiating the contract and agreed alternative payment arrangements, e.g. credit insurance on terms of payment via an *unconfirmed irrevocable credit* (see Chapters 4, 5, and 6).

The old saying 'there's many a slip twixt tongue and lip' applies very well to documentary credit transactions, and, of the problems one can encounter, many are unforseeable when starting out down the road to a successful transaction. It can help, however, to understand the route the credit takes from contract through the issuing of the credit to final payment to the exporter (see Figure 2.3).

One final area concerning the security afforded by exporting via a documentary credit is that of 'the banks' and in particular 'the issuing banks'. It is generally agreed that a major reason for using documentary credits is to transfer the exporter's risk from his buyer to a bank, thereby reducing his risks. Thought should be given to such questions as the following:

1. How did I receive the credit: via an advising bank or direct? If the answer is direct, another question arises: is the credit genuine? Fraud is not unknown and any credits received direct from an overseas bank should be taken for authentication to your company's bank.
2. What is the company's total exposure (in orders and shipments) to any one bank in a given country? Should the exporter be setting a credit limit on a bank? He may have set a credit limit on his buyer, *but he has transferred his risks to the bank!*
3. Is the credit truly 'confirmed?' Give some thought to the credit which is 'confirmed' by the branch or subsidiary of the issuing bank, and ask the question: 'Am I getting any security by paying the confirmation charges?' (Very often an exporter's cost.) Also, for those exporters with a whole turnover credit insurance policy, ask the additional question of will the credit insurer consider it a *true* 'confirmation', or will he treat the credit as unconfirmed and collect a premium? The exporter could end up paying both confirmation charges *and* a credit insurance premium.

There are two additional pieces of advice to close this section:

1. Do not, if it can be avoided, accept documentary credits where the production of any document called for under credit is outside your control.
2. Remember, under documentary credits, banks buy documents from you, not goods. If you do not expect to get away with supplying shoddy goods to your buyer, why should you expect the bank to buy shoddy documents? More banking relationships are soured by this than many realise. Banks do not exist to bail out your incompetence.

Bills of exchange and promissory notes

Documentary collections with or without the security of a letter of credit are most often made by means of a bill of exchange, to be accepted by the buyer (or in some cases his bank), in exchange for the negotiable shipping documents. To a much lesser degree the practice of handing over the documents in exchange for the buyer's promissory note is sometimes used. Before delving further into this subject, however, it is worth noting a few relevant points:

1. Despite the use of a bill of exchange or promissory note in the collection procedure, it is only a true documentary collection if the exporter has

BILL OF EXCHANGE NO. ________ (Amount in figures) ________
Place and date of issue________________________________ 19____
At/on (either 'at' sight or 'on' a date) ______________ for value received,
pay against this bill of exchange to the order of ______________
(Drawer/Seller) ______________ the sum of
(amount and currency in words) ______________
This bill of exchange is payable at ______ (Place) ______
DRAWN ON

(Name and address of drawee)	(Name of drawer and authorised signature)

Figure 2.4 Bill of exchange

control over his goods until the buyer either pays, accepts the bill of exchange or issues the required promissory note. Where no shipping documents are involved the procedure is called a 'clean bill collection'.

2. One could have a documentary collection without the use of either a bill of exchange or promissory note, i.e. the shipping documents are forwarded via the exporter's bank to the buyer's bank requesting immediate payment in exchange for the shipping documents. This is known as 'cash against documents' (CAD). If the exporter sends the documents directly to the buyer's bank, it is known as a direct collection, but the principle is the same.
3. Goods, and in particular high-technology, light-weight, non-bulky items, are now more likely to be delivered by means that make it more difficult for the exporter to retain control, e.g. air freight or parcel post. The exporter, in this situation, may wonder what is the point in drawing a bill of exchange on his buyer, if he has no 'lever' (the negotiable shipping documents) with which to ensure payment or acceptance of the bill of exchange. The answer can be drawn from the following main points defining bills of exchange and promissory notes and of which the exporter should be aware.

Bills of exchange

The UK Bills of Exchange Act of 1882, which is the world model, defines, in Section 3, a bill of exchange as:

> *An* unconditional *order in writing by one person to another, signed by the person giving it, requiring the person to whom it is addressed to pay on demand or at a fixed or determinable future time* a sum certain in money *to or to the order of a specified person, or to bearer.*

This forms the basis of the many versions given as examples in publications, bank guidance booklets, etc., but to be true, valid and legally enforceable bills of exchange they must contain all the points in the foregoing definition (see Figure 2.4).

The bill of exchange should be treated like money, and it should contain nothing which impairs its validity or leaves room for misinterpretation.

Dishonoured bills of exchange

A bill is deemed dishonoured if it is not accepted by the drawee, or if it is not paid by him. Such a bill must be protested or noted. 'Noting' means obtaining a minute on the bill by a notary public and is dated and initialled by him or her at the time of refusal to accept or pay.

A formal protest is initiated by the notary public only when the matter leads to legal action. Since the law with regard to 'protesting' differs in many countries, however, some of which call for a formal protest within a specified period, it is now common practice for exporters to include in their collection instructions, the order to protest upon non-acceptance or non-payment.

Claused bills of exchange

The adding of clauses to collect monies in addition to the stated value of the bill is quite common, e.g. 'plus interest at x% p.a. from date hereof, till date of payment' or 'payable with banker's charges'. Care should be taken, however, to try to live within the legal definition of the 1882 Act: 'a sum certain in money'. It follows that in the examples relating to interest and bank charges, there is an 'uncertain amount of money' to be paid. Better, perhaps, to be specific in the amount of interest to be collected and the amount incorporated in the certain value of the bill. Better also that instructions relating to the payment of bank charges be clarified in the sales contract and incorporated into the instructions to the collecting bank.

Types of bills of exchange

There are basically two types, under which many variations fall.

SIGHT BILL OF EXCHANGE

The 1882 Act defines a sight bill as follows:

1. A bill which is expressed to be payable on demand, or at sight, or on presentation.
2. A bill in which no time for payment is expressed.

The most common name for a sight bill is a sight draft. The expressions 'bill of exchange' and 'draft' have identical meanings.

PROMISSORY NOTE NO. ______________ (Amount in figures) ______
Place and date of issue ______________________ 19 ______
On ______ (date) ______________ against this promissory note,
I/We promise to pay to ______________________ or order,
the sum of ______ (amount and currency in words) ______
for value received ______ ______ (Name and address of issuer) ______
Payable at ______ (Place) ______ ______ (Authorised signature) ______

Figure 2.5 Promissory note

USANCE BILL OF EXCHANGE

Sometimes referred to as a 'time bill' or 'term bill', the usance bill is payable on a specified date in the future or on a determinable date in the future, e.g. 180 days after sight. Legally the bill *ceases* to be a bill of exchange if it has an uncertain due date such as '180 days after inspection of the goods on the buyer's premises', or '*after* sight', or 'on or before arrival of vessel', etc.

Promissory notes

Promissory notes (see Figure 2.5) may be preferred by some buyers or countries to bills of exchange. A promissory note is defined as an unconditional promise in writing by one person to another, signed and issued by the maker (the buyer) agreeing to pay on demand or on a specified future date a sum certain in money to a specified person, or to the bearer of the note.

The promissory note is not as common as the bill of exchange, and, from the exporter's viewpoint, is less desirable. The main difference is that the exporter organises the bill in the format he wishes, but has no real control over the wording of the promissory note which is issued by his buyer. His only control is to be specific in his instructions to the collecting bank as to any clauses or conditions which the note should or should not contain.

Promissory notes are, however, common in trade in Japan and many Japanese houses use this instrument. It is also a valued tool in the world-wide forfaiting market.

The invoice

Since the vast majority of readers world-wide will have access to a fairly local Chamber of Commerce (or similar institution), there is a ready-made service for advice and assistance in export documentation and procedures.

This section will, therefore, deal with certain aspects of the invoice which can cause expensive problems further down the line rather than concentrate on the exact description:

1. Do not assume that your stock of invoices designed for the local market will be appropriate for export!
2. One of the most common *faux pas* is to take for granted that, because your distributor or agent converses with you in your language his customs and excise organisation will have the same ability. Your cargo may have to wait until the officials find time to sit down with their translation dictionary, the customer has to wait for clearance and the period for payment expressed on your invoice extends. You may not have been in breach of the underlying instructions but that does not stop the delay from occurring. To avoid this it is important that the classification number for goods subject to customs' tariffs is quoted on the invoice. It is best to approach your customs and excise to establish the correct Customs Cooperation Council Nomenclature (CCCN): a standard accepted in most parts of the world.
3. The terms of payment should be explicit and reasonable. 'Payment thirty days after date of invoice to our bank (or our company address)' may appear reasonable, but if the shipment was from the United States to an Australian port it is more than likely that the customer, to comply with these terms, would be paying *cash in advance.* You have three options:
   (a) ensure the end customer is aware that the terms stated are your strict terms of trade;
   (b) amend the terms to read: 'Payment received in our bank *x* days from receipt of goods, at the (specific) Australian port', and price the goods accordingly;
   (c) leave the terms as they are, be aware there will be a delay and price accordingly.

   Obviously, amending your terms to what is reasonable before invoicing will ensure a greater possibility of follow-on business.
4. State the basis of sale; this should agree with the arrangements in the underlying contract.
5. Quoting discount for 'prompt payment' is undesirable, unless it is established as to where, and by what date, payment is to be received in order that the discount applies.

   Local invoices have been seen used for export with the statement retained at the bottom: '2.5 per cent discount if payment received within thirty days'. Within thirty days from when? To what does the 2.5 per cent apply? Goods? Total value of the invoice, including freight cost? In what currency? If the customer pays in local currency within the specified period, but his central bank is not immediately able to convert this to the currency of the invoice, and a delay occurs, is the customer still able to claim the discount?

It is best, by far, to negotiate discount (if any) within the contract price and let your invoice remain silent, allowing your credit insurance to look after the possibility of transfer delays.

6. Some countries require a specially printed 'customs' invoice' for exports over a certain value. It is used as a check to ensure that no duty liable is avoided. Others require a 'certified invoice' which is a commercial invoice carrying a detailed statement as to origin and value.
7. A minority will also require commercial invoices to be legalised by the customer's consulate in the seller's country before the goods will be allowed entry.

Transport documentation

Although transport documentation has undergone many changes in recent years, the *Maritime Bill of Lading* (B/L) retains its position as the most common transport document for the export of goods. The factors that cause it to remain a prime document are numerous, and relate to the organisation of payment through the banking system:

1. It is a document of title: the vital ingredient to the payment arrangement is that it describes ownership and when and where ownership is transferred.
2. It is a shipment receipt: providing for details such as, condition of the goods and, in certain instances, their position on board.
3. It is evidence of the contract between the exporter and the shipping company.

A 'clean B/L' is one on which no additional statement has been added or superimposed. In essence, any addition to the B/L would be to indicate some defect in the description or condition of the goods under consignment.

The *'combined transport'* and *'through container'* documents cover the eventuality of a multiplicity of transportation to eventual destination. It should be noted that although the purpose of both is the same, the liability on the carrier is markedly different and careful checks should be initiated to avoid ambiguity.

A *'received for shipment B/L'* indicates that the carrier has received the consignment for shipment. With the growth of containerisation the goods may well be delivered to some central source to become part of a full container load. It will then be transported to the designated port for shipment, at which time the 'received for shipment B/L' can be endorsed to become a *'shipped bill'*.

An *'air waybill'* (AWB; air consignment note) is also widely used, especially for high-value smaller items and urgent deliveries. It is, however, non-negotiable and as such does not carry the same legal power as the B/L; thus it is easier for the customer to gain access to the goods without going through the various financial checks. In some instances the seller will consign the goods to the overseas bank rather than to the end buyer in order that payment may be effected before physical access to the goods is obtained. This, of course, is not always feasible as it implies that the bank has storage facilities and is willing to accede. Therefore AWBs are regarded with caution by international banks.

'Railway consignment notes' can be used for transport by rail but these again are not documents of title and are non-negotiable.

Should you use a forwarding agent then the shipper/carrier may require the following:

1. *'Export cargo shipping instruction'* – to confirm bookings.
2. *'Standard shipping note'* (SSN) – to hand over to the collector.
3. *'Dangerous goods note'* – used instead of the SSN when the goods are classified as dangerous. The precise nature of the goods should be noted on the form.

Certificates

Although some certificates have been mentioned elsewhere in this chapter, a few of the most common are noted below.

Certificate of origin

The certificate of origin is required by some importing authorities to confirm where the goods originated. Any misrepresentation by the seller could result in the whole being rejected under any credit insurance claim (see Chapters 4 and 5).

Insurance certificate

To avoid future problems, the contract between the buyer and seller should indicate which party pays to cover the goods while in transit. An exact description as to which risks are covered should also be included. At some later date, what each party thought was meant by some ambiguous description in the contract will only benefit the legal profession. Most of the terms are abbreviated to FOB/CIF/C and F, etc., and a full description can be obtained by a study of Incoterms (international rules for the interpretation of export terms used in overseas trade, formulated by the International Chamber of Commerce). An exporting company of long standing will normally have 'open' or 'floating' cover for all its overseas sales. In this case an insurance certificate is usually enough. Should the contract, however, stipulate that a full copy of the policy is required, then compliance is necessary.

Blacklist certificates

Blacklist certificates are issued to evidence that the goods did not originate in an area blacklisted by the buyer or his country. One should make careful note as to whether the blacklist extends to the carrying vessel or its country of registration.

Other certificates

Certificates can be required to cover any contingency the buyer or his customs authority wishes, and the rule is to ensure that you can comply before final contracts are signed.

Depending upon the circumstances you could, in addition to the above, be requested to supply certificates of health, quality and inspection, in any combination. This latter certificate can cause heartache if not dealt with in a regulated manner. A good example is when the government of a country decides to contract with a third party for the inspection of the goods before shipment. The terms of reference can be wide-ranging, taking in quality *and* value-for-money checks. It is best, when aware of this requirement, to make arrangements for the goods to be inspected in good time to ensure the 'clean report of findings' is issued well in advance, since a delay in shipment could incur penalties through the underlying contract.

The cardinal rule with certificates of any kind is immediately to establish, with the buyer, which issuing authority is acceptable. On many occasions time and effort has been wasted in arranging for certificates to be issued by an *external* source when careful study of the contract conditions indicated that your own *internal* certificate would have sufficed.

It is not apocryphal to state that, in the past, the writer has been asked to supply certificates certifying that the certificate in question is a valid certificate. Exporting can be fun!

Bonds and guarantees

Definition

A bond or guarantee may be required for a multiplicity of purposes, but is normally defined as guaranteeing the good faith of the selling company to comply with a submitted tender or accepted contract. The seller must exercise extreme caution before accepting, or agreeing, to any bond whatsoever since inability to comply with the tender or contract will undoubtedly result in the bond being legitimately 'called'.

Description

Bonds are more strictly defined under five main headings:

1. *Bid bond* – issued to a customer to show the seller's real interest and ability to take on board the resultant contract. Obviously the customer will have expended time and energy in perusing the various tenders and the seller's subsequent failure to accept the contract will result in loss of time and perhaps revenue. The bond would be legitimately 'called' in recompense for this. This is virtually the only occasion when a bid bond can be called fairly and it is important that wherever possible the issued bond should be conditioned to this effect.
2. *Advance payment bond* – as the name implies, this type of bond is issued to guarantee the return of cash advanced by the customer if the seller does not comply with the criteria laid down in the contract. Normally, they would be issued conditional upon the receipt of the cash from the customer into the seller's account or by other defined routes.

   They can, and should, be arranged to be reduced pro rata to say: 'shipments made or services rendered', the exact where, when and how being a vital part of the instructions agreed by both parties.
3. *Performance bond* – this refers to performance of the contract conditions and should not be confused with 'warranty', i.e. the performance of the goods. These are the likely vehicles for permitting the transfer of cash due from the seller, owing to an inability to comply with the ongoing contract. It is important that these are most carefully worded to avoid any ambiguity or unnecessary risk, and the penalties should be conditioned upon some evidence which must be agreed at contract stage.
4. *Retention bond* – normally, in a goods and services contract, the customer will negotiate a retention of x% of the total contract value until a period of time after acceptance. In some cases it is felt better for cash flow purposes to issue a retention bond and receive the cash 'up-front'.
5. *Carnet* – there is a special category of bond, normally called a 'carnet' although other terms can be used, but its basic function is to guarantee to the overseas import authorities that goods temporarily exported (for exhibitions, etc.) will be re-imported.

It is recommended that a bond should not be issued if the following conditions hold:

1. It does not bear a fixed validity date, or in exceptional cases, a point in the future fixed by a contractual event.
2. It does not bear a fixed value.
3. It contains a 'top-up clause'. This is where the customer claims the right to draw down any percentage of the bond and it is then 'topped-

up' to the original value. Automatic reinstatement of a bond can, in the hands of an unscrupulous buyer, become a seller's nightmare. This is especially true when it has been issued through a correspondent bank in the buyer's country and right of redress is limited.

The minimum information required to establish a bond would be the following:

1. The beneficiary.
2. The value.
3. Percentage of total contract value or bid.
4. Validity.
5. Contract or bid reference number.
6. Description of goods.
7. Final date for issue.

In addition, any other relevant information should be noted, such as the following:

1. Special wording (required by either party).
2. Specific correspondent bank.
3. Pro rata deductions, etc.

The actual non-clementure of bonds can vary (i.e. bid or tender), thus it is always best to establish the intent rather than rely on titles.

Routeing and security of bonds

Having considered the main types of bond, it is prudent also to look at the methods by which these can be issued. Figure 2.6 illustrates the ramifications of each. These, for ease of understanding, are split into three main headings:

1. *Direct* – bond/guarantee issued on the seller's 'paper' and sent directly to the customer.
2. *Via a bank in the seller's country* – seller indemnifies his or her local bank which issues the bond on its paper direct to the customer.
3. *Via a local correspondent bank* – as for 2, but the seller's bank issues instructions to, and indemnifies, a local bank which will issue the bond to the customer.

As can be seen in Figure 2.6, the costs escalate by the amount of intermediaries used, as does the risk. Obviously, there is minimal risk of unfair calling of the bond when it is issued on the seller's paper since the customer would have to establish his right to payment in the courts of the seller's country.

There is certainly more risk involved in using a major bank as guarantor rather than a company bond and the reason for this is the 'simple' or 'on

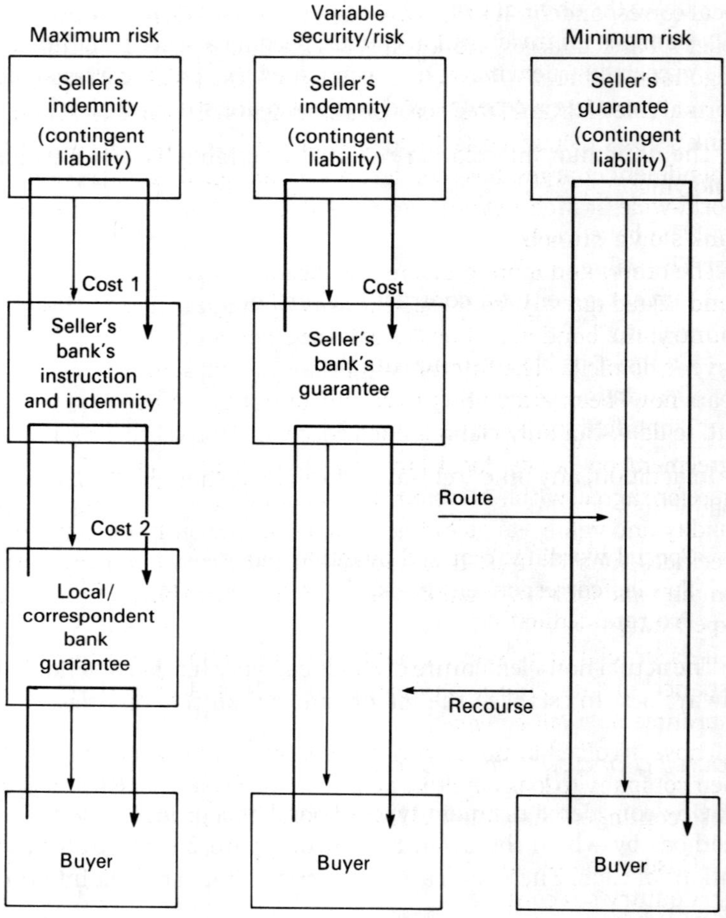

Figure 2.6 Routeing and security of bonds

demand' bond. If the customer cannot be persuaded to accept an arbitration clause in the bond and it is accepted by the seller as 'payable on first demand' then the bank is obliged to pay the customer *without necessarily advising the seller in advance.* A good relationship with the bank involved is, therefore, paramount.

However, if it is at all possible, an arbitration clause should be attempted since at least the seller has the opportunity to put his case. Obviously it would be best for arbitration to take place in the seller's country or, at least, a neutral area.

It would appear that, at face value, there is little difference between issuing a bank guarantee from the seller's country and issuing it through a local correspondent. It has, however, two distinct disadvantages. While the seller's bank charges are known in advance and can be the subject of negotiation, there is no such restriction on the local correspondent. As a normal rule of thumb, the local correspondent will be in excess of the seller's bank's costs. These costs include cable charges, quarterly charges and amendment charges. It is therefore an advantage to use a bank with a good world-wide branch network in order that the bond can be issued via the bank's own branch.

The other, and more problematic, disadvantage, is the fact that while a bond issued directly from the seller's bank remains under the law of that country, the bond issued by a local correspondent transfers the risk to the buyer's domicile. The International Chamber of Commerce has, for many years now, been attempting to reach consensus on bonds and guarantees but, to date, can only claim limited success. Since there is no international agreement on bonds, local law will apply. The seller and customer can therefore agree, within the contract, to condition the bond as to arbitration, validity and value, etc., all to no avail if the law of the customer's country precludes such clauses. It is known that in certain countries bonds will remain valid for many years; others admit to no arbitration but their own. Expert advice is vital.

It is crucial that sales, commercial and finance personnel take the issuance of guarantees seriously and do not accept the request for a guarantee as a *fait accompli.*

Those involved in the day-to-day operation of bonding are obligated to their company to look carefully at all factors affecting risk before agreeing to these contingent liabilities. These include the following:

1. Customer's record.
2. Country's record.
3. Local law and regulations.
4. Banks involved.
5. Currency.

Figure 2.6 also indicates clearly that, should a bond be called, the recource/liability rests with the organisation requesting the bank to issue on their behalf. Thus, the bond remains a contingent liability on the seller's books until release. The bank's risk rests on the ability of the seller to pay in the event of a 'call'. Since bonds issued can have an effect on bank borrowings it is encumbent upon the company's personnel to ensure their timely return.

Points to note

1. Check whether insurance cover against the unfair calling of your bond is available.

2. In the event a customer advises that he 'never received the bond issued' or 'the bond is mislaid', ensure that a release from the first bond is received before instructing the bank to issue a new document, otherwise double liability will occur. If it is a large-value bond it could, as already advised, have an adverse effect on the bank's borrowings.
3. In the United States, the practice is to offer 'stand-by' letters of credit as an alternative to bonds and guarantees.
4. Ensure that the commercial and sales departments are instructed to advise immediately it is known that a guarantee is required. The more time for *checking, vetting and instructing,* the better will be the end result.
5. Remember, overseas customers do not always work the same hours (or days) as domestic customers, and holidays differ markedly. In addition, the bank may have difficulty in communicating your instructions immediately to the correspondent bank.
6. Even if the exact value of the bond is not immediately available, the personnel responsible for bonds should still be made aware of the requirement. The preparatory work can then be undertaken well in advance of instruction to the bank.
7. If a bond is issued in a currency other than the currency of the seller, then it is advisable to update the exchange rate on a regular basis.

   Should the bond be 'called' then the exchange rate ruling on the date the bond was 'called' will normally be used. If these are not updated regularly then fluctuations in exchange rates could cause a nasty shock!
8. Take advice from the bank if uncertain of any clauses contained within the bond.

3

Official export credits and the Single European Market

MALCOLM STEPHENS
Chief Executive of ECGD and President of the International Union of Credit and Investment Insurers (the Berne Union)

Introduction

In export credit insurance, as in so many areas the Single European Market means different things to different people. The one certainty is that it will bring about significant change. However, it would probably be rash to try to predict with any degree of certainty just what is going to change and how.

It is, perhaps, helpful to distinguish at the outset between two increasingly different kinds of export credit:

1. First, short-term credits where exports are sold on up to two years' credit. The great bulk of such export credits for most EC export credit insurers is in respect of exports to Organisation for Economic Cooperation and Development (OECD) countries. For many, for example, the Export Credits Guarantee Department (ECGD) in the United Kingdom, a large percentage of current short-term business is for sales to buyers in other EC countries.
2. Second, medium- and long-term credits. These are credits in respect of exports of capital goods or projects with a minimum maturity of two years. For most credit insurers, the bulk of such credits will be for sales outside the OECD, often to developing countries. The terms of such credit are the subject of international agreement – the OECD Consensus – which sets minimum interest rates, maximum lengths of credit and minimum downpayments.

One important consequence of this distinction is that the diverging roles of government and the private sector in relation to these two categories are leading to significant change. In the United Kingdom, for example, competition for short-term business is growing. Not only is there competition between the public sector (ECGD) and the private sector (e.g. Trade Indemnity plc), there is also developing competition between UK entities and companies from other EC countries and elsewhere (e.g. the United

States) setting up operations in the United Kingdom. However, for medium-term business, the role (and desires) of the private sector – including the banks – seems limited. There is, therefore, fairly general agreement that the support of medium- and long-term export credit extended to developing countries will remain an area for governments. However, as is set out below, this does *not* mean that it is an area where the Single European Market will produce no changes for export credit. Indeed, it is an area where the last few years of this decade are likely to see substantial change.

Export Credits Guarantee Department

The Export Credits Guarantee Department is the oldest export credit agency (ECA) and has helped in various ways with the establishment of over half the more than forty ECAs in thirty-four countries which now exist. Most major credit schemes, including Eximbank in the United States, are completely or partially modelled on the ECGD. It was set up in 1919, and its original rationale was to encourage trade with the Soviet Union and other countries of Eastern Europe. Its activities grew in scope and volume but it was not until the 1960s that its growth began in earnest. It currently (1990) covers about 25 per cent of the United Kingdom's loans and exports. Short-term business is largely handled by its Cardiff operation and nine regional offices and its project business from its London headquarters.

For most of its seventy-one years, the ECGD's major activity has been the issue of insurance policies covering the main commercial and political risks in exporting. These cover the risk both that the buyer will not pay and that some political event (e.g. a country running out of foreign exchange) will prevent payment being made. In the last twenty-five years, the ECGD has also played an increasing role in facilitating the availability of finance from the banks to support exports. In the area of short-term credit, this can take the form of arrangements enabling exporters to assign the benefits of their ECGD policy to a bank or it can take the form of ECGD issuing what are, in effect, 'wholesale' insurance policies to banks who then 'retail' the cover to individual exporters, often through local branches. In the case of medium-term credit, the most common arrangements are where ECGD facilities are issued direct to financing banks. These have two main purposes: first to provide a guarantee of repayment of loans extended by the banks to borrowers/buyers overseas and second to provide a means of supporting fixed rates of interest. The terms of such lending (e.g. in regard to minimum rates of interest, minimum downpayments and maximum lengths of credit) are, as noted above, governed by international agreement amongst the major exporting countries under the OECD Consensus. In recent years, the Consensus interest rates have been subject to several increases to bring them closer to commercial or market interest rates.

The Single European Market: insurance developments

One problem with any discussion about the forthcoming Single European Market is that no single event will take place. Rather, there are a cluster of developments and EC Directives which, taken together, will make significant steps towards the creation of the Single Market and satisfy the requirements of the Treaty of Rome in respect of state aids and the creation of a common commercial policy (Articles 92–4 and 110–16) as these apply to official export credit insurance. However, even this can be misleading since it will not, for example, mean that sales from a company in the United Kingdom to a buyer in France will somehow cease to be exports. Neither does it mean that such sales will have become risk free – the whole range of buyer and commercial risks will continue to exist even if political risks are significantly reduced.

However, in looking at overall developments and likely developments in this area, it is possible to pick out some general trends.

Greater internationalisation

First, there will be greater internationalisation of activity. This takes various forms. More and more exporting companies operate from a number of EC countries. Production, etc., is diversified and can usually be redirected or adapted, for example, to financial changes or potential benefits. Thus, it is nowadays rather more difficult to be specific about what constitutes national goods and services and thus what constitutes national exports. This development seems certain to increase in scope and scale. This presents a challenge to ECAs which may traditionally have operated on the basis of supporting solely identifiably national exports. It also presents a challenge to companies since it offers the possibility of organising or structuring sales from within a multinational group on the basis of having some freedom of choice of where and on which agency or institution to concentrate the desired credit insurance cover.

In addition, internationalisation extends beyond the exporting companies themselves; it also has an impact on credit insurers. Commercial pressures and competition opportunities, coupled with EC moves on freedom of establishment, mean that an increasing number of insurers are looking to offer credit insurance facilities to customers outside their traditional areas. Directive 73/239/EEC (First National Life Insurance Directive) provides a framework for companies to exercise freedom of establishment. It sets up a harmonised regime for the authorisation and financial supervision of insurance undertakings and, in particular, provides for insurers with head offices in one member state to establish branches in another. In other words, an insurer in, say, the Netherlands is now free to offer, and may now feel perfectly confident about offering (i.e. selling), insurance to companies in Germany and the United Kingdom. In addition, there are signs that some insurers who have not previously offered credit insurance as part of their product range may now be doing so. The potential competitive impact of these developments is enormous and will inevitably force the pace of changes which would otherwise have taken longer to materialise.

When is an export not an export?

Second, whilst as I have said above that cross-border sales within the EC will not somehow cease to be exports, it is surely inevitable that such sales will become less like exports and more like domestic sales. In other words, we will probably enter a period where there will be three main classes of sales:

1. Domestic sales (e.g. from Birmingham to Glasgow or from Rouen to Lyons).
2. Exports (from the United Kingdom to Kenya or from Germany to Algeria).
3. Intra-EC sales (e.g. from Birmingham to Lyons or from Rouen to Glasgow).

Taken together, these two developments (i.e. greater internationalisation of production and of insurance availability and some blurring of the traditional distinction between exports and domestic sales) will almost certainly mean both that more companies will be interested in credit insurance as a single packaged product (and thus less interested in separate arrangements for exports and domestic sales) and that more insurers will look to respond to these marketing and product development opportunities and to sell such products outside their traditional national borders.

The intense competitive pressures which have been a feature of export credit insurance in recent years have pressed on prices, margins and profitability. This in turn has led the ECGD and no doubt others to look critically at costs and to maximise the return from fixed overheads. Expanding the portfolio of profitable business is the obvious, but difficult, way forward. The liberalisation of the European market may provide the means to make this a reality. While it is difficult to predict the future – and, in comparison with banking, the rather less global nature of the insurance market may suggest otherwise – my feeling is that because of the international nature of their business, the export credit insurers have both the skills and the systems to capitalise on what looks like a unique and golden opportunity for them. At the risk of oversimplification, it could be said that the risks presented by transactions and the underwriting skills needed to assess them are the same irrespective of the location of the credit-giver. Put even more simply, whether a buyer in Rouen is taking credit from a supplier in his own country, from Germany or from the United Kingdom, the risk to be assessed by an underwriter in, say, the Netherlands, is the same. Indeed, where the underwriting process has been significantly computerised – an area where the ECGD likes to consider itself a world leader – those programmes should be readily adaptable to provide customers anywhere with the speed and quality of service to which customers in the United Kingdom have become used without any deterioration in the underwriting out-turn.

A level playing field

Third, and again spurred on by these two factors, there will be greater interest in the concept of a 'level playing field'. This, too, will have various manifestations. It will lead the private insurers to look very carefully (and critically) at areas where they compete with public insurers. And, secondly, it will cause insurers to look at how freely they are allowed to set up and compete in other EC countries. For example, in the first context, if – as is currently the case – private sector insurers are required to maintain certain reserves or margins which public sector credit insurers are not required to maintain, or if private sector insurers are subject to tax when public sector insurers are not, then it is obvious that the private sector insurers will complain about unfair competition and point to the potential effects of such differences of requirement or treatment on premium rates and thus on competition. This takes no account of the arguments that private sector insurers may make about their needing to answer to shareholders whilst public sector insurers may be subject to political requirements, etc., to support exporters rather than to operate commercially.

The second point is also important, namely the extent to which it is possible for an insurer in, say, Italy to establish a business and sell insurance (either direct or through brokers or agents) in, say, Spain. Insurers may argue that until all barriers, etc., are dismantled, the concept of a free market or a single market in insurance within the EC is meaningless. But some insurers would also argue that, even though EC Directives, etc., are making significant progress in dismantling barriers, competition will not be fully free or equal until, for example, there is some greater degree of harmonisation in other, but related areas, i.e. in common treatment of tax in relation to the treatment of provisions and reserves on solvency margins.

Distortions of competition

Fourth, there is – especially in the area of medium- and long-term credit – increasing interest in the *differences* between the various national schemes within the EC. Some may argue – and have traditionally done so – that there is 'richness' and advantage in such diversity or differences, and that attempts to harmonise arrangements are sterile or stultifying or doomed to failure whilst so many other commercial and financial factors differ between EC countries.

However, two interesting and important questions seem to be arising with increasing frequency:

1. Are the differences in the availability of cover for particular overseas countries between different public export credit insurers in the EC now so wide as to represent a potential distortion? In other words, if an exporter in Spain can get export credit cover for, say, an export to Cuba, whilst the agencies in, say, the Netherlands and the United Kingdom do not offer similar cover to Dutch or UK exporters, is this unfair competition or a restriction of competition? Similar questions could arise in regard to differences in premium rates: if, for example, British premium rates for, say, five years' credit to Algeria were to be twice the level of Italian premium rates. This kind of question has increasing force as differences about market limits on the level of new business acceptable to individual agencies increase and as the disparities in premium rates grow.
2. Is it 'proper' for agencies to offer cover only to national exporters or should an EC exporter be allowed to shop around to any agency in the EC? In other words, if an EC agency has medium- and long-term cover for, say, Poland, then should this not be equally available to exporters in any EC country and not restricted to its national exporters?

A single institution

Some people have argued that the only effective way to tackle these questions is to move at once towards establishing a single agency or institution or the creation of a common European facility to cover all medium- and long-term EC exports. They argue that only in this way can competition between EC exporters be fully equal or absolutely fair and that only then can 'distortions' in terms of the availability and cost of export credit insurance be removed. Supporters of this view claim that only with such an institution can EC exporters hope to match the kind of support received by Japanese or American exporters and that the current arrangements for handling a multi-sourced bid from EC countries are cumbersome and thus time-consuming to organise. Some might even go so far as to argue that, until such a simple institution exists, the EC will not be a 'true Community'.

There is, of course, a range of counter-arguments. Many of these revolve around the view that it is not desirable to produce a solution until it is clear just what the problem is! It is argued that a range of arrangements already exist for supporting EC multi-sourcing in the area of projects and medium/long-term credit, especially the reciprocal arrangements under which an agency in one country takes in goods and services from other EC countries and treats them in exactly the same way as 'national' exports.

These arrangements can cover up to 40 per cent of the value of export contracts and so offer considerable scope for multi-sourcing. In addition, in the case of short-term credit many agencies are now very relaxed about covering non-national goods and services. Finally, reinsurance and co-insurance between different EC ECAs is perfectly feasible and already happens.

What next?

It is of course invariably easier to spell out problems than it is to suggest solutions. However, there are, perhaps, now some pretty clear signs – especially in the United Kingdom – of the shape of things (i.e. changes) to come.

First, the then Secretary of State for Trade and Industry (Nicholas Ridley) made a statement to the UK Parliament on 18 December 1989. The text of this is given in the appendix to this chapter. What it means is that, subject to the necessary legislation being approved by Parliament, some very radical changes are in prospect and should be largely set in place before the Single European Market.

First, the ECGD, after seventy or so years of operation, will be split into two parts. The two parts will mirror the distinction between the two different kinds of export credit discussed at the beginning of this chapter, i.e. short-term credit and medium- and long-term export credit. The ECGD's short-term business underwritten by the Insurance Services Group will be taken into a free-standing government-owned company. Second, this company will be privatised as soon as possible after its establishment. Third, for the first time, such business will reinsure with the private reinsurance market. Indeed, the aim will be to secure private market reinsurance to the maximum practicable extent. Fourth, to the extent that private market reinsurance cannot meet all the company's needs (e.g. for some political risks), then the government will consider providing reinsurance for a transitional period of up to three years. The aim will be to seek to develop further the appetite and capacity of the private reinsurance market during this period.

Key reasons for this change are the kind of factors identified earlier. The following are examples:

1. To reduce the level of government/state involvement in an area where the majority of the business (i.e. risks) are commercial.
2. To facilitate the development of a level playing field and thus to increase the 'equality' of competition between insurers.
3. To offer the possibility of extending the product range of the new company beyond the traditional one of insurance of UK exports. There is a reluctance to extend the activities or the product range (and thus the area of competition with the private sector) of a government entity.

4. To recognise not only the developments that are taking place in the credit insurance needs of companies operating within the EC, but also the changing pattern of competition between existing and new insurers attempting to meet such needs.

It is clear from this that, subject to the necessary legislation being approved by parliament, the Single European Market will see a significant reduction in the level of 'official' involvement in export credits in the United Kingdom. The changes will, arguably, be greater than anything else which has happened to the ECGD in its long and, I hope, distinguished history. But I also hope that they will not produce any adverse changes for UK exporters.

There is also the possibility that, in adopting this radical approach, the ECGD might go further and faster than its equivalents in other EC countries. As I have already made clear, an important element in the decision to change the ECGD's status was the need to create a level playing field between the providers of export credit insurance who are currently to be found in both the public and private sectors. The Treaty of Rome is even-handed between private and public sector undertakings, as long as the latter conforms to the disciplines of the private market and there are no hidden subsidies. So there is no EC requirement for the provision of export credit insurance to be wholly private. Nevertheless, in an area where the private sector 'disciplines' go beyond simply staying solvent, satisfying your shareholders, paying tax and observing relevant companies' legislation but extend to matters such as the need to comply with national and EC insurance supervisory requirements and the need to hold equalisation reserves, the question must arise as to whether a level playing field can ever properly be created unless all providers of short-term credit insurance are genuinely private. Certainly, pure government status such as the ECGD currently has, or some half-way house in which the public sector mimics private market practice, is probably, indeed almost certainly, unlikely to prove a tenable long-term position. Whether the ultimate shape of the market is determined by unilateral action of governments (currently, virtually all the EC governments are taking or considering taking action that will push their agencies more towards the private sector) or by the ruling of the EC Commission or the Court of Justice, is difficult to predict. The certainty is that, five years from now, the playing field will be more level and fewer of the players will be wearing the national strip.

As for project business, the major changes are likely to be concentrated on the way that the ECGD manages and prices its medium- and long-term political risks. Whilst – potentially – these changes (which will generally fall under the umbrella of its portfolio management system) will be of great significance, they will not be directly linked with, or attributable to, Single European Market factors. However, the other questions raised earlier about differences in the availability and cost of medium-term export credit covering both the pros and cons of a 'common facility' on single institutions are, I would judge, going to be the subject of increasing interest in Brussels and elsewhere. This could lead both to some harmonisation in the terms of cover provided by the various Community ECAs and to some increase in the amount of cover one ECA will be willing to give to exports from other countries which are the subject of sub-contracts from the main contract the ECA is covering. I think, too, that we could see some greater cooperation between ECAs in joint (or co-) insurance arrangements and also, in due course, risk sharing. In my view, all these developments are much to be preferred to the establishment of a single new EC institution.

The Single European Market, then, presents a range of changes and challenges for all involved with export credit. Perhaps the one certainty in this area is that none of us who work in it will have any doubt that we are the recipients of the Chinese proverb about living in interesting times!

Appendix: text of a statement to the British Parliament by Nicholas Ridley

Based on the findings of the Kemp Review of future status options for ECGD, the Government has decided that the two main ECGD businesses, that is the Cardiff-based Insurance Services (covering exports on short term credit) and the London-based Project Group (handling exports of projects for capital goods on medium term credit) should be split and run as separate organisations. The Government's intention is that Insurance Services be converted into a company and that private capital should be introduced quickly thereafter. These changes are being made to enable ECGD to take advantage of the opportunities offered by 1992 and to meet the increased competition which will arise. They will also ensure that its intra Community business is maintained. Equalising the legal and economic framework for credit insurance in Europe, with Private Sector capital, is a necessary condition for fostering UK trade within the Community.

The company will follow the normal practice of credit insurance companies operating in the commercial market in the use of reinsurance. The Government's aim is that this should be obtained from the private market. However, I recognise that in relation to certain of the political risks currently covered by Insurance Services there is at present insufficient private market capacity. Thus in order to maintain facilities for exporters, the Government is prepared to see a transitional period of up to three years from the date of the introduction of private capital during which a reinsurance arrangement will be in place between HMG and the company. During this period the company will work to complete adequate reinsurance arrangements with the private market with the aim of phasing out residual Government reinsurance.

When the new company is formed, the intention is that staff who transfer to the company should do so on broadly comparable terms to those which they presently enjoy as Crown Servants. ECGD staff will be asked whether they wish to remain within the Civil Service or to transfer to the new company. ECGD will use its best endeavours to meet their wishes where these are consistent with the business needs of ECGD and the company.

These changes will require legislation at the earliest opportunity. It is the intention that the new company is established on 1 April 1991. Advisers will be appointed shortly to assist ECGD in carrying out necessary preparatory work.

Over the last three years, ECGD's Insurance Services has introduced major improvements to the range and quality of its services. It has developed a unique underwriting system and rapid credit limit service designed to meet the needs of its customers in the 1990s, particularly in the Single European Market. The changes I have outlined for the Insurance Services Group are vital to enable it to meet the challenges which will be thrown up by the Single European Market and so ensure that we develop further what is a significant national asset for our exporters. I am confident that the changes I am proposing are the best way to secure jobs for the future.

In relation to ECGD's Project Group, the Government has decided that export credit and financing support should continue to be provided. ECGD's project support activities will remain within Government, but the precise form of ECGD's organisation – whether it should remain a Department or acquire Agency Status – will be decided as soon as possible.

The Government is anxious to reduce the costs which have been associated with ECGD support for project exports in recent years. It will, therefore, continue to press hard internationally for multilateral agreement aimed at eliminating subsidies which distort export credit and aid. In addition, to reduce the risk of losses in the future, radical new methods for managing ECGD's political risk portfolio will be introduced. Substantial premium increases for project business will be necessary, especially for business in the higher risk markets to ensure that ECGD premiums are better matched to risk. I believe that exporters will accept the need for this and will regard it as preferable to the withdrawal of facilities.

The changes I have outlined are essential if ECGD is to be able to maintain and improve the quality of support it currently provides to UK exporters. The overwhelming majority of the representations which have been made by interested outside parties have fully supported these changes. I commend them to the House.

4

Export credits: the broker's view

ANDREW NEILL
International Director, The Credit Insurance Association Ltd

In the United Kingdom and the United States, the specialist credit and political risk insurance broker has developed a unique position in the commercial life of their respective countries, one which is often incomprehensible to outsiders. This incomprehension is particularly true of Japan and most countries in the European Community which do not place in brokers the importance attached to them in, for example, the City of London. It should be remembered that approximately 70 per cent of all UK insurances are placed through brokers whilst only 30 per cent are placed through brokers in the remainder of the EC. As brokers are also responsible for placing the majority of all domestic and export credit insurance, particularly in the United Kingdom, they have developed a leading role in this sector, and as such are qualified to comment, warn and observe on the changes that are likely to occur within their chosen field in the future. This is a market strength and feature largely unique to the United Kingdom but not yet developed in other OECD markets.

It is perhaps worth recalling what contribution a specialist can and should bring to a frequent user of export credit insurance, bearing in mind that traditionally this form of cover has largely been available from the public sector or public sector supported insurers.

Primarily the broker should become a commercial support on which the exporter can lean, to enable the latter to have instant access to market knowledge, risk assessment, commercial alternatives and become a general sounding board. All this should be based upon a sound commercial understanding, backed by regular training and a first-class information base. It is for these reasons that the broker has developed a niche in the United Kingdom as well as within an environment which was commercially sympathetic to such a role in the first place. This contrasts with continental counterparts, who have largely developed the role of agent, acting on behalf of the underwriting industry.

The broker has therefore encouraged the development of new products as well as new underwriters, which has lead to a wider sense of competition. This, although encouraging a lower premium spend, has nevertheless seen a continued expansion of premium income. Before looking at how this competition will become more international in the specialised field of export credits, it is perhaps worth looking at where matters currently stand.

The OECD consensus

The ability to obtain finance, preferably at competitive rates, has been crucial to the exporters of capital goods. The so-called OECD Consensus rules have codified the lengths of credit which may be extended for the sale of capital and quasi-capital goods. This OECD agreement has operated for many years. However, the rules have been changed, particularly in regard to the interest rate matrix where, generally speaking, subsidised finance is now only available for the sale of goods to poorer countries outside the OECD.

Each supplying country has developed its own methods for making available to exporters the cover against contract frustration and related finance. In the United Kingdom, the ECGD provides specific covers for project business and major capital goods contracts, as well as covering the export of related repetitive goods, by means of a supplementary spread policy attaching to comprehensive short-term policies. However, this system is undergoing change. In future, all contracts that necessitate the granting of credit in excess of two years will be underwritten specifically by the project side of the ECGD, which will remain as a government department and the vehicle for granting governmental support and implementing government policy. The newly privatised part of the ECGD will continue to provide cover for credit terms of up to one day less than two years as part of their 'spread' agreement with exporters. Privatisation will take place on 1 April 1991.

This 'new' private sector insurer will immediately find itself competing with other commercial organisations which are willing to consider credit terms of up to three years, and in certain circumstances even longer. Nevertheless it must be borne in mind that the banks will also be active in this field through their forfaiting and export finance departments. No government-subsidised finance is available for deals covered by the private sector, and this crucial area is therefore likely to remain the preserve of the officially supported export credit insurance schemes for the forseeable future. The possibility of the EC providing some form of centralised support cannot be forgotten either. This, however, is fraught with difficulty, as we shall see later.

Furthermore, it is the impact of self-regulated competition that will have the most substantial impact upon the way most exporters use or take advantage of the facilities available within the EC. Clearly those nations, such as the United States, competing with the Community have perhaps the most to gain or indeed lose from this consolidation, depending on whether more or less support is given to European exporters as a result. Although it is too early to say, it is likely that the opportunity for the obvious subsidisation of exports will decrease and thereby make some contribution to the lessening of trade competition. How will this come about?

EC Directives

The root of the change is not the creation of the Single European Market, but more obviously the Directives issued by the European Commission which relate to the insurance industry, and therefore by implication, the insurance of trade credits, be they on short or long terms of payment, within a domestic or export market.

The most important Directive was that of 22 June 1988, which in turn amended an earlier Directive of 24 July 1973. These Directives related to 'the coordination of laws, regulations and administrative provisions relating to direct insurance other than life assurance and laying down provisions to facilitate the effective exercise of freedom to provide services'.

The Second Non-Life Directive

The so-called Second Non-Life Directive does not apply to public sector organisations, but as we shall see it has had a profound effect on state-supported or state-controlled export credit insurers. It is, perhaps worth looking in some detail at the major provisions of the Directive:

1. *Freedom of establishment.* This gives the right to a company, with its head office in one member state of the Community, to operate in another member state.
2. *Freedom of services.* A company with its head office in one member state has the right to provide services in another member state without being established there. For example, a Dutch insurance company has the right to offer cover in the United Kingdom from its domicile in the Netherlands.
3. *Large risks and mass risks.* These risks are deemed to apply to the larger industrial companies and are defined as follows:
   (a) marine, aviation and transport risks;
   (b) credit and surety ship insurance;
   (c) property and casualty insurance, where the insured is of a certain size. Policyholders must meet certain thresholds calculated by reference to their balance sheet and the numbers of their employees which should exceed 500.

It is important to appreciate that all credit insurance, whether or not it is purchased by a small company, is covered by this Directive and, as such, is treated as a large risk.

Home country and host country rules

Home country rules apply to the country of origin of the provider of the services concerned, whilst the host country's rules are those of the country where the service is provided. If, for example, a UK insurance company is providing cover to a French company, it will be necessary for the UK company to comply with the requirements of the United Kingdom's Department of Trade and Industry by informing the Department of its intention to provide services in France.

Similarly the UK country must comply with the regulations of the French authorities which will require sight of certificates from the Department of Trade and Industry in the United Kingdom confirming that the insurance company has minimum solvency margins, and that there are no objections to its providing services for which it is authorised.

The French authorities will also require that the company states the nature of the risk it proposes to cover.

It can be seen that there are ample opportunities for bureaucratic delay and frustration available to a protectionist-minded state, notwithstanding the apparent freedoms established by the Directive. Despite this, a genuine freedom to shop around for cover has been established, and there is now the possibility that an international group can have one policy covering all risks in the various member states of the community. Sadly this freedom is not complete as yet for the implementation of the Directive is delayed for the Irish Republic, Portugal, Greece and Spain. The process as far as it applies to these states commences in 1995 and will not be concluded until 1998. Further complications exist in such areas of taxation (the French Revenue collects 30 per cent of premiums for example), compulsory insurance, where a state imposes the obligation to take out insurance which must comply with the specific provisions relating to that member state, and in the law of contract where only in cases of marine, aviation and transport risks are insurance companies entitled to choose the law under which the contract of insurance is written.

Other problems exist of a more 'political' nature. France, which has complied with the necessary enabling legislation, has imposed a restrictive regime for mass risks, unlike the Netherlands and the United Kingdom which have indicated that they will treat mass risks in the same way as large risks.

In contrast the Italian government has delayed passing the appropriate enabling legislation. As background it should be remembered that the Italian authorities direct insurers to invest in Italian government stocks and therefore may not wish to see their control in this area diminished. However, the European Commission has made it clear that it is fully behind the liberalisation of the insurance market and will therefore continue to insist that the appropriate legislation is passed in all states as soon as is possible. In addition, there is a desire to work towards a common licence for insurance companies within the EC, which will lead eventually to a true free market.

Governmental support

All this will therefore theoretically enable potential users of credit insurance to choose with which insurer they place their business regardless of nationality. State-owned insurers were excluded from this Directive. Matters are further complicated though, because the status of some insurers, who fulfil the role of the state, and by implication can become a tool of government policy, is ambivalent since they remain private companies. This inevitably means that some of their less flexible competitors can feel disadvantaged. It is for this reason that steps are being taken to 'privatise' the UK ECGD's insurance services group. As we have seen, the ECGD will remain in existence, whatever it might be called, in two forms. First, as an organisation fulfilling the role of a state insurer for extended credit contracts, either as a supplier or buyer credit facility and the vehicle for guaranteed finance to UK exporters, and second as the aforementioned privatised body, with governmental reinsurance for political risks being sustained for three years after its change of status.

In most EC countries a virtual monopoly has existed for the providers of export credit insurance. It was, however, only with competition that the ECGD was able to change sufficiently to face the changes that lie ahead. This competition came from the private sector, mainly from the United Kingdom's prime provider of domestic credit insurance, Trade Indemnity plc. Trade Indemnity was successful in developing a substantial portfolio of short-term export credit business, as a result of an attractive, simple policy wording, a political risk reinsurance treaty and good timing. This enabled it to exploit the then difficulties which the ECGD was experiencing, to provide competitive cover and a better service. Trade Indemnity has also gone on to develop a book of new business both within the United Kingdom and elsewhere. To survive, other than as an instrument of government, the ECGD had to compete, and it is to its credit that it has done so. There are other private credit insurers in most developed markets, both for export and domestic trade, although the range of services they offer varies significantly. In the United States, export business, other than that supported by Eximbank, can be insured by the Foreign Credit Insurance Corporation of America (FCIA) or by the American International Group (AIG). Domestic credit insurance in the United States is also undertaken by American Credit Indemnity and Fidelity and Deposit.

Harmonisation

It is with the inevitable need to harmonise state-supported insurance as well as to establish a form of united support for finance that the greatest difficulties lie. The view of other OECD countries, particularly the United States, Canada, Australia and Japan, will become increasingly loudly stated if their worst fears are met in the establishment of some supra-export credit insurer in Brussels, attempting to pursue a central policy, but at the same time becoming prey to the demands of large multinationals and regional as well as federal interests. It is difficult enough to realise the particular regional interests within one country, without attempting to equate the demands of a manufacturer, say in Calabria or Greece with a competitor in Ulster or Brittany. It is for these reasons that such an organisation will take years to be established, if at all.

These extreme regional examples perhaps demonstrate a fundamental weakness of the EC, in that, if it is not possible to equate such demands, the creation of such a body will become impossible. This in turn will not lead to the harmonisation of policy throughout the Community, and will further delay not only the implementation of the freedom of services now allowed but also the opportunities arising from the creation of the Single Market.

Mergers

The various export credit agencies (ECAs) within the European Community present a mixed picture in terms of structure, ownership and policy, but even this is changing. Compagnie Francaise d'Assurance pour le Commerce Exterieur (COFACE) is developing closer links with its private sector counterpart, Société Francaise d'Assurance Credit (SFAC). Hermes Kreditversicherungs in Germany and the Dutch Nederlandsche Credietverzekering Maatschappij (NCM), whilst being part of the private sector, are, like COFACE, backed or reinsured by their governments for political risks, and are collaborating with COFACE in the joint ownership of a credit investigation company. Both Hermes and NCM are seeking business from companies across the Community's frontiers, and are beginning to market their products actively, by taking advantage of the flexible broking market in the United Kingdom, to offer both domestic and export coverage to UK companies.

Elsewhere, the Italian agency Sezione Speciale per l'Assicurazione del Credito all'Esportazione (SACE) is soon to collaborate with the private sector insurer Societa Italiana Assicurazione Crediti (SIAC), and in Spain Compania Espanola del Seguros de Credito a la Exportacion (CESCE) is facing the possibility that its traditional monopoly for export credit insurance could be abolished.

This is all very well, but exporters will be penalised if the providers of cover fail to remember some of the harsher facts of economic life of the past fifteen years. There has been a 'political' dimension to claims, which the recent expansion in economic activity and the breaking down of accepted political borders has tended to obscure. Substantial sovereign debt losses have been accumulated by most ECAs in Central and South America and in Central and Western Africa as well as a result of such dramatic events as the Iranian revolution. The privatisation or restructuring of ECAs may be a common currency, but these accrued losses cannot be ignored by the governments involved in supporting or encouraging the trade which led to these debts in the first place. By writing off the debts they will stand accused of subsidising their exporters at the taxpayers' expense, but to carry the losses forward as an 'asset' on a balance sheet will lead to a false valuation being put on the assets of the insurer, with all that implies for its rating and reputation.

Potentially two sectors could suffer from these changes, real or imagined. First the exporter of capital goods will find it increasingly difficult to obtain the support which was forthcoming with little argument in the 1970s and 1980s; and second those potential users of the products in the less developed countries will suffer the consequences of this restricted support. Conversely, exporters of goods to OECD countries on short terms of credit will find an embarassment of riches with a range of competing commercial underwriters vying for their business, at least in the early years, following the freedoms engineered within the EC. Inevitably competition will lead to underwriter mergers across state borders, which will gradually mean that choice will lessen and rates harden.

The role of the broker

Where does this leave the broker? It is tempting to think that with the developing plethora of underwriting markets, the broker will become even more essential to industry, and be instrumental in bringing new underwriters to new markets in North America, the Far East, the former Eastern bloc and elsewhere in the EC. Even the most dedicated specialist will find it hard to expand at anything other than a haphazard rate. This is because he or she will be dealing with insurers who are not used to the flexibility of approach offered by a widening market. With one or two exceptions the insurers will be inexperienced in dealing other than direct with their clients and will therefore feel threatened by the sense of competition a broker will bring to their business. In addition, the complexity of different laws, languages and cultures applying to the various covers will be a natural impediment to the flexibility the broker and sophisticated user would theoretically perceive and anticipate.

Nevertheless the role of the broker in this sector will become crucial. It will be necessary for one professional to understand and market the products available to industry. Above all, it will become increasingly vital for a proper risk analysis for an insured or potential insured to be undertaken regularly. A company needs its exposure to risk analysed frequently, and the means of mitigating these risks explained and cover negotiated on its behalf in the most cost-effective way, which will lead to the provision of protection of these risks in the way anticipated. This is not a plea for the broker, but a statement that, at last, one of the 'Cinderellas' of the world-wide insurance industry is beginning to assume its rightful position as the ability to offset financial risks becomes more widely understood.

5

Short-term schemes

JOHN HOLLOWS
Head of International Trade Services, Barclays Bank plc

Introduction

The purpose of this chapter is to summarise the finance schemes available from UK and several international banks to support exporters trading on short-term terms of trade (usually up to and including 180 days from shipment or delivery of goods), backed by export credit insurance. For the exporter who has never used these schemes, it is intended that this chapter should give a clear statement of the benefits and the pitfalls in order that a better-informed decision can be taken. For the exporter who has made regular use of these schemes, it is intended that this chapter should outline all the options currently available in order that the exporter can be satisfied that he is using the most suitable scheme.

Schemes such as those outlined in this chapter are being developed by many national insurers. With the advent of the Single Market in the early 1990s, potential exporters in virtually all OECD countries, including the United States and Japan, should be able to access them.

Background

Many of the current national schemes have their origin in a scheme offered by the Export Credits Guarantee Department (ECGD) of the UK government known as the Comprehensive Bank Guarantee scheme (CBG). It is worth, therefore, briefly explaining what this scheme was and why it was withdrawn between 1985 and 1987.

The CBG allowed exporters who had arranged export credit insurance with the ECGD to borrow from their banks against the backing of a 100 per cent guarantee from the ECGD. This guarantee assured the bank that, in the event that payment was not received from the buyer within 180 days of the due date for payment, the ECGD would unconditionally reimburse the bank for the full amount of the payment due, plus interest.

Where the bank claimed under the CBG, the exporter had to refund the ECGD with the full amount of such claims under a 'recourse agreement'. The exporter was then able, within the terms of his insurance, to submit a claim on ECGD and receive 90 or 95 per cent of the original sum (excluding bank interest).

The scheme could accommodate business conducted on open account terms as well as business where the buyer's payment obligation was evidenced by way of bill of exchange or promissory note. The agreed interest margin of 0.625 per cent above the bank's base rate was very attractive for all but the largest exporters.

The CBG allowed many exporters to access larger lines of credit than would otherwise have been the case at a more favourable rate of interest. Again, although the banks sometimes complained about the relatively fine interest margin agreed, they, too, appreciated the unconditional and 'undoubted' nature of the security. Unfortunately the ECGD too often found that, having reimbursed the bank the full amount due plus interest, the exporter was unable to stand recourse upon him or her or claim on his or her insurance effectively. As a result, and in the face of rising losses, the ECGD announced in October 1985 the phased withdrawal of the CBG over two years.

When this announcement was first made, it was thought by some in the export community that the willingness of banks to lend to exporters would be severely curtailed. Some predicted that the UK export effort as a whole would be significantly hindered. In fact, the opposite was true. Many banks quickly devised new ways of delivering short-term export finance. Moreover, the keen element of competition that was introduced thereby had such an effect that, now as never before, there are (a) a very wide variety of bank schemes available to choose from, and (b) many banks and other financial instructions actively promoting such schemes to exporters. Unlike the CBG, all these schemes are backed by ECGD insurance only (*not* ECGD guarantees to banks). It is important to understand, therefore, what this insurance cover provides.

Export Credits Guarantee Department insurance

The ECGD was established in 1919 and continues to operate under Act of Parliament. Its defined purpose is to encourage trade with other countries for the benefit of firms carrying on business in the United Kingdom. See Chapter 3 for the similarity with most other export credit agencies.

It was to operate at no net cost to the taxpayer and this has been achieved for much of its history. In the last ten years, however, the Third World debt crisis and other problems have given rise to substantial deficits in many ECGD programmes, especially in respect of medium-term debt (credit terms of two years or more). Nevertheless, the short-term insurance-only programmes currently (1990) operate in surplus. About 7,000 exporters hold ECGD policies and insure £13bn worth of short-term exports with ECGD each year.

The standard ECGD policy is known as the Comprehensive Short-Term Guarantee (CST). It usually provides a *90 per cent commercial indemnity* against commercial losses including the following:

1. The insolvency of the buyer.
2. The buyer's failure to pay (within six months) for goods accepted.
3. The buyer's failure to take up despatched goods (where the ECGD agrees that legal action would serve no useful purpose).

It also provides a *95 per cent political indemnity* against political causes of loss including the following:

1. A general moratorium on external debt declared by the buyer's government.
2. Any other action by the buyer's government which prevents performance of the contract.
3. Political events, economic difficulties and other measures outside the United Kingdom which prevent payment being made.
4. War and other events preventing performance of the contract.

ECGD's charges are normally made up of (a) an annual premium payable in respect of ECGD's administrative costs in maintaining the policy, and (b) a turnover or risk premium payable monthly against an exporter's declared turnover. Usually ECGD insures all an exporter's turnover but, for a price, a restricted spread of business can be considered.

It is important to stress that ECGD will only meet claim payment if (a) the exporter fulfils his contractual obligations to his buyer(s), and (b) the terms and conditions of the ECGD policy are adhered to in all other respects.

Financing: the basic structure

Provided ECGD insurance, of the type described above, is available as security to the bank, finance can be arranged using one of the short-term schemes which are described in more detail below. It is important in the first instance, however, to understand how banks view such schemes when assessing credit and, in particular, when determining the facility limit and the price.

When contemplating a financing facility for a company in respect of domestic receivables, the banker will often seek to secure his position by way of a general charge over the undertaking of the company. This is usually known as a debenture and incorporates a first fixed charge over the book debts of the company. In the event of the company's failure, a receiver can be appointed to collect the receivables and realise other assets with the primary objective of repaying the indebtedness of the bank.

In assessing what limit to agree, and pricing issues, the banker will have regard first and foremost to the credit standing of his customer and the security available. This assessment will have particular regard to the net worth of the company, historic trading performance and future prospects.

Providing the banker can be satisfied on these points he will often agree a facility limit which will include a debenture or 'margining' formula. An example of such a formula might be that, within an overall facility limit, a bank will typically lend to a maximum of *50–75 per cent of the value of good domestic debts*, provided such debts are no more than thirty days overdue.

By and large, credit insurance is not regarded as significantly improving the bank's risk. This is not to say that such an attitude (towards credit insurance) is correct or advisable. It is rather a comment, from experience, of attitudes currently prevailing amongst bankers involved in lending in respect of domestic receivables.

With the benefit of export credit insurance, however, and using the short-term schemes which are the subject of this chapter, the banker structures the finance so that, in assessing the risk, he can look to the following:

1. First and foremost, a range of good overseas buyers, preferably 'well spread' (for example, with no more than 25 per cent of the total exposure outstanding against any one buyer).
2. Second, and in the event that a buyer defaults, good export credit insurance arranged by the customer or the bank, depending upon the scheme.
3. Third, and in the final resort, the customer himself, and only then if he is in breach of his financial agreement with the bank.

Using this approach the banker may be prepared to do the following:

1. Lend more than would otherwise be the case – usually 90 or 100 per cent of the value of receivables financed.
2. Lend at a finer interest margin given that the perceived risk may be less in the banker's eyes owing to the presence of government-backed export credit insurance.

Before considering the various schemes in detail, it will be helpful to review why exporters use such schemes. In other words, what customer needs are the banks seeking to satisfy in offering these schemes?

Why use a short-term scheme?

Of course, as we have established already, these schemes are essentially financing arrangements. As such they represent one of many options open to the exporter to finance his overseas receivables. For example, the exporter may borrow from his bank using a simple currency overdraft. Again the exporter may ask his bank to discount bills of exchange drawn on and accepted by his buyer(s).

Many exporters complain, however, that they find it difficult to obtain sufficient finance to support their export turnover. This complaint may arise out of historical reasons; in the past, and outside traditional ECGD-backed schemes, bankers have tended to place less security value on overseas receivables compared with domestic receivables.

In this context, it is also important to be aware that many exporters report that (a) they have to offer longer terms of trade when tendering in export markets, and (b) the incidence of significant payment delays is greater in export markets. For these reasons, many exporters are attracted to the short-term schemes because, as explained above, the banks may be prepared to agree to higher lending limits at finer interest margins.

In addition, some exporters look to short-term schemes to help minimise the risk of non-payment by buyers. For this reason many schemes are advertised as providing *non-recourse or without recourse finance.* It is very important, however, to define precisely what is meant by these terms, since almost certainly they do *not* mean that the bank will never seek repayment of certain advances from exporting customers.

These schemes are without recourse to the exporter *provided* the following terms are satisfied:

1. The exporter fulfils contractual obligations to buyer(s).
2. The exporter properly maintains the export credit insurance policy (if this is the exporter's responsibility under the scheme).
3. The exporter complies with the other terms and conditions of the financial agreement or facility letter with the bank.

Otherwise the bank may seek to exercise recourse to the exporter in respect of certain advances, or all advances.

As such, it is usually more appropriate to describe these schemes as 'limited-recourse' or 'essentially non-recourse' schemes. It is also pertinent to mention that, by and large, banks can only offer this benefit with the involvement of ECGD or some other export credit insurance.

Following on from this, and given the essentially non-recourse nature of the finance provided, some auditors are prepared to regard these schemes as providing *'off-balance sheet'*. In other words, the finance provided does not appear with the other current liabilities in the exporter's balance sheet. It is rather regarded as a cash payment to the exporter by the bank on shipment (when the advance is usually made).

This is an important benefit for some exporters who are keen to present their published balance sheet and accounts in the most favourable way. Of course the auditor in each case will wish to examine carefully the detailed terms and conditions of the financial agreement to ensure that it meets the auditor's exacting professional standards. Some international auditors report the limited recourse liability as a contingent liability, and agreement should be sought at an early date.

The schemes in detail

Having considered the general principles involved, we now turn to a more detailed review of the particular features and benefits of each of the main schemes. Our purpose is to compare the different structures and approaches in the schemes themselves. In this respect we shall divide the schemes into two main groupings:

1. Schemes backed by credit insurance arranged and managed by the exporter ('exporter-insured schemes').
2. Schemes backed by credit insurance arranged and managed by the bank ('bank-insured schemes').

Exporter-insured schemes

The schemes under this heading may conveniently be divided as follows:

1. Schemes where the exporter's credit insurance is assigned to the bank.
2. Schemes where the bank's name is added to the exporter's credit insurance by way of endorsement.
3. Schemes where a professional credit insurance policy manager is used by the exporter to assist in the arranging and managing of the insurance.

ASSIGNMENTS

For many years exporters have been able to 'assign' all or part of the benefits of their credit insurance to a bank. Often this has been in support of overdraft or other general credit facilities made available by the bank.

In these circumstances the 'assignment' is more properly defined as a letter of authority addressed by the exporter to the insurer instructing the latter to pay claims to the bank in the event that any claims become payable under the policy.

There are various types of letters of authority accepted, for example, by the ECGD including whole policy, single market, single buyer and single transaction. Banks prefer the whole policy approach because it is considered to provide the best security and also excludes any other bank from offering finance against the backing of the credit insurance policy. Exporters, on the other hand, may prefer the flexibility of giving letters of authority in respect of certain risks only. Amongst other things this may enable the exporter to split banking arrangements.

Features

With the benefit of an acceptable letter of authority, the banks have structured schemes which provide finance on shipment as to 90 per cent of the invoice value. In the event of non-payment by the buyer, the bank finances the claims waiting period (usually six months from the due date) and the advance is repaid from the proceeds of the claim.

Interest is normally payable quarterly in arrears, having been calculated on the daily balance outstanding. There may also be fees payable in respect of the administrative costs of arranging for each drawdown under the facility and monitoring repayment in each case.

Benefits

Apart from the general benefits mentioned above, *the exporter benefits* from the *freedom* which this approach gives him to manage his own insurance arrangements without 'interference' from the bank. He may also welcome the *flexibility* of assigning the policy to more than one bank.

The *bank benefits* from the *additional security* provided by the credit insurance. Banks recognise, however, that this security is only as good as the exporter's management of insurance arrangements. If the exporter breaches the terms and conditions of the credit insurance policy, *no claim will be payable* and the bank is powerless to intervene. In these circumstances recourse would be had by the bank to the exporter.

For this reason, some banks have restricted the use of this particular scheme to their very best exporter customers, where they consider that the expertise and resources available to manage the credit insurance policies are sufficient and proven.

EXPORT CREDIT ENDORSEMENTS

Under this approach, an endorsement is attached to the exporter's credit insurance policy. This endorsement recognises the bank's interest in financed contracts and gives the bank the right to receive the proceeds of claim payments. There are various endorsements, including, for example, the following ECGD endorsements:

1. Sales to finance company.
2. Export finance short term (EFST) (exporter as manager).
3. EFST (bank as manager).

The sales to finance company endorsement is used where the bank chooses to be the undisclosed principal in the export transaction. In effect, the bank buys the export goods from the exporter, who sells those same goods to the buyer on the bank's behalf and on an undisclosed basis. We shall come back to this structure when we consider legal aspects later, not least as this concept has now been challenged in law with potentially devastating effect.

The other two endorsements have been more widely used over the last two years. The words in brackets signify who manages the insurance on a day-to-day basis. With the 'bank as manager' endorsement, the bank manages all aspects of the insurance on the exporter's policy in relation only to financed contracts. With the 'exporter as manager' endorsement, the exporter continues to manage all aspects of the insurance until such time as the bank gives notice to the insurer that, from that moment on, it wishes to be responsible for the insurance arrangements (e.g. the submission of claims) in respect of financed contracts only.

Benefits

Again, depending on which endorsement is used, the *exporter* may have the *freedom* to continue to manage his own insurance arrangements. Using the EFST endorsements, however, the *bank* will consider its *security position* to be superior to that prevailing when an insurer's letter of authority only is used. As such the bank may be willing to grant higher overall lending limits for the export finance facility and consider a finer interest margin.

EXPORT CREDIT POLICY MANAGERS

In recent years some companies, predominantly involved in overseas debt collection, have begun to offer policy management services to their customers. The need was identified when these companies found that, having failed to secure full repayment of an insured debt, customers were unable to sustain claims under their policies because some term or condition of the insurance had been breached.

Accordingly, these debt collection companies obtained 'master policies' from the credit insurer and then allowed their customers access to such policies. Usually such customers must insure all their exporter turnover through the company's master policy.

Under this arrangement, the policy manager is responsible for, amongst other things, the following:

1. Obtaining credit limits on buyers.
2. Validating copy invoices against limits.
3. Making declarations.
4. Making premium payments.
5. Reminding the customer of overdues.

The policy manager will also be willing to arrange for that part of the master policy applicable to a particular exporter to be assigned to that exporter's bank. Furthermore, the policy manager may be willing to agree special arrangements with that bank to confirm to the bank that particular invoices have been declared to the credit insurer.

Benefits

The *exporter* receives professional *help and support* with the management of the insurance arrangements. This may be of especial importance to smaller or first-time exporters. At the same time the *bank* has the *comfort* of knowing that its security (the policy) is being properly managed.

Bank-insured schemes

We shall consider these schemes as follows:

1. Export finance house schemes.
2. Smaller exports schemes.
3. Finance for exports schemes linked to the EFST guarantee issued by the ECGD.

EXPORT FINANCE HOUSE

In the 1970s a great deal of short- and medium-term export finance business was arranged by intermediaries known as confirming houses. These companies had their own ECGD policies. They 'confirmed' to the exporter that payment would be made on shipment provided the exporter produced the agreed documentation. The confirming house then arranged finance for the credit period with a bank, against the security of an ECGD banker's guarantee.

In the late 1970s many banks acquired their own confirming houses. These continued to operate as wholly-owned subsidiaries of the parent bank. As a result, the parent bank continued to enjoy the security of the ECGD's banker's guarantees. In this new guise, these bank-owned confirming houses became known as export finance houses.

At the same time, the ECGD's experience with confirming houses and export finance houses began to deteriorate. This was partly a result of the developing Third World debt crisis. It was also a product of 'adverse discrimination' by exporters. By this we mean that exporters tended to put their least favourable risks to the confirming houses and export finance houses to handle. The result has been that many of these companies have had to curtail or even discontinue their activities against the backing of government insurance and guarantees. Nevertheless, most banks continue to offer export finance house facilities albeit without the benefit of the ECGD's banker's guarantees on the short-term side.

Features

Such a scheme gives 100 per cent finance on shipment, against presentation of agreed documentation. The bank concludes all government insurance arrangements. The bank will also usually have a financial agreement with the overseas buyer. In the event of non-payment by the buyer, the bank bears the uninsured portion of loss (usually 5 or 10 per cent). Charges can be all for the account of the buyer, all for the account of the exporter, or some combination of the two.

Benefits

The *exporter benefits* from *100 per cent essentially non-recourse finance.* In the event of non-payment by the buyer, there is usually no come-back to the exporter provided the terms and conditions of this contract have been fulfilled with the buyer. The approach is also *simple* and *inexpensive*; the exporter does not have to make any insurance arrangements or pay a premium on all export turnover.

The *bank benefits* from the comfort of knowing that the *insurance is in its own name.* As such, it is not exposed to the risk that a third party, i.e. the exporter, might invalidate the insurance.

Given the comparatively high incidence of the buyer default under export finance house schemes in recent years, exporters may well find that, at present, the fee structures proposed by banks for particular facilities are relatively high. Again, the bank and the insurer will usually impose the strictest criteria when approving credit risk, especially private buyer risk.

SMALLER EXPORTS

This scheme was first introduced in 1979 with the small or first-time exporter in mind. The concept was to provide simplified access to government cover and finance for exporters who might be reluctant to conclude their own insurance arrangements direct.

Initially the scheme was restricted to exporters having an export turnover of £500,000 per annum or less. Subsequently this threshold has been raised to £1 million or even £2 million in some cases. Exporters are not required to put all their export turnover under the scheme.

Features

The scheme gives 100 per cent finance on shipment, against the presentation of agreed documentation. The bank concludes all government insurance arrangements. The exporter continues to deal direct with the buyer; there is no direct finance contract between the bank and the buyer. In the event of non-payment by the buyer, the bank bears the uninsured portion of the loss (usually 5 or 10 per cent). All charges are for the account of the exporter and include an interest margin (often 1.5 per cent above the bank's base rate) and a flat invoice fee to cover insurance premium and other costs (often in the range 2–3 per cent).

Benefits

The *exporter benefits* from *100 per cent essentially non-recourse finance.* His primary responsibility is to fulfil the terms and conditions of his contract with his buyer. The scheme is also *simple* to operate and gives him *selective access to government insurance* (i.e. he does not have to declare, and pay premiums, on all his export turnover to the insurer). As such, the scheme is an excellent way for the smaller or first-time exporter simply to obtain insurance cover and finance together. Of course, it is also worth commenting that smaller or first-time exporters are often most in need of insurance cover and finance.

The *bank benefits* from the comfort of knowing that the *government insurance is in its own name.* It also has an excellent means for assisting two key target markets: small firms and exporters.

Although all banks tend to offer this scheme, some have incurred substantial losses. These have arisen as a result of contractual disputes and the commercial failure of buyers. This highlights the need, on the bank's part, to ensure that the exporter is still capable of fulfilling contractual obligations, despite being comparatively small.

FINANCE FOR EXPORTS

This scheme was introduced in 1985 in the wake of the announced withdrawal by the ECGD of the CBG scheme. The main thrust for its introduction came from some banks which were reluctant to continue to finance exports against the assignment only of exporter ECGD policies. These banks were concerned that their principal security, i.e. the ECGD insurance policy, should be in their name and under their direct control.

Features

The scheme gives 90 per cent finance on shipment, against the presentation of agreed documentation. The bank concludes all government insurance arrangements. The exporter continues to deal directly with his buyer. In the event of non-payment by the buyer, the uninsured portion of the loss (usually 10 per cent) is for the account of the exporter. All charges are for the account of the exporter. The exporter must agree to declare all his export turnover under the scheme or an agreed spread.

Benefits

The *exporter benefits* from obtaining *insurance cover and finance from the same point.* As with other bank-insured schemes, his primary responsibility continues to be to fulfil his contractual obligation to his buyers. The *bank benefits* from *direct control of the insurance arrangements.*

Some banks have found this scheme onerous to administer given that the exporter must declare (and the bank must handle) all the exporter's turnover or an agreed spread. Nevertheless many exporters continue to view this scheme as an excellent way of obtaining insurance cover and finance from a single point.

LEGAL ASPECTS

The precise legal construction of each facility varies from bank to bank and from scheme to scheme. The reasons for these variations are not always clear. To some extent, however, they arise as a result of the extent to which the particular bank is relying upon the facility letter itself to secure title to the overseas receivables.

Some of the most common constructions are as follows:

1. Advance against assignment of debt.
2. Debt purchase.
3. Discount without recourse.
4. Goods purchase or undisclosed principal.

Probably all these approaches give the bank adequate title to the overseas receivables as against the exporter, so long as the exporter continues to trade. The position is less clear in the event of the failure of the exporter and the appointment of a liquidator or receiver. For this reason, some banks choose separately to secure title to the overseas receivables by way of duly registered assignments or debentures.

Particular mention needs to be made of the goods purchase or undisclosed principle approach. This has already been referred to above when discussing ECGD endorsements and, in particular, the sales to finance company endorsement. Some banks and finance institutions adopted this approach because they considered that, having technically purchased and given good value for the goods to be sold by the exporter, they had effectively avoided any charge held by any other bank over the exporter's receivables. Recent legal decisions suggest that this approach is flawed. As a result, some banks are moving away from this approach.

The exporter will, of course, wish to review the legal aspects with his own legal advisors. In particular the exporter will wish to establish the following:

1. What documents need to be presented to obtain drawdowns under the facility?
2. What instructions for payment must be given to the buyer and quoted on the invoice?
3. What charges are payable and when?
4. What arrangements are agreed to allow for negotiations with the buyer after shipment, for example for the issue of credit notes or the extension of the due date for payment?
5. To what extent does the bank need to monitor the management of the insurance policy?
6. In what circumstances may the bank exercise recourse to the exporter?
7. What provisions are made in respect of currency invoices and for currency advances?
8. When may the bank terminate the facility and what notice must the bank give?

If the exporter and/or his legal advisors are not satisfied with one or more clauses of the proposed facility letter, the matter should be raised with the bank. Many banks are prepared to consider proposed amendments.

Ultimately, if the exporter is not satisfied with the bank's response in this area, an approach to an alternative bank should be considered. At the risk of repetition, it should always be remembered that bank competition in this area is very keen.

Auditing aspects

We have mentioned already that some exporters make use of these schemes to obtain access to off-balance sheet finance. In this area it is important to understand that each auditor will use professional judgement in the particular circumstances of each case. It is impossible, therefore, to generalise.

It is noticeable, however, that auditors are stricter in their requirements than was the case two or three years ago. They will tend to pay particular attention to the following two features:

1. The strength of the recourse clause, if any, in the agreed facility letter.
2. The treatment of interest charges.

It is recommended that exporters seek written advice from their auditors in this matter. If this benefit is important, confirmation of treatment by the auditor should be sought well in advance of the financial year end.

Other insurers

So far we have referred extensively to ECGD export credit insurance. It is necessary to mention, however, that other underwriters are now offering comparable insurance programmes. In particular, Trade Indemnity PLC has been providing such insurance for over five years now and is reported to be underwriting exports worth about £3bn per annum already (compared with ECGD £13bn per annum). Non state-owned credit insurers are able, particularly in the short-term field, to service exporters world-wide and multi-sourcing.

Trade Indemnity has an advantage over the ECGD at present in that, in addition to export credit insurance, it can also offer its policyholders comprehensive UK domestic credit insurance programmes. Indeed this remains Trade Indemnity's core business with UK sales underwritten each year amounting to something in the region of £30bn per annum.

The bank schemes linked to the assignment of ECGD policies managed by exporters, are also generally made available now against the assignment of Trade Indemnity export credit insurance policies. Trade Indemnity has not so far moved into the area of bank-insured schemes in any significant way.

Banks are also adapting schemes to accommodate insurance provided by other underwriters including American International Underwriters, Pan-financial, Namur, NCM (Dutch underwriter) and Hermes (German under-writer). Some of these underwriters specialise in 'catastrophe' cover. This involves a layer of cover above an annual aggregate first loss, with a comparatively modest maximum liability. For comparison, traditional ECGD cover is sometimes described as 'ground-up' cover in that a 90 or 95 per cent indemnity is offered in respect of all risks, with a comparatively substantial maximum liability.

Short-term schemes are less readily adaptable to 'catastrophe' cover. Nevertheless most banks now have some experience of structuring finance against the backing of such cover.

Export Credits Guarantee Department privatisation

The UK government has announced its intention to reconstitute the Insurance Services Group of ECGD, responsible for short-term programmes, as a public limited company. This will take place in 1991 or shortly thereafter. Subsequently it is the intention to introduce private capital. This should enable the ECGD to begin to compete more effectively with other European underwriters. In particular, the ECGD will be free to provide cover in respect of UK domestic risk and cover to non-UK suppliers. Some exporters fear, however, that prices are likely to rise and cover will become more restricted in some high-risk markets. The banks are monitoring developments closely. They are anxious to see the new company properly capitalised, otherwise they may be forced to consider whether their current exposures under the ECGD-backed short-term schemes can be justified.

Conclusion

The market-place for short-term schemes is currently very dynamic. Given the backing of credit insurance, the financing business is very attractive to banks. As a result, the range of options available is expanding whilst the promotional effort remains at a high level. All this is good news for the exporter seeking finance. Provided careful thought is given at the outset to what is required, most exporters should be able to obtain the most appropriate financial package.

6

Credit insurance from the private sector

TERRY BRIDGMAN
Director of Reinsurance, Trade Indemnity Group plc

Background

For most of the twentieth century the provision of credit insurance by national export credit agencies has been taken for granted. Whenever risks have loomed, those in business and bankers involved in international trade have leant heavily on the security it provides, knowing that should their overseas customers become insolvent or foreign government action prevent payment getting through they would be reimbursed for up to 90 per cent of their losses.

But now the situation is changing rapidly. Public sector credit insurance, especially for short-term trade, is fast becoming a thing of the past. Governments are keen to rid themselves of loss-making export credit schemes, both to reduce the burden on their treasuries and to comply with international demands for free, unsubsidised trade.

Ironically, just when national export credit agencies are being dismantled, the need for credit insurance is greater than ever. With new markets opening up all around the world, international trade is increasing. It has been left to private sector credit insurers to fill this gap.

There are advantages and disadvantages to this scenario. The main disadvantage is that exporters and importers can no longer rely on limitless government coffers, which have enabled many contracts to be signed in the face of considerable commercial and political risks. Gradually, artificially low lending rates are being phased out. In July 1988, for example, developed (Category 1) countries were removed from the Consensus system of subsidised rates of interest. The days of unquestioned, unconditional guarantees have also passed, and national agencies have been instructed to become more commercially-minded, and therefore selective in offering security – the United Kingdom's ECGD, for instance, owing to uncommercial decisions in the past now has provisions against bad debt totalling £3.2 billion. The action now by governments of further reducing their backing for export credits is disheartening to many who are involved in international trade.

A major advantage is that the private sector has introduced the concepts of service, creativity and flexibility to the credit insurance market. This ability to react quickly and innovatively to exporters' needs is very welcome, as the nature of international trade is changing rapidly. The emergence of flourishing economies in the Far East, a barrier-free Europe and new markets in Eastern Europe has brought different trading conditions and new, unfamiliar risks.

Although in the long term there will be many opportunities for trade and investment with Eastern European nations, at present their economies are in upheaval and there are almost no reliable indicators of companies' creditworthiness. To trade profitably with this part of the world requires extensive market knowledge and tight credit control procedures. Instability in the Middle and Far East and Africa means that political risk is hard to predict and therefore expert knowledge and insurance cover are essential.

Even Western Europe, where there is little or no political risk, is facing uncertain times. The Single Market will lead to fierce competition and in 1990 over 100,000 companies are expected to become insolvent in the EC alone. Other predictions suggest that as many as 50 per cent of all EC firms could either become insolvent or be taken over after the creation of the Single European Market. So commercial risk is increasing.

The decline in the number of projects in Third World countries has led to increased emphasis on inter-OECD trade. Whereas the terms of trade with the developing countries almost always involved various forms of security, such as letters of credit or escrow accounts, OECD business is normally done on open account, where there is no inherent security of payment. With more and more customers asking for more frequent, smaller shipments of goods to fit in with new 'just-in-time' supply and distribution methods, letters of credit (l/cs) are becoming unfeasible, as well as unpopular. To draw up an l/c for each shipment would involve a disproportionate amount of documentation and expense.

In all the above instances, it can be seen that information and efficient credit procedures are needed, as well as credit insurance. A significant advance made by certain private sector insurers has been to integrate credit insurance into the whole credit management process. It is always better to avoid bad debts in the first place, rather than claiming on insurance. Claims take up management time and even if 90 per cent of losses are reimbursed, that still leaves 10 per cent to be borne by the exporter, or the bank if the exporter goes out of business.

The role of credit insurers

Four main areas are involved in credit management. These are: establishing the ability of your customers to pay; monitoring that ability; maintaining cash flow budgets; and dealing with recalcitrant payers.

Credit insurers provide help on all these fronts. Their overriding concern is not just to reimburse firms for the money they cannot retrieve from a customer in receivership or liquidation, but rather to see that their client companies either avoid such losses in the first place, or at least minimise their losses when they are otherwise locked into historical dependent supplier situations.

Ascertaining a customer's creditworthiness

One of the most important factors in reducing trading risk is securing comprehensive information on existing and potential customers to discover the likelihood of being paid on time. But ascertaining a customer's creditworthiness requires other data besides that which can be gained from a historical balance sheet. Trading pattern and payment record, not only to a single supplier but also to the sector generally, are also important. To this one must add all the trends in the customer's industry sector as a whole. To complete the picture requires facts on local, regional, national, continental and even world trends.

Taking as an example an electronics and computer manufacturer in a provincial town, one can illustrate the impact of various factors on the appraisal of the company's future creditworthiness. The balance sheet may, for instance, look weak, with relatively little capital backing. However, on further investigation it may become clear that the firm has a full order book and pays its suppliers promptly. A glance at industry figures would show that electronic and computer manufacture is a growing sector where failures are running at a low rate compared to other sectors. Regional trends, on the other hand, show that the number of insolvencies in the area is the highest in the country, and the national outlook, with declining consumer demand, anticipates the greatest impact will be on particular areas of this sector. Continuing the analysis on the next level, one would see that developments in Europe, with the Single Market imminent, bring increased opportunities. Yet, finally, the world-wide view indicates the very real chance of increased opportunities in Europe being snapped up by companies in the Far East, which hold a very strong position in the electronics and computer field and have been investing heavily in Europe.

Even this simplistic analysis shows the wide range of data that needs to be gathered and interpreted to make a sound decision on whether to do business with consumer electronic firms in provincial towns. This example also shows that, as different bits of information can, taken alone, lead to contradictory judgements on a customer's creditworthiness, it is dangerous to work from snippets of data. For example, companies dealing with some of the troubled household names featured in the Press in 1990, might have been happy to extend them a large amount of credit in 1989, seeing that they were all amongst the European Top 500. Many firms that did so, acting on one piece of data alone, now regret their action.

Credit insurers' livelihoods depend on their ability to predict which companies, in which industry sectors, in which markets, are going to become insolvent. To aid them in this task they gather micro- and macro-economic information every day from myriad sources around the world.

Trade Indemnity PLC has led the world in the development of private sector export credit and political risk insurance. It has, for example, information on over a million UK companies on its own database and has access to similar databases throughout the world, through cooperation agreements with other credit institutions. The insurer also has an economics intelligence team, whose sole task is to gather data on industrial and economic trends. This information, along with statistics on bad debts and failures, is published in Trade Indemnity's *Quarterly Economic Review*.

Teams of underwriters at Trade Indemnity specialise in particular industry sectors, monitoring the fate of individual companies and trends in that sector throughout the world. There are also teams of underwriters monitoring country risks to provide political risk cover.

A unique aspect of the information credit insurers have at their fingertips is the data from their day-to-day business. Through their clients, insurers have information on companies' levels of trading, how much they owe and how promptly they pay their suppliers. Very often the insurer will see world economic trends developing abroad before they affect the home market.

It is clear, then, that very few people can boast of having as much up-to-date information and expertise as credit insurers when it comes to assessing creditworthiness.

Determining credit levels

Companies that use a credit insurer benefit from the competitive advantage provided by their credit insurer's unrivalled data. Underwriters will check their clients' existing and potential customers and then use their specialist knowledge to suggest appropriate credit levels for each customer.

In many cases, it will become apparent that a customer is financially stronger than was thought and more credit can safely be extended, thus increasing overall turnover and profitability. Companies can trade up to the insurer's credit levels confidently, knowing that the underwriter will back his judgement with cash.

Minimising credit risk

As well as having access to detailed information, it is important for companies to have good internal credit procedures. When a company first takes out a credit insurance policy, the insurer will look at its credit management system in relation to its business and, if appropriate, suggest techniques for improving cash flow. Several insurers also have collections divisions for dealing with late payers. An insurer usually has a fair amount of clout, since a company that refuses to pay may affect its credit rating, which could reduce its ability to get insurance cover and credit.

Although good information and efficient credit control can minimise credit risks, certain bad debts are unpredictable. For instance, no one can foresee when there will be an outbreak of *Salmonella* or mad cow disease, which puts egg producers and butchers out of business. Or there may be a new invention, which puts manufacturers of suddenly obsolete goods out of business. Alternatively, companies may suffer through the domino effect. This is where a large company goes bust and causes a chain reaction of failures through all its suppliers and their suppliers and so on. Government coups, wars and suchlike which may also stop payment getting through are also often hard to predict (e.g. Iraq's invasion of Kuwait).

This is where credit insurance comes in. It acts as a backstop, ensuring that a company will not fail or suffer a sharp decline in profits, owing to unforeseen customer failures.

Defining credit insurance objectives

Before a company takes out a credit insurance policy, however, it should analyse its risks and consider what level and type of protection it needs.

First, it is necessary to identify which risks need to be insured. A company may wish to insure all its business, or just a portion of it. The latter may involve cover for a defined geographical area, such as all non-European markets; the sales of a particular product; or perhaps the company's top ten customers. One can also choose to insure against the insolvency of suppliers. If vital supplies do not arrive, very often a contract cannot be fulfilled and, in any event, substantial deposits will be lost. If an exporter already has a secure form of payment from its customers, it may wish to insure only against losses arising from foreign government action, such as restrictions on foreign exchange or an import embargo.

The objectives of insuring credit must then be defined. Most firms will be eager to avoid going bust, but they may also wish to protect profits, and results. Non-protection could well adversely affect the short-term share price. Alternatively, the objective may be to instil discipline into subsidiary companies, by ensuring they adhere to the insurer's proposed credit limits on all contracts over a certain value. Or one may wish simply to benefit from the insurer's data on existing and potential customers.

Having considered the risks and objectives, a company must decide on the level of indemnity required. The target may be to be reimbursed for as close to the full value of losses as possible. Or a large company may decide to stand a part of any losses itself. It may be desirable to be covered for a portion of the loss on each contract insured or to be paid in full for all losses, over and above a pre-set level, that occur within the financial year.

Choosing a policy

The next step is to choose the policy that best suits your needs. In recent years, since the private sector entered the credit insurance field in earnest, the range of credit insurance products has increased dramatically.

The standard credit insurance policy covers a company's whole turnover, with up to 90 per cent of each loss being reimbursed within thirty days of proof of insolvency. The concept of whole turnover is nowadays very flexible and can comprise all sales of a particular product or all sales to a certain market or group of markets.

Whole turnover cover usually contains a 'first loss' clause. Here all losses above a certain level are covered by the insurer. The insurer and the client will also agree on a 'discretionary limit', stating a contract value level above which company executives must refer to the insurer for a check on the customer's creditworthiness and a credit limit.

'Excess of loss' policies work on a different basis, covering all losses above a certain aggregate threshold. The threshold can be set to reflect the degree to which the company wishes to self-insure, but which in any case must be high enough to reflect the catastrophe protection which this cover is designed to provide. There is no discretionary limit and the company is left to run its credit management by itself. This type of cover is popular with large corporations, who only need to protect against extreme losses.

Large one-off deals can be insured using specific contract cover and there is also a special policy to protect against supplier risks. Political risk insurance, which guards against governmental action, can be added to commercial risk cover or taken out separately.

One of the most significant developments in private sector credit insurance recently is the trend towards pan-European policies covering all of a company's domestic and overseas business under the terms of one policy.

A combined domestic/export policy has several advantages. First, it is simple to document and operate. Until recently it has been necessary for a company that does both domestic and export trade to negotiate two policies with separate underwriters. Now, only one negotiation is required and one set of paperwork. Second, by combining domestic and export, companies end up with a larger policy, which normally commands better terms. Firms with a small volume of export sales, which alone is too small to interest the insurer, can tack this portion on to their domestic turnover under the combined policy and cover it at a reasonable cost. The same thing can be done for firms which mostly export and only have a small amount of domestic business.

A combined policy is especially helpful to companies that want to grasp the opportunities of the Single European Market. It will break down the division between home and export markets, enabling companies to develop the correct frame of mind to trade throughout Europe.

Pan-European cover has been available for some time from niche players in the credit insurance market, but it is only now that it is becoming more widely available. Trade Indemnity, the largest private sector export credit insurer, has a policy called Multi-Market, which combines cover for all business in Europe and OECD countries. Trade Indemnity has combined the best aspects of domestic and export policies for Multi-Market. Traditionally, export policies have had a lower first loss clause, while domestic cover was extended to a larger portion of the company's total business. The Multi-Market policy offers the option of no first loss at all and reimburses up to 90 per cent of each debt. Another advantage is that domestic underwriters with specialist knowledge of various trades and export underwriters familiar with overseas markets, work together on each Multi-Market policy. The domestic underwriter, however, will remain the sole point of contact with the client.

If a company cannot find an existing type of policy that suits its business, private sector insurers can tailor-make cover. In fact, the private market is willing to insure any risk as long as it makes commercial sense.

The cost of insurance

Premiums are often worked out on a different basis in the private market. The standard credit insurance premium is a charge on turnover, usually a fraction of 1 per cent. But as well as a charge on turnover, cover can be costed on the level of risk, which may be low even though volume is high. Excess of loss cover is costed on a different basis again: a tranche of cover, with set lower and upper limits, is bought at a fixed rate. The exact cost obviously depends on the level and nature of the risks involved. If a company chooses to offer a good spread of business to an insurer the premium will be lower than if only high-risk contracts are included. On a standard policy, the level set for first loss will affect the price. The addition or omission of political risk cover will also substantially alter the final cost.

In many instances the cost of credit insurance is less than a company's contingency fund for bad debts. Furthermore, credit insurance is a calculable cost, which once budgeted for avoids any nasty surprises in terms of losses because of customer insolvencies.

Public sector insurers

Public sector insurers do not offer the same flexibility as the private market. For instance, combined domestic and overseas cover is usually not available, since public schemes have been wholly geared to supporting exports and do not deal at all with business in the home market. In fact, the very existence of government-run export credit agencies in intra-European trade is out of keeping with the spirit of the single market.

Some argue that technically trade within Europe will be classed as domestic business rather than exports. If this were so, then the national agencies would not be allowed to cover trade between EC countries under their present constitutions. Others believe that backing from a government agency will represent unfair competition and consequently be disallowed. Several EC countries are already starting to hand over insurance of European business to the private sector. Some believe that the remaining high-risk exports to the developing countries, which are uninsurable in the private market, should be handled by one supra-national European export credit agency, offering the same terms to all EC exporters.

As government support for international trade is slowly removed, cooperation between banks and credit insurers, who have traditionally worked together to assist exporters, is increasingly important, for neither alone can shoulder the full burden of providing security for exports.

The role of banks

Amidst the increasing competition for corporate business, the banks have found themselves taking more and more trading risks off their customers' shoulders and on to their own balance sheets. Gone are the days when the norm was finance given with either full recourse to the client, and/or a charge on assets, and/or an unconditional guarantee from an export credit agency. Non-recourse finance is often the order of the day, whether it be factoring, forfaiting or receivables purchasing.

Credit insurers, of course, have always dealt in risk. But they have moved closer to the banks in providing a wider range of flexible, or tailor-made, products, catering for the differing needs of all sizes and types of company. Furthermore, insurers are increasingly stressing the use of security as a means of obtaining financing, often on better terms.

There is, naturally, the potential for conflict between banks and insurers, each offering alternative solutions to covering trading risks. But the course that both, thankfully, seem to be pursuing is cooperation. The greatest benefit is clearly where resources are pooled and both sets of services are complementary. Many banks have developed special schemes in conjunction with credit insurers for export receivables.

When assessing how much to lend and at what rates, banks tend to look at the value of a firm's assets. Outstanding credit normally accounts for 40 per cent of a company's current assets. Therefore, if a firm is insured against bad debts, it is a better risk to the bank and this should be reflected in the terms of the finance offered. Essentially, both companies and banks benefit from the insurers taking a share of the risk. Many credit committees judge the value of insurance directly to the bank as of greater value than any assignment of the companies' interests, because performance of the insurance policy conditions is then within their own control.

In any event, the advantages of insuring trade credit have long been recognised in the export field. Banks traditionally have close links with national export credit agencies. Indeed, many of the banks' export financing schemes are based on either the exporter's or the bank's own export credit insurance policy.

The assistance that credit insurers can give to banks is now an important factor in maintaining growth in world trade. With their balance sheets not yet fully recovered from the battering they have taken because of the Third World debt crisis, banks are being squeezed by new, tougher capital adequacy ratios being adopted world-wide. This is beginning to restrict the areas and the extent of bank lending, as financiers are being forced to look increasingly to higher-margin business.

Insurers can provide valuable extra capacity. This can be done by 'securitising' or 'enhancing' certain assets on the banks' balance sheets. Bonds, for example, are seen as contingent liabilities and thus use a large chunk of the bank's capacity, historically at too low a price. The purchase of insurance can be used to improve the percentage weighting of the asset which in turn improves capacity. This allows the bank to take on other profitable business. The premium need not be high and can probably be catered for within the increased margins that are in any event necessary.

Trade Indemnity has worked on several deals with banks, ranging from one-offs to broad policies. An umbrella policy was set up for Midland Bank as part of its Midfes (finance for exports) scheme. Under the scheme, Trade Indemnity undertook to reimburse the bank in the event a claim could not be sustained by the exporter: for example, if a client invalidates his insurance or fails to perform on his policy.

Assessing the insurer's ability to cover the risk

The ability of an insurance company to cover large risks is a matter of major concern for the customer over the security of its protection. 'Will the claim be paid?' is a question not always deemed necessary when dealing with governmental ECAs. The movement of export credit support away from government into the private sector will inevitably mean that companies have to assess the strengths of competitive insurers – in the same way as they do for their customers.

The customer is helped in his assessment by the fact that insurance companies are subject to public regulations over liquidity and insolvency ratios to liability (among many other issues), which depend on capital strengths and/or adequate reinsurance support for their operations. There is much concern about the private sector carrying the political risks involved in many export credit transactions. Reinsurance support is particularly relevant here.

Although such political risks have been written since the mid-1970s by Lloyd's of London, American International Group, PanFinancial Ltd and the Pool d'Assurances des Risques Internationaux et Speciaux (PARIS), they have tended to supply protection for single contracts and thus complementary support to that given by national agencies. They did not attempt to provide true alternative coverage. It was Trade Indemnity who pioneered the full private sector export credit alternative in 1984 and who persuaded the international private sector reinsurance market to add its considerable capacity support in 1990.

The role of brokers

The increasing number of services available to cover trade risk means that there are solutions to most risk problems. The only difficulty might be in keeping track of all the options. This is where brokers come in.

Specialist credit insurance brokers offer advice and administrative assistance when choosing, negotiating and renewing policies. Unlike many intermediaries in other fields, specialist credit insurance brokers must measure up to certain stringent criteria. They must be committed to credit insurance, displaying expertise in credit and risk management. They have to have trained staff who can provide the right level of professional advice.

These brokers can often help companies to choose a policy best suited to their needs, owing to their detailed knowledge of the market and the various products available. Subsequently, the broker becomes the company's interface with the insurer. Claims are also a major function of the specialist broker, who ensures all the documentation is correct.

The future

Credit insurance is a vital part of international finance. Together, the forty insurers who belong to the Berne Union cover about $500 billion in trade credit around the world. This security protects exporters, importers and banks, and allows them to have confidence in increasing their levels of business.

The wider range of policies being introduced by the private sector has made credit insurance relevant to a greater number of companies and is helping them to adapt to a world that is changing economically and politically at a frightening rate. Added value services from the private sector mean that credit insurers not only protect the balance sheet, but also provide valuable information on companies and market trends which helps the sales and marketing effort.

Reduced support for international trade from the public sector is, of course, a great loss. But if bankers and company executives take time to find out what is now on offer from private sector insurers, they may well find that their businesses run more smoothly.

7

Long-term and project financing

ROSAMUND BLOMFIELD-SMITH
Assistant Director, J. Henry Schroder Wagg & Co. Ltd

When a company is seeking to provide finance in support of a proposal to undertake a turnkey project overseas, it is very likely to have recourse to one or more of the financing techniques discussed elsewhere in this book: many of the techniques are the same as those commonly employed in the financing of any other contract for the supply of capital or semi-capital goods. There are, however, some aspects, related particularly to the size and complexity normally associated with a turnkey project, that require special consideration. This chapter identifies those factors and seeks to give some guidance as to the financing techniques that may be appropriate.

Turnkey contracts for development projects fall into two broad categories: first, those to be undertaken by a public sector body or, more unusually, a major private sector entity, where full guarantees are available for the loans which are provided to finance the project and, second, projects, often undertaken on the basis of a concession of finite duration, for which bank or government guarantees are not available. It is in the second of these areas, often referred to as 'limited recourse financing' or 'pure' project financing, that the greatest complications arise. It is, however, helpful to address the problems of government-guaranteed project financing before moving on to the complexities of limited recourse financing: most of the basic financing techniques of the government-guaranteed financing can be used in both contexts.

Government-guaranteed project financing

There has been a marked decline over the last five years or so in the type of project for which many UK companies bid so successfully in the 1970s and early 1980s: major infrastructure or greenfield industrial projects in developing countries implemented on the basis of a turnkey contract let by the government of the country concerned and with a requirement for supporting finance for which the government concerned makes available its guarantee. Nevertheless some such contracts are still let and the terms of the financial package which is offered frequently have an important impact on the award of those contracts.

Analysing the customer's evaluation practices

The first step in developing a financial package to support a bid for a project is to analyse the basis on which the government or other entity calling for bids will evaluate the financial aspects of those bids. A proper evaluation process will involve a calculation of the present value of all payments which will be due under the loan or loans which are proposed, using a discount rate or rates selected by the buyer. In some countries all such payments, in whatever currency, are treated equally. More sophisticated borrowers will have a system of weighting currencies, normally by applying different discount rates to the various currencies involved.

Some buyers, particularly in the developing world, fail to undertake any kind of detailed analysis of financial offers and will look to, for instance, a high level of grant funding or a low interest rate or a certain currency and will fail to make a quantitative analysis of their relative merits. If evaluation is to be on a simplistic basis of this kind, it goes without saying that it is helpful to know this: it may well be possible to structure the financing package to accommodate particular whims, and it should be emphasised that, even when a buyer employs a consulting engineer to carry out a detailed technical evaluation of bids received, it is by no means uncommon in the Third World for financial offers to be evaluated on an extremely unscientific basis.

A slightly more sophisticated evaluation, which calculates the present value of all payments due but takes no account of different currencies, clearly favours low interest rate currencies such as the yen, and the exporter will wish to see his financial offer structured accordingly. Where a sophisticated financial analysis is to be carried out, it will be important to ascertain the basis on which the discount rates to be used for different currencies will be selected: there are almost always some which are, for one reason or another, more favourable than others in the context of market conditions at the time.

It is not just in the context of deciding in which currency to denominate a financing package that it is important to have information about the discount rates to be used in calculating the present value of a financial offer: it will affect a range of issues related to the timing of payments due from the buyer/borrower and it may well be possible to structure the financial offer to take maximum advantage of the evaluation methodology.

It is often not difficult to ascertain what methodology is to be used for evaluating financial offers. It is in a buyer's interests to make quite clear what he is looking for and how he will evaluate different alternatives, and the information is sometimes contained in the tender documents. When this is not the case, the importance of obtaining the maximum available information and, if necessary, making some informed guesses cannot be over-emphasised: failure to do this is all too frequent and obviously amounts to an exercise in shooting in the dark.

Officially-backed finance

Whatever the detailed methodology to be used in bid evaluation, finance subsidised by the exporter's government will usually – though not invariably – be favourably evaluated. In the case of UK exporters, this means that the main component of the financing package is usually finance backed by the ECGD. The ECGD facility most frequently used in the context of the financing of a major project is the buyer credit. In most cases where medium-term finance is required and in competition with the other bidders, official state finance is employed. All major trading nations have departments to carry out this task and the majority subscribe to the rules for competition agreed by the Berne Union. This applies in France as it does to Eximbank in Washington. The fundamental framework is largely modelled upon the ECGD.

THE BUYER CREDIT FACILITY

Under a buyer credit arrangement, the exporter appoints a bank to make a loan to his overseas buyer. The proceeds of the loan are disbursed by the bank direct to the British exporter, on the basis set out in the supply/construction contract and the buyer/borrower repays the bank over an agreed period. The ECGD enters into an agreement with the bank under which it (a) guarantees to make good to the bank any amounts of principal and interest not paid by the borrower and (b) pays to (or occasionally receives from) the bank the difference between the fixed and usually subsidised interest rate paid by the borrower and a market rate. The ECGD charges an insurance premium for its guarantee which is payable by the exporter and is normally included in the contract price (see Figure 7.1).

SUPPLIER CREDITS

Hitherto, almost all ECGD-backed loans made available to finance projects have made use of the buyer credit mechanism. The main disadvantage of the buyer credit is that it is a relatively cumbersome mechanism and evidenced by a full loan agreement, with the result that the negotiation of the documentation can be expected to last at least six months. The supplier credit, under which the bank makes funding available to the exporter for passing on to the buyer in the form of extended payment terms, is much

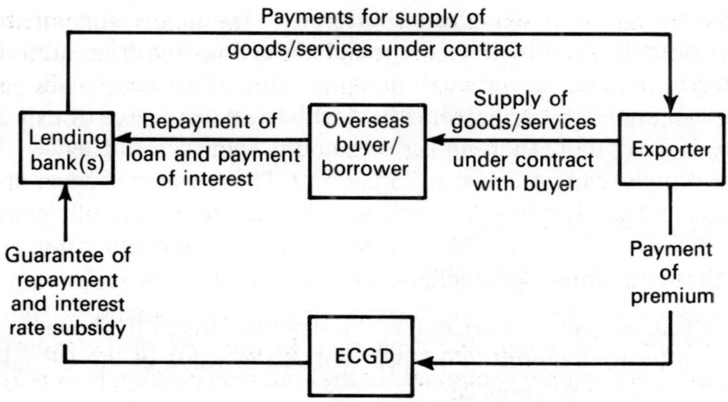

Figure 7.1 The ECGD-backed buyer credit

simpler than the buyer credit procedurally but has suffered from a number of disadvantages, of which the most important has been that, in the event of default by the buyer, the ECGD has had recourse to the supplier for 10 per cent of unpaid amounts. (In the case of a buyer credit, recourse can only be taken to the exporter in the event of proven negligence under the supply contract.) A further major difficulty is that progress payments, which would normally be a feature of the type of contract associated with a project, are difficult to accommodate within the supplier credit mechanism.

The ECGD has developed a new supplier credit facility which will not involve recourse to the supplier (except in the case of the latter's proven negligence). The progress payment problem remains, however, and the security requirements have been tightened so that the buyer will be required to provide the guarantee of a first-class bank. This seems likely to continue to limit the use which is made of the supplier credit mechanism, despite the improvements in the recourse arrangements, particularly as, with the requirement to provide a bank guarantee, the supplier credit will come into direct competition with the à forfait market (see Chapter 10) and may well be the less attractive of the two options. Exporters need to be aware of the supplier credit mechanism and watch how the new arrangements develop in practice but it seems likely that the buyer credit will continue to be the principal vehicle for making export credit available to a project.

TERMS AND CONDITIONS FOR CREDITS BACKED BY THE EXPORT CREDITS GUARANTEE DEPARTMENT

The terms available for an ECGD-backed credit – whether a buyer or supplier credit – vary according to the country of the borrower and are governed by the terms of the OECD Consensus on government-supported export credits to which all the major exporting countries subscribe. The Consensus stipulates the maximum percentage of the value of the goods and services from the country concerned which can be covered by export credit. This is never more than 85 per cent and in some cases (defence contracts, for example) can be as low as 75 per cent. The question of cover of non-UK goods and services is a grey area which needs to be carefully explored. In general terms ECGD may provide cover for one or more (but not usually all at the same time) of the following:

1. Local goods and services (i.e. those originating in the buyer's country) up to a maximum of 15 per cent of the value of the UK goods and services to be supplied.
2. Goods and services of EC origin up to a maximum of 30 per cent of the value of UK goods and services to be supplied.
3. Goods and services of third country (i.e. none of the above) origin, up to 15 per cent of the value of UK goods and services to be supplied.

In accordance with the Consensus, subsidised credit is no longer available for so-called 'rich' markets and the rest are divided into 'intermediate' and 'poor', with the agreed rate for 'intermediate' markets further divided so as to provide for a slightly higher interest rate for the repayment periods in excess of five years which are normally required for the financing of a project and a lower rate for credits with two- to five-year repayment periods. The rates are reviewed every six months against a basket of market rates. In recent years, during which sterling interest rates have often been high in relation to other currencies in the Consensus basket, particularly the US dollar, sterling-denominated buyer credits at Consensus rates have frequently contained a very significant element of subsidy. Where this has been properly evaluated by the overseas buyer, it has produced an important competitive advantage for the UK exporter.

These so-called Consensus rates are used for currencies in which the market rate at the time is the same or higher than the agreed rate. The Consensus also stipulates a commercial interest reference rate (CIRR) for all currencies, reviewed monthly. These rates can, in principle, be used for currencies for which market rates are lower than the prevailing Consensus rate but they are, in practice, rarely competitive.

Where an exporter is taking full responsibility for a project, the repayment period of the ECGD-backed facility will normally run from completion of the project and will be between five and ten years, sometimes producing a total life of thirteen to fourteen years. This is another area in which the Consensus rules permit some latitude and in which the exporter will need to work closely with his appointed bank to ensure that, as a minimum, the repayment period offered in support of his bid is no shorter than that of his competitors.

In exchange for giving its guarantee to the lending bank, the ECGD charges a premium to the exporter, normally included in the latter's price. The ECGD is currently reviewing the basis on which it charges premium in an attempt to ensure that the premium charged reflects the risks involved in individual cases. Like all the export credit agencies, the ECGD has had a poor claims record in recent years and premiums will rise significantly for some markets. A full evaluation needs to be undertaken, preferably using the buyer's methodology, of the relationship between the cost of premium and the benefit to be obtained from the subsidised finance before any decision is taken to opt for ECGD-backed finance.

Despite the premium charge, the ECGD-backed credit remains the basic tool of the exporter seeking to obtain project business in the developing world, very broadly defined and including countries such as the USSR, Hong Kong and South Korea to which that label may arguably not apply at all. It is not invariably the best solution, however, even in such markets and where it is, it may need to be used as part of a more complex financial package to ensure that the exporter derives maximum competitive advantage from its use. Some of the devices which may be used are described below.

Aid

The question of aid–trade–provision (ATP) funding is covered in detail in Chapter 11 but it is important to note here that the possibility of ATP funding must be examined at an early juncture. The sums available where ATP support is agreed – an outright grant for a minimum (and usually, it has to be said, also a maximum) of 35 per cent of the value of UK goods and services supplied, normally with the balancing 65 per cent funded by export credit on the terms discussed above (or the equivalent 35 per cent grant element structured together with the ECGD-backed credit in the form of a soft loan) – will clearly have an overwhelming impact on contract award: from the buyer's point of view, ATP support is tantamount to a 35 per cent reduction in the bidder's price.

Applications for ATP support are made through the Department of Trade and Industry. Unlike ECGD cover, which is allocated on a first-come, first-served basis, the limited ATP budget is allocated on the basis of the relative merits of different applications. Applicants are required to demonstrate that winning the contract to which the application relates would have important benefits for the development of the industry concerned in the United Kingdom, particularly in the context of employment and/or that it would have major commercial benefits in terms of opening up a new market, acting as a reference project for others in the same area, etc. Of far more importance, however, the applicant has to demonstrate to the satisfaction of the Overseas Development Administration that the project is 'developmentally sound', i.e. that it will be to the overall economic benefit to the country concerned and is a proper subject for priority treatment in the context of that country's development.

Application for ATP funding is a complex issue and an early start is essential: the data required for the application may take some time to assemble and both the formulation of the application to the committee which adjudicates the allocation of the funds and its subsequent passage through the committee can take some months, particularly if there are difficulties with the Overseas Development Administration's enquiries into the 'developmental' aspects of the case.

Multi-contract and multinational projects

It is sometimes the case that a major project overseas involves the award of several parallel contracts, all to British companies. The financing of these contracts is normally effected through a government-backed project line of credit. This involves the establishment of a single loan facility on a buyer credit basis which is available for disbursement to all the exporters concerned rather than just for one. From the exporter's point of view this does not present any special complexities.

In the 1970s, project lines of credit were quite common but the increased internationalisation of project business and greater sophistication of buyers means that they are now less so: it is more and more frequent to see the different parts of, say, a major power station, awarded to companies from different countries. Where these contracts are placed in parallel, rather than under the umbrella of a single overall turnkey contract, the financing of the ones for which the exporter is not responsible is of no concern to the exporter (except insofar as they set precedents which the buyer may expect matched for the parallel contracts).

The complexities arise when the exporter is bidding for a turnkey contract and decides that, either because the goods concerned are not available in the home market or because they can be more cheapily supplied from overseas, he wishes to place substantial sub-contracts overseas. He may be able to finance these under his government-backed buyer credit under the arrangements for the financing of EC and third country supply described above. If the amounts involved are substantial, however, the bidder for the turnkey contract will need to ensure that separate credits are available in support of the different contracts.

It is normally best for the exporter to ask his bank to make preliminary enquiries as to the credit likely to be available to his buyer from countries in which he has possible sub-contractors in mind. In this way, he can exclude from the outset sub-contractors whose governments have no – or hopelessly insufficient – cover available for the market concerned. More detailed enquiries and lobbying are, however, normally best carried out by the potential sub-contractor who would normally be asked to submit not only his price and technical specifications but also details of the credit which he can offer in support of his bid.

The main contractor must then carry out a full present value calculation of the proposed financing, including the impact of the currency in which it is proposed that the loan should be denominated, obviously as far as possible using the methodology which the ultimate client will adopt.

Commercial bank funding

Buyers will usually ask for finance in respect of 100 per cent of the proposed contract price. Where this is so and where aid is not available to bring the government-supported funding up to 100 per cent of the value of the contract, the raising of the uncovered element may present considerable difficulties. The funds will certainly need to be raised in close conjunction with the syndication of the export credit, with banks awarded a pro rata share of the more attractive export credit in exchange for agreeing to put up some of the unguaranteed funding. It is in cases such as these that the exporter will need to make full use of the banking relationships he has built up!

For more creditworthy borrowers, export credit will not necessarily be the most attractive option when the cost of the credit insurance premium is taken into consideration, and for the richest markets no subsidy is, in any case, available (although that may not necessarily make it desirable to dispense with the credit insurance guarantee). Where export credit is not the best option, and assuming the buyer is sufficiently creditworthy to attract unguaranteed lending, a range of options will need to be examined, some discussed in detail in other chapters. These options include the following:

1. A floating rate Eurocurrency loan.
2. A fixed rate Eurocurrency loan.
3. A floating rate Eurocurrency loan plus an interest rate swap facility, producing a fixed rate.
4. A bond issue, normally at a fixed rate.
5. An à forfait financing.

The most commonly used of these is the commercial Eurodollar loan but this suffers from the disadvantage that fixed rates of interest are rarely available and the more usual floating rates mean that buyers are unable to calculate the overall cost of the borrowing at the outset. It is sometimes possible to swap a floating rate obligation into a fixed rate one. There are, however, risks inherent in such an arrangement which will mean that it is not available for borrowers of marginal creditworthiness, and there are also costs. More seriously, the long and unpredictable drawdown period associated with the financing of the type of contract normally associated with a project, can make a swap prohibitively expensive. There are, however, possibilities such as a single swap into a fixed rate at the end of the drawdown period and these will need to be examined.

The various types of bond issue are complex and are normally handled by the exporter's bank. Where sovereign borrowers are concerned, a significant degree of creditworthiness will be required for a bond issue to be made in the international markets but, particularly in some of the fast-developing South-East Asian markets, a bond issue in the local market may be a possibility. Again, however, the long drawdown period associated with projects can present problems.

The à forfait market is discussed in detail in Chapter 10 and should not be ignored in the context of the financing of projects. In general, however, this market can find it difficult to handle the staggered drawdown periods and the extended repayment periods usually required to finance large projects. Again, this is one option which should be examined and which will have application in some cases.

Currency

The issue of currency is a key one, particularly for more sophisticated borrowers. In any consideration of this issue, however, it is of paramount importance to take into account a buyer's evaluation procedures: the aim must always be to offer a currency which will evaluate favourably under that methodology while, of course, taking account of the exporter's currency requirements and protecting him from exposure to exchange rate fluctuations.

The provision of finance in a currency other than sterling may lead the exporter to denominate his contract in that currency. If this is so, he must clearly hedge the currency risk in the forward market, with all the problems (and potential costs) associated with the following:

1. Currency fluctuations between the date of bid submission and contract signature.
2. Rolling over the forward contracts when drawdown is late for any of the reasons common when major projects are undertaken overseas.
3. Cancellation of the forward contracts in the event of termination of the supply contract.

It is often better to allow a mismatch between the currency of contract and that of the financing. In this case, the exporter is exposed to the risk that the currency in which his contract is denominated will appreciate against the currency of the loan so that the loan is insufficient to fund the contract. This risk can obviously be mitigated by setting the loan amount high enough to allow for a measure of currency fluctuation but the borrower will have to pay commitment commission on the increased amount and, if sophisticated, will evaluate such payment to the detriment of the bidder.

A partial solution to this problem, available in some more creditworthy markets, is a multi-currency loan facility: such a loan can be drawn, at the borrower's option, in a choice of currencies. An option to convert the principal amount of the loan into another specified currency following completion of drawdown is also a possibility. Such facilities are by no means invariably available and the range of currencies is limited.

An alternative is to swap a loan denominated in the exporter's preferred currency into the preferred currency of the buyer/borrower. When a project is involved, this can normally only be done at the end of the drawdown period but it may, nevertheless, be attractive. Like the interest rate swap discussed above, the currency swap has risks and costs associated with it and for unusual currencies it may be difficult to find an appropriate swap partner. However, the swap can have significant cosmetic attractions when combined with an ECGD-backed buyer credit at times when sterling interest rates are significantly higher than Consensus rates, as they have frequently been in recent years. At such times, if the sterling-denominated buyer credit is swapped into a low interest rate currency such as the yen, the subsidy inherent in the buyer credit can lead to a very low or even negative interest rate in yen with obvious marketing advantages.

All the options for making financing available in currencies other than the preferred currency of the exporter have problems associated with them and some of them are only feasible in a narrow range of instances. The issue is of paramount importance in the context of a closely contested bid, however, as is the need to avoid exposure to exchange rate fluctuations by the exporter, and the options must be explored to the full at an early stage.

Multinational funding agencies

This chapter addresses the way in which an exporter can use financing to obtain a competitive advantage in bidding to undertake a major overseas contract. It is worth mentioning the multinational funding agencies and banks such as the World Bank, the Asian Development Bank, the European Investment Bank (EIB) and the like, if only to note that they have nothing to offer the bidder in this context. All these agencies operate under strict guidelines for competitive tendering and the applications for funding by them must invariably emanate from the borrowing country. Funding is made available to the borrowing government on terms agreed with it and is equally available to finance contracts with all bidders (or at least all those covered by the agency concerned). It is helpful to maintain close links with such agencies and to be aware of the projects for which bids are likely to be called as a result of the availability of finance from them, but it is important to dispel the frequently encountered view that it may be possible for a bidder to secure support from such a source to the exclusion of his competitors.

The build–own–transfer model

There is a growing tendency, in a number of countries around the world, to seek a greater involvement by the private sector in projects which have hitherto been in the domain of the public sector. The terminology and the exact arrangements vary from one country to another – build–own–transfer (BOT), build–own–operate (BOO), concession-based financing, franchise financing are some of the terms used but the principle remains the same: to grant to a private sector company a concession to build and operate the facility concerned and usually, though not invariably, return it to the government granting the concession at the end of a finite concession period. The term BOT is used loosely here to imply any of these arrangements and the principles involved are also applicable to the financing of industrial and other projects which are not the subject of a concession from government but which are, nevertheless, undertaken by single project companies, unsupported by government or parent companies. In all cases the financing techniques employed are referred to as 'limited recourse' or 'pure' project financing.

Probably the best known of the BOT projects is the Channel Tunnel, the largest project undertaken this century. There are a number of other examples under construction or discussion in the United Kingdom, which is regarded as the model for arrangements of this type: the crossing of the Thames at Dartford, the second Severn Crossing, light rail schemes in cities such as Manchester, Bristol and Birmingham and the many schemes for private power generation (the latter not strictly concession-based but very much part of the same trend).

Markets and sectors

In general, countries which seek to implement the BOT model exhibit the following:

1. A political disposition (usually a right of centre government) to encourage the private sector.
2. A major requirement to invest in infrastructure projects.
3. An inability, or at the least an unwillingness, to pay for that investment.

The promotion of the BOT concept is now widespread in both the developed and the developing world and it is helpful to keep a look out for countries that exhibit these characteristics.

The BOT mechanism has been used, or seriously considered for use, in a number of sectors but the most usual are the following:

1. Power generation and transmission.
2. Transportation projects, widely defined to include rail and light rail projects, bridges, tunnels, roads, airports and ports.
3. Water supply and sewage treatment.

Organisational structure

A BOT arrangement involves the award to a company, established especially for the purpose and referred to here as 'the concession company', of a concession to build a facility and operate it for an agreed period. This concession agreement is the key to the implementation of the project: it will confer important rights on the concession company but is likely also to impose significant obligations.

The concession company lets a contract or contracts (a single turnkey contract is normally required) for the construction of the facility and the supply of equipment, and another for its operation. Unless the market for the project's product or service is beyond any doubt (and sometimes even when it is not), the concession company will also need to enter into arrangements which secure a stream of revenue for the project, normally in the form of long-term sales agreements. It will also need to enter into long-term agreements for the supply of other necessary inputs for the project: power and other utilities, fuel and raw materials, as the case may be.

The concession company contracts loans to enable it to meet the capital cost of constructing the facility and repays them out of the cash flow of the project. Many of the funding techniques used for government-guaranteed projects can be used but the key difference lies in the security available for the lenders, which is in the anticipated cash flow of the project itself. In a true BOT or limited recourse financing, there are no financial guarantees from government or parent companies at all (see Figure 7.2).

Debt/equity structure and the use of grants

The required level of capitalisation of the concession company is dependent on the financial projections for the project and the degree of risk associated with those projections. For low-risk projects, such as a power station with a power sales agreement to a creditworthy state-owned power distribution utility, the percentage can be very low and there are examples of projects in the UK transportation sector where there is virtually no equity. A more normal debt/equity ratio would be in the 4:1 range and the government letting the concession will sometimes insist that the group seeking to undertake the project contributes equity to about that level in order to

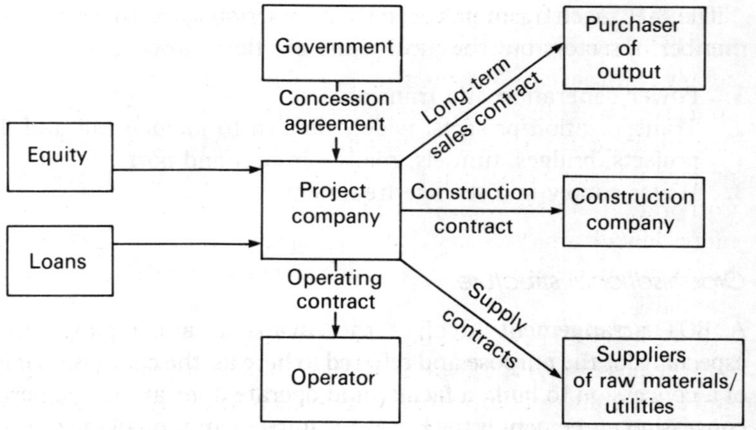

Figure 7.2 The BOT structure

demonstrate its commitment to the project. It cannot be emphasised strongly enough that each project has to be considered on its merits and that, in some instances, 50 per cent or more of the capital costs of the project may have to be contributed in the form of equity in order to enable debt to be raised for the balance.

Many infrastructure projects are, on their own, insufficiently robust financially to attract private sector lenders and equity investors. This applies particularly to some of the types of transportation projects for which the BOT model has been used. This does not preclude the use of limited recourse financing provided that funding, normally in the form of a non-repayable grant, can be made available to support the required proportion of the capital costs of the project. Such an arrangement can have attractions for government: the level of grant is stipulated at the outset and the government has no further obligations towards the project. Anomalies arise when the level of grant needs to be very high and the government concerned may then want to retain a significant degree of involvement in the project.

It goes without saying that the level of available grant funding will have an important impact on the debt/equity structure.

Equity

The sources of equity available for a project depend very much on the degree of risk inherent in the project, itself often a function in large measure of the country in which the project is situated.

In countries in which there is a significant degree of political and macro-economic risk, the raising of the equity for the project may present serious difficulties. It will almost certainly be necessary for those who expect to benefit from the project in other capacities, such as through construction or supply contracts, to contribute a large part of the equity. The government concerned will often insist on taking a shareholding, though is more likely to contribute this in kind, for instance in the form of the land on which the project will be constructed, than as cash. The International Finance Corporation (IFC) is an important potential source of equity in some of the more difficult markets and local entrepreneurs may welcome an opportunity to invest in a project which benefits from foreign management standards.

In developed countries and when the risk profile of the project is low, it may be possible to raise equity in the financial markets from institutional and even individual investors. Where such funding is available, it is often better to avoid high levels of equity in the hands of those who will construct or operate the project: there are numerous examples of problems arising from too close a relationship between the concession company and its suppliers.

Debt

All costs of the project, including interest accruing during the construction period, which are not covered by the equity in the concession company or a grant have to be funded by debt. Because the concession company which will act as the borrower for this debt does not have any resources other than the project itself, it is particularly exposed to fluctuations in two key variables: exchange rates and interest rates. It is important that it should not undertake any significant degree of risk in either of these areas.

The risk of fluctuations in exchange rates is handled by ensuring that the concession company only enters into contracts to make payments, whether to contractors, suppliers or operators, or to banks and equity investors, in the currency in which its revenues will be denominated. In some cases, this may involve quite complicated currency baskets with the agreement for the sale of the output of the facility denominated in a range of currencies to match the obligations of the concession company. It follows that if a project is of the type that the revenue stream is made up of a large number of small payments from the local population, such as a railway or toll road project, very serious difficulties will be encountered if it is not possible to raise debt finance for the project in the local financial markets.

The need to insulate the project from fluctuations in interest rates places an even greater value on fixed rate funding than is the case with government-guaranteed projects, but the potential sources of such funding are usually more limited than for a government-guaranteed project and export credit will play an important role. In cases where the other risks associated with the project are relatively low, it may, in fact, be possible to finance a BOT project with floating rate funds: the revenues of the project will rise in line with inflation, thus covering that element of the interest payments and leaving the project exposed only to fluctuations in real interest rates, which are likely to be very much less than those in nominal rates.

Security

The structuring of the security package for a limited recourse financing will normally be handled by a bank or financial advisor but it will have important implications for the group developing the project concerned.

The development of the security package involves the identification of all the risks associated with the construction and operation of the project and the removal of these risks from the concession company to the greatest extent possible. The package will normally incorporate the following:

1. A full set of financial projections for the project, demonstrating that it can reliably be expected to yield enough revenue to service debt on the basis of ratios of available cash flow to debt service obligations acceptable to lending institutions for the whole of the period when debt is outstanding.
2. The conclusion of arrangements for the securing of an income stream for the project. This is a key element in the financing arrangements and, in the case of a manufacturing venture or, for instance, a power station, would take the form of a long-term contract for the sale of an agreed level of output at an agreed price. In some cases, particularly public transport projects, a degree of market risk has to remain with the concession company. When this is so, lenders will require detailed studies of the market carried out by a reputable – and independent – entity.
3. Conclusion of long-term contracts for the supply of necessary raw materials and utilities for the project.
4. Receipt of all necessary planning, environmental and other governmental and local authority approvals.
5. Signature of construction/supply contract or contracts. This is an important area for the project sponsors whose primary interest is normally in the construction contract and/or the supply of equipment. Lending banks will wish to see that the risk of the project being completed on time and to budget rests with the recipient(s) of the supply and construction contracts to the greatest possible extent. This normally implies a single turnkey contract, placed with a financially sound company which, through the turnkey mechanism, bears the risks of failure by smaller sub-contractors.
6. Operating and maintenance agreements which place the maximum possible degree of operating risk on the recipient.

Sources of debt finance

EXPORT CREDIT

The requirement both for long repayment periods and for a fixed rate of interest mean that, for most BOT projects, some kind of government-supported or multinational agency funding will form an important part of the debt package. All these sources have shown reluctance to bear the increased risk associated with a project financing, but most of the major export credit agencies now have a framework which, at least in theory, can handle these risks. The United Kingdom's ECGD's scheme has three options, involving it in the acceptance of varying degrees of risk:

1. Cover for the pure political risk of the country concerned.
2. Cover for political risk plus other clearly specified risks related to failure by the government of the country in which the project is situated to meet specific obligations in relation to the project.
3. Full cover for all risks of non-payment by the concession company.

In the third case, cover is for a maximum of 60 per cent of the value of the loan, with the bank's lending under the ECGD facility required to finance the balancing 40 per cent and premium rates are high.

The relative merits of the different schemes have to be considered in the light of circumstances relating to each project but it is worth noting that the majority of applications to the ECGD are under the first or second of the schemes described above.

SYNDICATED GUARANTEE FACILITY

In the case of many of the multinational agencies, lending has to be guaranteed by the government of the country in which the project is situated, making it unsuitable for use in financing a BOT project. There are increasing signs of flexibility, however, and all the possibilities need to be examined.

Some agencies, such as the EIB, are increasingly willing to bear the project risk after its completion. In this case, a syndicate of commercial banks can sometimes be arranged to bear the pre-completion risk, by giving their guarantee to the lending agency during the period in which the project is under construction. On satisfactory completion, their guarantee falls away and the whole risk is borne by the lending agency.

COMMERCIAL BANK LENDING

For historical reasons, commercial banks have a longer experience of assessing the risk of lending to projects than export credit agencies and may well, as a result, look more favourably on the risk of the project itself. When a project is in the developing world, the problem is more often with the political and economic risk of the country. It is important to note that it is only in the most unusual circumstances (when the whole of a project's output is to be sold to international buyers and it can in other ways effectively be isolated from the economy in which it is operating) that banks will lend to a project company in a country where the government is such that they would not lend to it for the same period. The relatively short lives and floating rates of interest which characterise most bank lending to the developing world are also important problems but, in the more credit-worthy markets, the lending techniques discussed for use in connection with government-guaranteed projects will all need to be examined.

LEASING

Under many jurisdictions, single project start-up companies are not very tax efficient and there can be significant tax benefits in leasing equipment to the project company rather than selling it. The attractions or otherwise of leasing are, of course, wholly dependent on the tax regime involved and also on the degree of risk associated with the project.

Advantages and disadvantages for the exporter

From the exporter's point of view, the BOT model has one big potential advantage: the fact that it is more often possible to negotiate a contract, and often one which is attractively priced, than it is to obtain a government-guaranteed contract by negotiation in today's market. There is also an increasing tendency for governments to call for bids on a BOT basis which will mean that the exporter has to bid on that basis if he wants the work at all.

In such a case, the exporter will need to consider his position very carefully because there are also some serious risks associated with a BOT project.

BUSINESS DEVELOPMENT RISK

The first of these is the business development risk. Because of the need to undertake detailed work on the financial viability of the project, which in turn implies sufficient work in its engineering and design for detailed prices to be determined, a company wishing to negotiate a concession for a BOT project will need to incur very substantial costs before there is any certainty of success. In many countries this problem is compounded by the fact that the government granting the concession has a limited understanding of the complexities involved and no organisational mechanism for dealing with them. The resultant delays frequently run into years with obvious implications for the cost of the business development effort.

CONTRACT RISK

The second problem for the exporter comes with the terms of the supply/construction contract. Many contractors fail to realise that the requirement for a 'fixed price', a concept they have learnt to be comfortable with in the context of a government-guaranteed project, means exactly what it says where a BOT project is concerned. Minimal scope for price variations and very heavy penalties for late delivery or completion impose risks on the contractor which are considerably in excess of those to which most are accustomed.

EQUITY RISK

Finally, there is the equity risk. In more developed countries, the contractor may not be required to take an equity stake in the project. However, in the developing world and in any instances in which the contractor hopes to negotiate a contract, he is likely to be required to take a significant stake in the concession company. It may or may not be possible to sell this stake on completion of the project or when it has been operating satisfactorily for a few years: the higher the risks, and hence the less attractive to the original contractor of a continuing equity investment, the more difficult the sale of the investment will be.

A BOT financing may indeed offer the possibility of a negotiated contract but it involves very substantial risks and considerable complexities which are only touched on here: any contractor intending to become involved in such a project will want to make a full and early assessment of these risks in close conjunction with professional advisers.

8

Aircraft finance

TOM BUDGETT AND GRAHAM MCBAIN
Clifford Chance

The financing of aircraft is a major industry in which expansion looks likely to continue well beyond the millennium. For example, Boeing estimates that between 1988 and 2005 an open market of $342 billion worth of new orders will be placed to meet world traffic demands.

Aircraft finance is also an area where the involvement of lawyers and the law is considerable.[1] Given that many transactions are tax-based, the documentation tends to be voluminous and complex. Furthermore, a number of transactions are in the nature of cross-border financings and, thus, the complications of potentially competing laws arise. Finally, there is a variety of national registration requirements, EC Directives and International Conventions which invariably must be taken into account when dealing with the financing of aircraft.

The purpose of this chapter is to set out, in simple terms, some of the legal issues affecting aircraft and their financing under English law.

The registration of aircraft

In accordance with the terms of the Chicago Convention, to which most countries of the world are signatories, aircraft cannot be registered in the aircraft register of more than one sovereign state at any one time – though the state of registration may be changed. Furthermore, aircraft will take the nationality of the state in which they are registered.[2]

In the United Kingdom the register in which aircraft are registered is the United Kingdom Nationality Register of Civil Aircraft (the 'UK Aircraft Register'), which is maintained in London by the Civil Aviation Authority (CAA), a government department.[3] In the register will be registered all aircraft which intend to fly under the flag of the United Kingdom. Perhaps, surprisingly, there is no statutory definition of an 'aircraft'. However, it will cover balloons, airships, kites, gliders, aeroplanes and helicopters.

Not all aircraft may be registered in the UK Aircraft Register. Under the terms of the Chicago Convention states are permitted to establish rules providing what aircraft may, or may not, be registered. Most states do this on the basis that the aircraft owner or lessee must have some connection with the state of registration – and the United Kingdom is no exception. Basically, only the following aircraft may be registered in the UK Aircraft Register:[4]

1. Aircraft *owned* by qualified persons.
2. Aircraft *demise chartered* to qualified persons.
3. Aircraft owned by an unqualified person *residing* or *having a place of business* in the United Kingdom where the CAA is satisfied that the aircraft may properly be registered.

'Qualified persons' include the Crown, Commonwealth citizens, Irish citizens, British protected persons, Commonwealth bodies having their principal place of business in any part of the Commonwealth and firms carrying on business in Scotland.[5]

This list of qualified persons appears rather a mixture and is the result of history and the British Empire – when registration of aircraft owned by Dominion or Commonwealth citizens or companies was permitted where the states in question had not themselves established independent aircraft registers. Today, the CAA is very reluctant to permit the registration of aircraft owned by Commonwealth citizens or bodies and, as a result, registration in the UK Aircraft Register is generally restricted to UK citizens or companies – whether as owners or demise charterers of the aircraft.

Registration and its effects

As indicated, registration is necessary for the aircraft to be accorded UK nationality. On registration the aircraft will also become subject to UK legislation relating to aviation, including all the requirements relating to airworthiness, operation, crewing, etc.[6] Registration is made by the filing of a completed application form with the CAA and the payment of a fee.[7]

Deregistration of the aircraft will be made at the request of the party who applied for the registration of the aircraft, or by the CAA where that applicant no longer satisfies the prerequisites for registration. There is no fee charged.

The financing of aircraft

Before considering the nature of aircraft leases and mortgages in detail it is worth considering the principal methods commonly used to finance the acquisition of aircraft.

Funds provided by a financier will be in the form of either *debt* or *equity*, that is, in the form of a loan or its equivalent (debt) or in the form of capital to a company to acquire the aircraft (equity).

Loan and mortgage

The financier will provide funds in the form of a loan. That loan will generally be secured by a mortgage over the aircraft and an assignment of insurances. The relatively high cost to the airline of this method of financing means that it has become less popular. However, it is often an element of more complex structures designed to secure to the airline other benefits, such as tax benefits. An example may be given. In Ireland (under the Corporation Tax Act 1976) interest paid to an Irish resident lender on a loan which is dependent on the results of the borrower's business may be treated as a distribution for tax purposes. As a result, while the interest payable on the loan is not a deduction for the borrower, the interest payments are not taxable in the hands of the lender. Given the large amounts involved in aircraft finance transactions such a tax saving can be significant.

Lease financing

This has been a popular method of financing over the last ten years, particularly tax-based lease financing. A third party lessor buys the aircraft and leases it to the airline. The lease is in the form of a finance lease (also called a 'full payout lease'). The nature of a finance lease is discussed below (see the section on types of lease). However, it basically comprises a lease in which all the risks and rewards of ownership in respect of the aircraft are transferred to the lessee.

The tax benefits of a finance lease are that the lessor is usually able to claim tax allowances in respect of the capital cost of acquiring the aircraft (called 'capital allowances', see the appendix to this chapter). This enables the lessor to shelter its taxable profits (or those of the members of its group). The lessee will also share in the benefits of these tax allowances in the form of reduced rental payments.

The availability of tax-based leasing in the United Kingdom has reduced in the last few years. The 100 per cent first year capital allowance of the whole of the purchase price of the aircraft in the year in which the cost was incurred has now been reduced to a 25 per cent writing down allowance on a reducing balance basis (see the appendix). Furthermore, the benefit of such allowances to a UK tax-paying lessor is now calculated at a 35 per cent corporation tax rate (from 52 per cent). Thus, the benefit that can be passed on to the lessee in the form of reduced rentals has been cut to 1–2 per cent of the capital cost (from 5–6 per cent when the allowance and corporation tax rates were higher).

Hire purchase financing

Under the hire purchase agreement the hirer will pay hire charges (similar to the rentals paid by the lessee under the finance lease). The hirer also has an option to purchase the aircraft at a specified time during, or at the end of, the hire period.

Although there appears to be little difference between the hire purchase and the finance lease agreements they have very different tax consequences. Capital allowances, in the case of hire purchases, may be claimed by the hirer (rather than the lessor in the case of the finance lease). Furthermore, the availability of these capital allowances may be accelerated.

Because of this a UK-based airline may take advantage of what is popularly called a 'double dip' – that is a transaction in which tax benefits may be claimed in more than one jurisdiction. Thus, capital allowances may be claimed in one jurisdiction by the seller (and owner) of the aircraft and in another by the hirer of the aircraft under the hire purchase agreement. The opportunities for double dips are rare and will usually only exist for a limited period of time.

Option financing

With diminishing benefits from tax-based leasing the operating lease has become increasingly popular. There are various reasons for this. Operating leases are flexible and permit the lessor to re-use or re-lease the asset at the end of the lease term. Operating leases will also be accounted for on the balance sheet of the lessor and, therefore, are 'off balance sheet' in relation to the lessee. Furthermore, operating leases have been incorporated as an element of a method of financing popularly known as 'option financing'. Under a typical option financing structure the aircraft will be bought by the UK lessor (who will be able to obtain the capital allowances). The aircraft will then be leased to the lessee for the economic life of the aircraft (usually eighteen to twenty years). However, there will be cancellation rights exercisable on specific dates (e.g. every five years) with no obligation or only a limited obligation to pay the outstanding balance of the lease payments (which will comprise the outstanding capital cost of the aircraft). Because of this option this type of lease is popularly known as a 'walk-away' lease.

If the lessee chooses to return the aircraft on the specific dates (popularly known as 'window' dates) the intention is that the capital cost of the aircraft will be recovered through its sale. However, what happens if the sale proceeds are insufficient to meet this cost? There will be a shortfall. Who covers this? This answer is, usually, not the lessor or lessee. In order to provide the flexibility that the lessee desires it is inappropriate that the lessee bear all of this cost. Nor should the lessor, since it is usually only in the transaction to enable the option financing structure to be set up. As a result, the risk is usually taken by the manufacturer of the aircraft or by a combination of the manufacturer and the financiers. They do this by way of asset value underwriting (AVU). This underwriting is designed to meet the shortfall between the sale proceeds (the residual value of the aircraft) and the outstanding amount owing under the lease. However, it is not designed to cover other risks, such as the damage or destruction of the aircraft. These will be covered by other forms of insurance.

The amount payable in respect of AVU will usually be taken between the manufacturer and the financiers and will be taken in the form of portions (slices). The precise way in which it will be apportioned will depend upon the particular aircraft and the particular financing structure. There may be as many as five or six slices, the first slice usually being taken by the lessee.

Leasing

Aircraft leasing, in particular cross-border leasing, is a growth area. Much of it is tax-based and, therefore, dependent on the tax laws prevailing in the relevant jurisdictions. In this section the legal aspects of leasing will be dealt with, together with a brief reference to the various tax benefits that may arise under English tax law in relation to leases and hire purchase agreements.

The nature of leases

Aircraft leases are like leases in general under English law, that is, they comprise contractual obligations. As such, in order to be valid there must be an offer and acceptance together with consideration (consideration basically means the provision of money or money's worth for the entering into of the contract). Aircraft leases may arise orally though, invariably, they are in writing.

The terms of leases are not regulated by statute in the United Kingdom and therefore the parties may generally agree such terms as they wish.

The UK leasing industry

As with the terms of leases, the UK leasing industry is not regulated by any specific legislation. Instead, the lessors involved in various different kinds of equipment leasing have formed various trade associations to represent their interests and to promote good conduct and practice in the leasing industry. One such association in the United Kingdom is the Equipment Leasing Association (ELA) which regulates its members through a code of practice. There is a similar organisation in relation to leasing in other European states (Leaseurope) of which the ELA is a member.[8]

There are no statutory licensing requirements to conduct leasing business, and, more particularly, aircraft leasing business in the United

Kingdom – though UK leasing companies will be regulated by the provisions of the Companies Acts 1985–9 and the general provisions of English law in relation to matters such as negligence, misrepresentation, etc. Given that leasing companies are not regulated by statute in the conduct of their leasing business there are no prerequisites for eligibility and, as a result, both banks and non-financial enterprises may conduct leasing business. Indeed, the major part of 'big ticket' leasing conducted in the United Kingdom is effected through the subsidiaries of UK and US banks.

Types of lease

Aircraft leases are usually distinguished as being either *operating* leases or *finance* leases. There are no detailed statutory definitions of either operating or finance leases under English law. However, their definition is based on their commercial purpose.

Under the *operating* lease the lease rentals are not intended to amortise the capital outlay incurred by the lessor when the aircraft was purchased. Instead, the capital outlay and profit are intended to be recovered through the re-leasing of the aircraft and/or its residual value on its eventual sale. Furthermore, the operating lease is not a method of financing the acquisition of an aircraft but simply a hiring for a specified period. As a result, substantially all the risks and rewards of the ownership of the aircraft will remain with the lessor and the lease period will usually be considerably shorter than the economic life of the aircraft. Finally, the operating lease will be reflected in the balance sheet of the lessor and not the lessee.

Under the *finance* lease, however, the lease rentals are intended to amortise the capital costs of acquisition (and interest thereon) as well as to provide profit. Furthermore, it is usually the lessee who chooses the aircraft to be leased and who bears the costs of repairs, maintenance and insurance. Thus, the intention is that substantially all the risks and rewards associated with the ownership of the aircraft are transferred to the lessee. Accordingly, the lessee is usually granted a purchase option to purchase the aircraft at the end of the lease period or on earlier specified dates – unless the granting of such a purchase option would prejudice any tax benefits otherwise available to the lessee (in which case provision is normally made for the sale of the aircraft to a third party and for all, or a very high, proportion of those proceeds to be paid to the lessee by way of a rent rebate). Finally, the finance lease will be reflected in the balance sheet of the lessee and not the lessor.

Operating and finance leases are similar, however, in that it is intended that the legal ownership of the asset remains at all times with the lessor and that only possession passes to the lessee. Operating and finance leases should be distinguished from other agreements which may appear similar to them but have different legal (and tax) effects. A *hire purchase agreement* is an agreement that contains an option to purchase the equipment on the payment of the purchase instalments. A *conditional sale agreement* is similar to a hire purchase agreement save that title will automatically pass on the payment of the final instalment or satisfaction of the stipulated conditions and there is no separate option to purchase. A *credit sale agreement* is similar to a normal sale agreement in that title to the equipment will pass immediately to the purchaser. However, the purchase price will be paid off in the form of a loan together with interest.

It can be seen that hire purchase, conditional sale and credit sale agreements are legally different from leases in that, in the case of the former, *both* title and possession to the equipment will pass. In the case of leases (whether operating or finance leases), title will not pass to the equipment and the lessee merely has a right of possession. The legal differences have important tax and accounting consequences.

Registration of leases

No legal provision is made for the registration of leases in any public register. Thus, the CAA will not permit the registration of leases in the UK Register of Aircraft. Nor will leases be registrable in the UK Companies Charges Register, that is the register in which certain types of charge or mortgage entered into by UK companies or overseas companies carrying on business in the United Kingdom are registered. The exception is where the lease contains language which has the effect of creating a charge over the aircraft – which would be unusual.

The effect of this is that there is no public register in which the parties to a lease may give notice of it to third parties.

The mortgaging of aircraft

The financing of aircraft often involves the owner granting a right over that aircraft to a third party as security for a debt or other obligation. In the United Kingdom the most common form of security granted over an aircraft is a mortgage.[9]

Under English law the effect of the mortgage is to assign (i.e. transfer) the title of the owner in the aircraft to the mortgagee until the debt or other obligation is repaid or satisfied. This assignment is a conditional one and the owner will have the right to recover title to the aircraft on the payment of the debt. However, the mortgage will also contain a power of sale (usually this is expressed as a term of the mortgage but, if not, it will be implied) which will be exercisable if the mortgagor fails to pay the debt in accordance with the mortgage or otherwise breaches its terms.

It is possible to register an aircraft mortgage so as to give notice of it to third parties. It will be registered in the UK Aircraft Mortgage Register. This register is also maintained by the CAA in London. An application form must be completed and a fee will be payable.[10]

In the case where the mortgage has been granted by a UK company or by an overseas company carrying on business in the United Kingdom the mortgage must also be registered with the UK Companies Register of Charges or else it will be void.

The benefits of registering the mortgage in the UK Aircraft Mortgage Register (registration is optional) are considerable. A registered mortgage will have priority over unregistered mortgages and subsequently registered mortgages. The CAA will also indemnify any party suffering loss in respect of an error or omission in the Register or a copy of the Register.

Liens and statutory rights of detention

It should be noted, though, that the registration of an aircraft mortgage will not give that mortgagee priority over certain other types of security right, such as liens and statutory rights of detention.

Liens basically comprise a right to hold on to property until payment of a debt. Aircraft liens will arise in various situations, such as when work is performed on the aircraft which has the effect of increasing its value (a possessory lien) or on its salvage (a salvage lien). Statutory rights of detention will arise in respect of unpaid airport and air navigation charges (including those of Eurocontrol), unpaid taxes and on the transport of prohibited goods (explosives, drugs, etc.). These liens and statutory rights of detention are not capable of registration in the UK Aircraft Mortgage Register. As a result, they may suddenly spring upon the owner or lessee of an aircraft as an unpleasant surprise.[11]

The 1948 Geneva Convention

Aircraft may also be subject to security rights and mortgages arising when they were previously registered on a foreign aircraft register or whilst they were abroad. Will they be recognised in the United Kingdom? There is a Convention which has been entered into by a number of countries where the courts of those countries undertake to recognise such rights if they have been validly created in accordance with the law of another country which is also party to the Convention.[12]

The United Kingdom has not ratified this Convention, though countries such as the United States, France and Germany have. This means that an English court will not automatically recognise mortgages and other security rights created in foreign countries over the aircraft. However, in general English law will recognise such rights in any case.

Enforcing security rights

The next issue to consider is the means by which security rights, such as an aircraft mortgage registered in the UK Aircraft Mortgage Register, may be enforced before the English courts. In some jurisdictions the value of such a security right is very considerably diminished by the fact that the means of enforcement is difficult, or slow, or the judicial process is uncertain or corrupt.

In England the means of enforcing an aircraft mortgage is relatively straightforward and fast. If the mortgage debt is not paid or the mortgagor has otherwise defaulted in the terms of the mortgage then notice of default should be given. If the default is not then remedied a *writ* should be issued for the recovery of the mortgage debt.

Where there is a possibility that the aircraft may be removed from the jurisdiction so as to defeat any claim against it then the mortgagee may apply to the English court for an *injunction* – which, if successful, will prohibit the mortgagor from so acting. In the case where there is evidence that the mortgagor may attempt to defeat any claim against him by removing his other assets from the jurisdiction of the English court or otherwise disposing of them, the mortgagee may request that another form of injunction (called a *Mareva injunction*) be granted to stop the mortgagor from doing so.

Injunctions may be sought and obtained very speedily (and, in urgent cases, may be obtained without the presence of the mortgator before the court. The injunction is called, in this case, an *ex parte* injunction). The costs for making an application for an injunction before the English court are not usually large. Injunctions should not be sought lightly, however, since the mortgagee will be responsible to the mortgagor for any loss arising to the latter if the English court subsequently determines, at trial, that an injunction should not have been given.

The costs of the issue of a writ will also not usually be large.

The trial

If a writ is served and the mortgagor still does not pay the mortgage debt, the next question to be considered is how long the trial will take. There are some procedures that the mortgagee may avail himself of in order to obtain the judgment of the English court quickly. For example, if the writ is served and the mortgagor fails to acknowledge the writ or fails to serve a defence, the mortgagee may be able to obtain a judgment in default within two weeks thereafter. Similarly, where the mortgagee can show that the mortgagor has no valid defence, the court may proceed to summary judgment – which may occur within three months of the service of the writ.

However, where the mortgagee cannot take these remedies, the case may take two or three years to come to trial, given the general backlog of cases before the English High Court.

Selling the aircraft

In the case where the mortgagor has failed to pay the mortgage debt or has otherwise defaulted under the terms of the mortgage the mortgagee may take possession of the aircraft without judicial process. However, this does not usually occur. If the retaking was wrongful, damages payable by the mortgagee might be high, including those in relation to third parties, such as passengers. The CAA may also refuse to grant the mortgagee the requisite operating licences, airworthiness certificates and other permissions necessary for the continued flight of the aircraft. Instead, repossession of the aircraft is usually sought through the judicial process (by way of writ and injunction, see above).

Where the mortgagor has resisted the claims of the mortgagee and yet judgment has been given against it, the court may order the sale of the aircraft. The court may also order the sale of the aircraft prior to judgment in the case where it can be shown that there is likely to be a deterioration in its condition in the interim. The order for sale will be on such terms as the court may specify. However, the sale will usually be advertised to all interested parties (in the national Press and in relevant aviation articles) in order that they may have the opportunity to bid. The mortgagee will be entitled to bid. Sale will be to the highest bidder. Expenses of sale will be deducted from the sale proceeds prior to the claims of the mortgagee being satisfied.

The mortgagee may also request that the aircraft be sold by a private, rather than a public, sale and the English court will generally permit this where it can be shown that a higher price would probably be fetched as a result.

Insurance

Under English law, insurance over aircraft is not compulsory. However, in practice, the CAA will not permit aircraft to fly unless they carry adequate insurance. There are also important reasons why insurance is necessary:

1. *Payment obligations.* The payment obligations under the loan or any lease of the aircraft are usually secured by a security interest over the aircraft (whether by way of mortgage or otherwise). As a result, if the aircraft is destroyed or damaged, the insurance will be used to meet those payments.
2. *Third party claims.* Under English law the lessor, as owner, may possibly be liable for claims brought by third parties in relation to loss or damage caused by the aircraft or for product liability. Such claims are, potentially, huge. Therefore, it is important that insurance be taken out to cover this.

The usual types of basic insurance that are taken out in respect of aircraft are as follows, and are principally carried for most commercial airlines world-wide in the Lloyd's of London market.

Hull all risks insurance

This usually covers all the risks of physical loss or damage to the aircraft. It will not usually cover general wear and tear. Nor will it cover any loss of use, delay or grounding of the aircraft.

Hull, war and allied perils insurance

Normally separate insurance is taken out in respect of damage or destruction of the aircraft through war or similar acts (such as civil war, sabotage, hijacking, strikes, etc.) since these risks are generally excluded from the hull all risks insurance above. However, it is not possible to obtain cover against detonation of a nuclear weapon or war between the five great powers (United States, USSR, China, France, United Kingdom).

Third party liability insurance

This insurance relates to liability in respect of passengers, baggage and cargo carried on the aircraft and the liability of the aircraft for damage done to property or people outside the aircraft.

There are also a number of other forms of insurance that are commonly encountered in aircraft financing, such as the following two.

Political risk insurance

The hull, war and allied perils insurance does not provide cover in certain events such as the confiscation or expropriation of the aircraft, nor its deprivation, re-possession or de-registration. However, this can be covered by taking out political risks insurance. As to the meaning of some of these terms, confiscation is a discriminatory act where a government takes away the aircraft and is unlikely to return it. Expropriation is similar to confiscation but where, under international law, compensation is required to be paid. Deprivation is a discriminatory act depriving the owner of property owing to the owner being unable to obtain an export licence from the appropriate government authority, and thus being unable to export the aircraft.

Residual value insurance

There are two basic types of residual value insurance (RVI) available. Since the fair market value appraisal policy is more common, mention of it only will be made here. It provides for payment of an agreed value of the aircraft at a specified future date (the date usually being the termination date of the lease). If, at that date, the lessor determines that the actual market value of the aircraft is less than the agreed value, the insured party (often the lessor or lender) will be entitled to claim for the shortfall (providing that it otherwise satisfies the conditions of the insurance). In the event of a claim under the insurance the insurer is normally entitled to purchase the aircraft at the agreed value, if wished. This type of insurance is of use in that it provides cover against a decline in the aircraft's value throughout the lease term.

It should be noted, however, that a claim may only be made at the lease termination date. Furthermore, the insurance policy is normally tightly drawn and there are specified exclusions from cover (e.g. claims are normally excluded if the financier amends the lease (or related documents) with respect to return, maintenance, operation and other provisions).

Features of aircraft insurance

Finally, there are a number of features of aircraft insurance to which specific attention might usefully be drawn:

1. *Loss payee.* This clause will specify who is the loss payee, that is, the party nominated in the policy as being entitled to the insurance proceeds. Usually, the loss payee will be a lessor or mortgagee. Additionally, other beneficiaries of the insurance may be stipulated for and they are referred to as 'additional insureds'.
2. *Agreed value.* Insurance cover is normally at an 'agreed value'. That is, in the event of the loss of the aircraft the insurer will pay the agreed value specified although this may be more than the actual loss incurred. This will be of use to the financier since it will be known from the outset the amount of insurance payable and the financier will derive comfort from the fact that he or she will remain unaffected by any downturn in the value of the aircraft itself.
3. *Severability of interest clause.* The insurance policy will normally contain a clause which provides that 'The insurance shall operate in all respects, except in respect of the limit of liability, as if each insured were the subject of a separate policy'. The purpose of this clause is to provide that each insured party is not prejudiced by the acts or omissions of any other insured party.
4. *Cross liability clause.* The insurance policy will usually also contain a clause which provides that 'The inclusion of B to this policy as an additional assured shall not preclude the right of recovery hereon by A in respect of claims made against it by B'. The purpose of this clause is to retain the ability of the original insured (A) to recover claims against the additional insured party (B) in respect of any acts or omissions by that party.

5. *50/50 per cent clause.* This clause is intended to deal with the situation where it is not clear whether the loss will be covered by the hull all risks insurance or by the hull, war and allied perils insurance. A clause is therefore inserted to provide that, where a claim arises and it cannot be clearly shown under which policy the loss should be covered, the underwriters of each of those policies will contribute to 50 per cent of the loss and then settle the matter between themselves.
6. *A cut-through clause.* This is a clause which will arise when the original insurance is re-insured, whether in whole or in part. Its purpose is to enable the loss payee to recover the insurance proceeds directly from the reinsurers rather than through the original insurers. 'Cut-through' clauses are a difficult subject and their legal nature and practical effects have been questioned.

Notes

1. The principal legal textbook dedicated to aircraft finance in the United Kingdom is *Aircraft Finance: Registration, security and enforcement* by R. Hames and G. McBain, 1st ed. 1988 (2 vols) dealing with the registration of aircraft and aircraft mortgages and the enforcement of the latter in some fifty countries. See also *Air Law* by Shawcross and Beaumont, 4th ed. 1990 (with updates), Butterworths (general law of aviation); *Introduction to Air Law* by Diedericks, 3rd ed. 1988, Kluwer (introductory text); *Aviation Insurance* by Margo, 2nd ed. 1989, Butterworths.
2. Chicago Convention of 1944 on International Civil Aviation, articles 17 and 18. Over 150 countries are parties to the Convention.
3. The UK Aircraft Register is a central register for England, Northern Ireland, Scotland and Wales. The address of the Civil Aviation Authority is Aircraft Registration Section, Central Library, Civil Aviation Authority, CAA House, 45/59 Kingsway, London WC2B 6TE.
4. There are currently some 14,000 aircraft registered in the UK Aircraft Register including 743 aircraft with a maximum weight exceeding 5,700 kg, 2,363 microlights, 800 helicopters and 991 balloons.
5. For a more detailed explanation of these requirements and the mechanics of registering an aircraft on the UK Aircraft Register see Hames and McBain (note 1), chapter on England and Wales.
6. The basic legislation governing aviation is the Civil Aviation Act 1982 and the Air Navigation Order 1989 SI 2004.
7. Currently the fees, which are revised annually, vary between £26 and £95 depending on the weight of the aircraft.
8. In relation to leasing see the *World Leasing Yearbook*, Euromoney.
9. It is also common to provide for other forms of security, such as an assignment of insurances.
10. The fees for registering a mortgage range from £45 to £720. For a more detailed explanation of these requirements and the mechanics of the registration of an aircraft mortgage in the UK Aircraft Mortgage Register see Hames and McBain, (note 1) chapter on England and Wales.

11. An example is International Lease Finance Corporation, the lessor of four MD 83s to British Island Airways (which subsequently went into liquidation), which was presented in 1990 with substantial outstanding airport and airways charges which were apparently owed by the lessee and which had accrued as far back as 1983.
12. The Geneva Convention of 1948 on the International Recognition of Rights in Aircraft.

Appendix: UK tax considerations

As previously mentioned much of leasing is tax-based, that is, the leases (or hire purchase agreements) are so structured in order to take the benefit of tax allowances in the United Kingdom. Brief reference will now be made to various tax matters in so far as they may affect leases in the United Kingdom.

Capital allowances

Capital allowances are in the nature of tax depreciation allowances arising on the purchase of certain types of qualifying plant and machinery, including aircraft. A UK lessor purchasing an aircraft for leasing in the course of a leasing trade will usually be entitled to claim capital allowances providing that the purchase price has not been subsidised. The capital allowances currently comprise a 25 per cent writing down allowance on a reducing balance basis. Capital Allowances are established pursuant to the Capital Allowances Act 1990. Their availability will depend upon the precise structure of the lease, hire purchase, conditional or credit sale agreement in question.

Capital allowances may also be available in the case of cross-border leases (i.e. where the lessor is based in the United Kingdom and the lessee/end-user abroad). When the UK lessor is leasing to a foreign lessee/end-user at any time within ten years of the acquisition of the aircraft the writing down allowance may be reduced to 10 per cent or nil. There are exceptions to this, however.

Eligibility for capital allowances is a complex area subject to exceptions and to anti-avoidance provisions.

Value added tax

Value added tax (VAT), which is a tax charged on the supply of goods or services in the United Kingdom, is not payable on the leasing of commercial aircraft since the lease rentals are zero-rated (i.e. charged at a notional nil rate).

Corporation tax

Broadly speaking, a company engaged in a leasing business in the United Kingdom will be subject to UK corporation tax on the profits of that business as computed for tax purposes. The rate of corporation tax on such profits is currently 35 per cent.

Withholding tax

Lease rentals and instalment payments under hire purchase agreements do not attract UK withholding tax (UK withholding tax may apply to the 'finance charge' elements of payments under conditional or credit sale agreements, however).

9

Shipping finance

VICTORIA PARRY, PAUL TURNER AND
TONY CANNELL
Clifford Chance

Introduction

The outlook for the shipping industry today is optimistic. As a result of the slowing down in the world economy in the early 1980s together with the rise in oil prices, shipbuilding prices declined and consequently demand for new ships fell. At one point during this depression, the supply of new ships exceeded demand by 40 per cent. This had an effect on the second-hand market for ships, where demand increased. As a result today the world's shipping fleet is an ageing one and needs to be replaced. It has been forecast that 170 million dead-weight tonnage (d.w.t.) of oil tankers and 70 million d.w.t. of dry bulk carriers will be required by 1998. On current estimates, the cost of fleet renewal will require almost $103 billion of finance (source: Drewry Shipping Consultants Ltd). These figures deal with replacement of ships and do not take into account any increase in demand within the shipping industry.

The sea, shipping and ships have given, and continue to give, rise to a number of legal problems that are wholly different from those encountered with other forms of transport. Because of this, shipowners and seafarers (and their financiers) expect that when they bring their particular problems to a court of law, they will be answered in a way that satisfies their special needs.

Over time communities that had connections with the sea built up their own customary laws which often spread beyond their own boundaries – carried by the shipowners and seafarers (and their financiers) whom such laws were designed to help. In Northern Europe the laws of Visby and the Hansa communities of Northern Germany were widely used, and in the Mediterranean the laws of the Island of Rhodes were often referred to. However, in England, a separate maritime code of laws was developed – based upon the laws of Oleron, a small island off the mouth of Charente in the Bay of Biscay! By the end of the fifteenth century the basic principles of English maritime law had been established from this source.

Needless to say, English maritime law was also part of the laws of England's colonies and other overseas possessions and, moreover, when these in the due course of time obtained independence, such maritime laws were largely retained as part of the 'common law' basis of the legal system of the ex-colony or possession in question.

In addition to such common law systems, such as the United States, many of the concepts used in English maritime law have their counterparts in the maritime laws of non-common law jurisdictions – whether as a result of pragmatic absorption or simply the need to satisfy comparable problems by similar means.

This chapter sets out briefly some of the legal issues affecting ships registered under the British flag and aspects of their financing under English law.

What is a ship?

The Merchant Shipping Act 1894 (the 1894 Act) defines a 'ship' to include 'every description of vessel used in navigation not propelled by oars' and 'vessel' to include 'any ship or boat, or other description of vessel used in navigation'. The Department of Trade and Industry considers the definition of 'ship' wide enough to include units capable of movement at sea whether self-propelled or not (for example dumb-barges, pipe-laying barges, crane barges and vessels used as floating oil tanks) and also to include submersible and jack-up rigs (other than those required to be put on barges to move from one location to another). A ship under construction has been held not to be a ship.

In order for a ship to be a 'British ship' it must satisfy the requirements of Section 2 of the Merchant Shipping Act 1988 (the 1988 Act). That section treats, as a British ship, all ships registered in the United Kingdom on the register of British ships, the small ships' register and the fishing vessel register; it also includes a government ship, a ship registered in a relevant overseas territory (which includes Gibraltar, Hong Kong and Bermuda) and ships which are less than twenty-four metres in length.

The registration of a British ship

This section deals only with registration of a ship under the British flag. It should be noted, however, that a ship may possibly be registered under another flag and in deciding where to register a ship, the owner will take various factors into consideration, such as the following:

1. Ownership qualifications – many countries limit ownership of ships registered under their flag to their own nationals.
2. Costs of registration.

3. Restrictions on trade – for example for political reasons a ship flying the flag of one state may not be able to trade with certain others.
4. Corporation taxes, income taxes and other taxes.
5. Crewing requirements – including labour costs, trade union pressures and local labour legislation.
6. If there is intended to be a mortgage over the ship, the mortgagee's views will need to be taken into account. A mortgagee will be concerned about the system for registering mortgages, its effectiveness and speed, the availability of clear and consistent local legal advice, and the system of priorities between competing mortgages.

Finally it is worth noting that there are certain 'open registries' such as Liberia, Panama, Cyprus, Singapore and the Bahamas which are registries available to ships that are beneficially owned by persons other than nationals of that country. These are more commonly known as 'flags of convenience'.

Under the 1894 Act it was compulsory to register as British all ships (unless they were exempted) that were eligible for registration. However, it is now no longer so: HM Customs and Excise have indicated that a ship, which is eligible for registration as a British ship, will need to be so registered if it is intended that such ship will leave UK waters, fly the red ensign or be mortgaged (*Registering British Ships in the United Kingdom*: Notice 382 (HMSO, Jan. 1990)).

Who can own a British ship?

Section 3 of the 1988 Act lists the persons (individuals and companies) who are qualified to be owners of British ships. The list follows the divisions of British nationality as set out in the British Nationality Act 1981 and includes the following:

1. British citizens.
2. British Dependent Territories citizens.
3. British overseas citizens.
4. Persons who are 'British subjects' under the British Nationality Act 1981.
5. Persons who are 'British Nationals (Overseas)' under the Hong Kong (British Nationality) Order 1986.
6. Bodies incorporated in the United Kingdom or in any relevant overseas territory and having their principal place of business in the United Kingdom or in any such territory.
7. Citizens of the Republic of Ireland.

The 'relevant overseas territory' includes Anguilla, Bermuda, British Antarctic Territory, British Indian Ocean Territory, Cayman Islands,

Falkland Islands, Gibraltar, Hong Kong, Isle of Man, Montserrat, Pitcairn Islands, Sovereign base areas of Akrotiri and Dhekelia, St Helena and Dependencies, Turks and Caicos and Virgin Islands.

When can a ship be registered as a British ship?

Section 4(2) of the 1988 Act states that 'a ship shall be entitled to be registered if a majority interest in the ship is owned by one or more persons qualified to be owners of British ships . . . [by virtue of Section 3 of the 1988 Act].' For the purposes of ownership a British ship is divided into sixty-four shares. A ship can be owned by up to five individuals or companies. A sole owner will hold the sixty-four shares outright. 'Majority' in the context of Section 4 of the 1988 Act means thirty-three or more of the sixty-four shares. The 1988 Act does not require *all* the shares to be owned by qualified persons.

However, except in the situations listed in Section 4 of the 1988 Act, the 1988 Act requires that the majority interest in the ship must be owned by qualified persons who are *resident* in the United Kingdom. Where the majority interest is not resident in the United Kingdom, a *representative person* as defined in Section 5 of the 1988 Act must be appointed in relation to the ship. A representative person is either an individual resident in the United Kingdom or a body corporate incorporated in the United Kingdom and having its principal place of business in the United Kingdom.

Where and by whom can a British ship be registered?

Registration of British ships is performed by registrars. The 1894 Act lists the persons who may be appointed registrars of British ships, and this list includes officers appointed by the Commissioners of Customs and Excise at ports approved by the Commissioners, in the United Kingdom. Any port in the United Kingdom can be an approved port.

Every registrar of British ships must keep a register book. This contains details of the name of the ship, port of registry, details from the surveyor's certificate, details of ownership of the ship and details of all mortgages on the ship.

How is a British ship registered?

Section 10 of the 1894 Act lists the evidence required on first registration of a ship. It includes the relevant application form, title documents, certificate of survey and declaration of ownership. In addition, the Department of Transport must approve of the proposed name of the ship. Once the registrar is satisfied, he will issue a so-called 'carving and marking note' which shows the ship's official number and the details to be marked on the ship. When the carving note is returned and the fees paid, the registrar will grant a certificate of registry.

The certificate of registry sets out the particulars entered on the register. However, the certificate in itself is not proof of ownership; the register is the only true proof of ownership. To prove ownership either the register may be inspected or a signed extract of the register obtained. The signed extract is known as a 'certified transcript' and this details the ownership of the ship and any outstanding mortgages on the ship.

Once a ship has been registered and a certificate of registry issued, it is possible for ownership of the ship to change or the ship's master to change. In these cases the certificate of registry is endorsed with the change. It is also possible to transfer the registry to another UK port or to a port outside the United Kingdom, and to change the ship's name.

If the ship ceases to be a British ship or the ship is lost, then the registrar must be notified and he makes the relevant entry into the register book and the register will be closed. Proof that the register is closed is in the form of a 'closed transcript' or deletion certificate which shows ownership and outstanding mortgages at the time of closure.

Ship financing

There are a number of alternative sources of finance open to a shipping company seeking expansion (usually by way of the acquisition of a new or second-hand ship), namely the following:

1. Commercial loans.
2. Government-backed finance and subsidies.
3. Issue of shares or debentures or raising of loan capital.
4. Lease or equivalent asset finance.

Basic structure of a shipowning group

Generally in shipowning groups, each ship will usually be owned by a separate company. That company will hold no other assets than the ship. The shares in each shipowning company will be held by the group holding company whose only assets will be the shares in each shipowning company. The shares in the holding company will be owned by the beneficial owner of the group. Each shipowning company will usually be managed by the same management company, which is usually another company and part of the same group – although this need not be the case. This structure of single shipowning companies also reduces the 'sister ship' risk. This arises because so-called *in rem* legal proceedings can be issued against 'owners and other persons interested' in the ship in question and the ship need not be the ship in respect of which the claim/loss arose. It is enough that it is a sister ship, i.e. another ship beneficially owned by the same owner of the ship in respect of which the claim/loss arose.

The finance for the acquisition of a new or second-hand ship may be provided either (a) to the particular company acquiring the ship with guarantees from the other subsidiary shipowning companies and the holding company, (b) a loan to the holding company and guaranteed by all the subsidiary shipowning companies, or (c) a loan jointly and severally to each subsidiary shipowning company and guaranteed by the holding company. The most common circumstance is (a). Needless to say, the company acquiring the ship will mortgage it to secure its borrowings or, as the case may be, its guarantee.

COMMERCIAL LOANS

Most finance for the acquisition of new ships is provided by commercial loans. The finance is made available subject to adequate security being provided (which is dealt with below). One of the advantages of a commercial loan over other forms of finance is its flexibility in the sense that the terms and conditions of such loans can be negotiated with the lender, namely a bank or financial institution. The terms and conditions of such finance will be documented in the form of a *loan agreement*. Under the loan agreement the lender agrees to make a loan to the company purchasing the ship and that borrower covenants to repay the loan subject to certain terms and conditions. These will include, for example, the principal amount of the loan, the repayment dates and the rate of interest. The repayment dates can be more flexible than under government-backed finance. The rate of interest will usually be higher than under government-backed finance and will be a commercial rate of interest, for example, a floating rate such as the London Inter-Bank Offered Rate plus an agreed margin. The loan agreement will also set out the security which the lender requires, the representations and covenants to be made by the borrower and all the other conditions of the loan including events of default, which on their occurrence, entitle the lender to require the borrower to repay the loan immediately.

GOVERNMENT-BACKED FINANCE AND SUBSIDIES

Under the provisions of Section 10 of the Industry Act 1972:

> the Secretary of State [of the Department of Industry] may . . . guarantee the payment by any person who is an individual resident in, or a body corporate incorporated under the law of any part of, the United Kingdom . . . of any sum payable by that person in respect of principal or interest . . . for the purpose of financing the construction.

The loans are usually made by lenders such as banks or financial institutions at a fixed rate of interest. The rate of interest is lower than one would expect to find in a commercial loan, and the difference between the fixed rate and the commercial rate of interest will usually be made up by the Department of Trade and Industry.

ISSUE OF SHARES, DEBENTURES OR LOAN CAPITAL

Companies may also raise finance by an increase in their share capital. An English private limited company may be restricted in this way: first because existing shareholders may not be able to provide the additional funds, and second because an English private limited company is not permitted to advertise or offer the sale of its shares to the public. Therefore it may have to be converted into a public limited company to raise finance. A public limited company can increase its share capital either by a private placement through a merchant bank or by advertising or offering the sale of its shares to the public. Alternatively, depending on its capital structure, the company may be able to issue debentures or raise loan capital – often in the form of bearer or registered debt securities.

LEASE OR EQUIVALENT ASSET FINANCING

Like any other tangible asset, a ship can be the subject of a lease, hire purchase, conditional sale or credit/deferred sale or like arrangement. The permutations are numerous, but they basically revolve around a limited number of factors and may well also be tax-driven:

1. Is the owner (financier) of the ship to retain title to the ship at all times even on expiry of the agreement – such an arrangement being normally referred to as a lease agreement?
2. Is the operator (lessee/hirer) of the ship to have an 'option' to acquire title to the ship at certain times – such an arrangement being normally referred to as a hire purchase agreement?
3. Is the owner of the ship to retain title to the ship until all the instalment payments have been made by the operator and only then will title (automatically) pass to the operator – such an arrangement being referred to as a conditional sale agreement?
4. Is the owner of the ship to pass title to the operator on (say) signature of the documentation or on (say) payment of the first instalment – such an arrangement being usually referred to as a credit or deferred sale agreement?

Unfortunately there is a tendency for the terms 'lease agreement, hire purchase agreement, conditional sale agreement, credit sale/deferred sale agreement' to be used interchangeably and, accordingly, a document entitled 'a lease agreement' may well contain various purchase options in favour of the operator.

One common factor with all the foregoing arrangements is that the ship must, at least at the inception of the transaction, be owned by the financier.

If the ship is already owned by the prospective operator then the financier will often obtain title to the ship through a sale and leaseback transaction or an equivalent arrangement. However, in the case of a new ship, the financier will usually obtain title to the ship from the builder. In this case, the financier may contract directly with the builder – but it is more usual for the existing contract between the operator and the builder to be assigned or novated to the financier. In connection with this, the operator may well have a continuing function in order to supervise the completion of the construction of the ship and, effectively, to act as the financier's agent in that regard.

As mentioned above, the structuring of the transaction may well be tax-driven. Capital allowances may be available to the owner of the ship (see the appendix to this chapter). However, it should be noted that in the past credit sale/deferred sale arrangements have also been completed whereby the financier obtained other fiscal benefits. For example, the financier might be able to obtain a tax credit (or deemed tax credit) in circumstances where the relevant Double Taxation Convention enabled tax sparing to be utilised in respect of such transaction.

One general note of caution should be sounded with regard to transactions whereby the financier acquires ownership (for however short a space of time). Liabilities may well be easier to attach to an 'owner' than a mortgagee, e.g. in tort (civil wrong) for damages to third parties or by way of liability (statutory or otherwise) for oil or other pollution. For these reasons, the financier as owner will be particularly concerned to ensure that the ship is properly insured, and it may be preferable for the financier as owner to own the ship through a single purpose company rather than to risk all of its assets in the event of some claim against the ship or itself, as owner of the ship.

Security for ship financing

When a commercial loan is made or government-backed finance obtained, the lender (i.e. the bank or financial institution) will be concerned as to the type of security obtained and its adequacy, and to the methods of enforcement of that security.

The types of security fall into three main categories:

1. Mortgages.
2. Deed of covenants, insurances and earnings.
3. Guarantees.

Mortgages

The form of mortgage used depends on the nationality of the ship. Each flag has its own form of mortgage. In the case of British ship mortgages, Section

31 of the 1894 Act states that 'A registered ship or a share therein may be made as security for a loan or other valuable consideration and the instrument creating the security (in this Act called a mortgage) shall be in the form . . . of the First Schedule'. The registrar does not have to register mortgages that are not in the prescribed form. For this reason, in complex financings, it is prudent to ensure (in advance) that the registrar will accept the negotiated form of mortgage – especially in syndicated loan/credit financings where the benefit of the mortgage may be held by a security agent or trustee for the lenders.

There are two possible forms of prescribed mortgage for a British ship. One secures the principal sum and interest while the other secures an account current. The mortgage to secure an account current is more widely used owing to its flexibility, since, subject to the normal rules as to 'tacking' new loans and proper drafting, it can effectively secure further loans as well as amounts due at the time of execution of the mortgage, in addition to contingent liabilities such as counter-indemnities (for the issuance of letters of credit) and guarantees.

This prescribed form of mortgage is shorter than mortgages of other nationalities and it invariably refers to a collateral *deed of covenants* which sets out in detail the operational covenants, insurance and earnings covenants and other covenants relating to the ship and the maintenance of its classification (see below). The deed of covenants usually contains the assignment of insurances and earnings which is dealt with below.

International classification societies such as Lloyd's, Det Norske Veritas and American Bureau of Shipping issue classification certificates to international ships fulfilling the technical requirements necessary to qualify them for registration under a particular flag. A ship cannot trade internationally without a classification certificate and therefore maintenance of classification is vital to protect the value of the ship.

Mortgages on British ships are recorded by the registrar at the ship's port of registry according to the time they are given to the registrar. A mortgage (the 'first mortgage') recorded before another mortgage (the 'second mortgage') will take priority over the second mortgage even if the second mortgage was created before the first mortgage.

The mortgage must be presented for registration together with the prescribed fee at the ship's port of registry (as detailed on the ship's certificate of registry). The registrar will then *register* the mortgage by recording its details in the register, endorse the mortgage and return it to the mortgagee. Once registered, a certified transcript of the register can be obtained which sets out the date and brief details of the mortgage.

A mortgage will remain on the register until it is discharged. To discharge a mortgage, the endorsement on the reverse of the mortgage should be completed and presented to the registrar, together with the prescribed fee. The registrar will register the discharge in the register, endorse the mortgage accordingly and then return it to the mortgagee. Additionally a mortgagee can transfer the mortgage to another lender. To do this the transfer section on the reverse of the mortgage should be completed and presented to the registrar together with the prescribed fee. The registrar will register the transfer, endorse the mortgage accordingly and return it.

POWERS OF THE MORTGAGEE

The 1988 Act, Section 35, gives the registered mortgagee 'power absolutely to dispose of the ship or share in respect of which he is registered and give effectual receipts for purchase money'. A subsequent mortgagee cannot exercise his power except with the 'concurrence of every prior mortgagee'. The ability of the second mortgagee to have the ship arrested and enforce its public sale is of concern to prior mortgagees. Consequently, it is the practice to allow a second mortgage to be taken only in circumstances where a coordination agreement is entered into between the first and second mortgagees, giving the first mortgagee power to prevent action by the second mortgagee, unless the latter is prepared to pay off the debt to the former. A coordination agreement will also tend to abolish the problems associated with 'tacking' new loans onto the security and keeping the same priority for such new loans. Sections 39–46 of the 1988 Act detail the rules governing a sale by a mortgagee.

In addition where the mortgagor is an English company, the mortgage (and deed of covenants if it contains an assignment) should be presented for registration at the Companies Registry pursuant to the Companies Act 1985. If the mortgagor is a foreign company which has or may have an established place of business in England and Wales, the mortgage (and deed of covenants) should also be presented for registration.

MORTGAGES OF SHIPS UNDER CONSTRUCTION

In some jurisdictions it is possible to take a mortgage of a ship under construction. (Even where it is not possible, one may be able to take a standard chattel mortgage over the ship during construction – assuming that the mortgagor has some title to mortgage!) Such a mortgage will not necessarily be good security as the builder will almost certainly have a lien over the ship during construction for any sums due from the owner. Where a ship mortgage or a chattel mortgage is not possible or practical, the lender may be able to obtain an assignment of the shipbuilding contract as security, but this will often require the consent of the builder as the shipbuilding contract may prevent or restrict such security arrangements.

Deed of covenants, insurances and earnings

The deed of covenants, in the case of a British ship, is collateral to the mortgage. It will set out in detail the operational, insurance, earnings, classification and other covenants relating to the ship. As mentioned above, it will usually contain the assignment of insurances and earnings, although the assignments can also be dealt with by separate documents. The insurances and earnings are dealt with in further detail below. The covenants relate to the operation and use of the ship by the owner of the ship. Generally the owner must maintain the ship's registration under the British flag, ensure the ship is surveyed regularly and kept in good working order, maintain the ship's classification, etc. The owner is also required to do all things necessary to perfect and maintain the mortgage, including keeping on board the ship at all times a notice of the mortgage. The deed of covenants also sets out all the mortgagee's rights and powers of enforcement and other remedies including power to take possession of the ship, to sell the ship and to appoint a receiver on the occurrence of an event of default as are set out in the loan agreement. The deed of covenants usually contains a power of attorney whereby the owner/mortgagor irrevocably appoints the mortgagee as its attorney during the period of the security to do all acts which the owner/mortgagor could do in relation to the ship.

A lender will take security usually by means of an assignment of the present and future insurances of a ship because if the ship is destroyed the lender will have an interest in the insurance proceeds which replace it. The lender will also take security, by means of an assignment, of all the present and future earnings of the ship.

INSURANCES

The following are the main classes of ship's insurance:

1. *Hull and machinery.* This is the basic insurance covering the fabric of the ship. The value of the ship will fluctuate according to general market conditions. However, the lender/mortgagee will require that the owner/mortgagor maintains the insured value of the ship, on an agreed value basis, to at least 100 per cent of the loan being secured by the mortgage on the ship (usually the lender/mortgagee requires the amount of the insurances to be equal to either 120 or 130 per cent of the amount of the loan).
2. *Protection and indemnity.* Protection and indemnity insurance can be obtained through protection and indemnity clubs which are associations of shipowners formed to insure each other against marine losses. They cover third party liability risks; for example liability to officers and crew in respect of loss of life and personal injury. For oil tankers, there is a further form of mutual insurance, for which the tanker should be entered, known as 'Tovalop', derived from the 'Tanker owners' voluntary agreement concerning liability for oil pollution'. There is also a special type of loss of earnings insurance for passenger cruise ships.
3. *War risks.* War risks insurance is also placed with mutual insurance companies like the protection and indemnity clubs. War risks covers

loss or damage to the ship caused by civil war, revolution, rebellion, insurrection, mines, torpedoes, bombs, etc.

4. *Loss of earnings.* This type of insurance is taken out when the ship has entered into a long-term charter, and covers off-hire risks. This type of insurance is usually very expensive and lenders/mortgagees would not usually require it. However, if a loan was only to be repaid from an anticipated cash flow (to be guaranteed by a specific long-term charter) then loss of earnings insurance should be carefully considered.
5. *Mortgagee's interest insurance/protection insurance.* This type of insurance is to protect the lender/mortgagee in the event that the insurances in relation to any of the above insurance policies have been avoided because of some default by the owner who took out the policy. Such defaults will include breach of warranty, misrepresentations or non-disclosure of a material fact.

In connection with the assignment of insurances, the owner will normally covenant to keep the ship insured (usually for hull and machinery, war risks and protection and indemnity risks) in the required amount. The owner also normally covenants to pay all premiums and not to make any material alteration in the terms of the various policies. The assignment of insurances will also normally require that a notice of assignment is sent to the relevant insurers/brokers and, in turn, that a letter is received from them confirming that the relevant 'loss payable and notice of cancellation clause' forms part of the insurance policy. Such a clause states that all claims in relation to a total loss or above a certain amount shall be paid to the lender/mortgagee and claims below such certain amount shall be paid to the owner. The clause also requires the insurers to advise the lender/mortgagee if any material changes are proposed to be made to the policy, if instructions from the owner to renew the policy are not received or if the insurers intend for any reason to cancel the policy.

EARNINGS

A lender/mortgagee will also require an assignment over all the present and future earnings of the ship. Earnings includes all freights, hire and any other moneys which may be earned and payable to the owner. It also includes all moneys due under any charter or contract of affreightment. A charterparty is a contract between the owner and the charterer by which the charterer hires the use of the whole ship (a) known as a *bareboat charter* or *demise charter* or (b) together with its crew for a fixed period known as a *time charter* or (c) for a voyage or a series of voyages, known as a *voyage or consecutive voyage charterparty* or (d) at short notice of a then available ship, known as a *spot charter.* A notice of assignment will usually be given to the charterer (or the person paying the income) requiring that all charter-hire monies should be paid into a particular account – usually in the name of the owner with the lender/mortgagee. However, for shorter charters the lender/mortgagee may not give such notice immediately – but will reserve the right to give such notice to the charterer in future or if default occurs. It may also be desirable to take an assignment over the specific accounts into which the earnings are from time to time paid.

Under the assignment of earnings the owner also normally covenants to procure the due performance by any charterer of its obligations under the charter, and that the owner will perform its own obligations under such charter. The owner also covenants that on entering any charter or contact of affreightment that it will notify the lender/mortgagee and supply it with a copy thereof. The owner will then procure that all moneys will be paid into a specified account in the name of the owner. On the occurrence of a default all money is usually transferred to an account in the name of the lender/mortgagee.

Guarantees

A lender/mortgagee will often require a guarantee to be given by the borrower's parent company and/or from other companies within the same group as the borrower. This is the case if the loan has been made to the borrower on the strength of the credit of the guarantors.

A guarantee is a promise by one person (the 'guarantor') to answer for the present or future debt of a second person (the 'debtor', i.e. the owner/mortgagor/borrower), such promise being made to the person to whom the debtor is, or will become, liable.

The types of clauses to be found in a guarantee will often be similar to those in the loan agreement, for example covenants, representations and financial reporting requirements.

Enforcement of the security

In the event of the borrower's default under the loan agreement the lender/mortgagee will have to consider whether and how to enforce the security. In that respect he will have regard to the following:

1. Costs of enforcement.
2. The fact that the price obtained for a ship at a court auction may well be substantially lower than that in a private sale.
3. Prior claims on the ship.
4. Unsecured claims on the ship (since if the lender/mortgagee wishes to continue operation of the ship rather than sell it, it will be necessary to continue paying unsecured claims as they arise in order to prevent the ship from being arrested by creditors).
5. The ship's movements and employment.

PRIOR CLAIMS

The order of priorities of the proceeds of sale of a ship depends on the jurisdiction in which the claims against the ship are proceeding. Subject to the overriding discretion of the courts the usual English order of priorities is as follows:

1. The Admiralty Marshall's costs of effecting and maintaining the arrest and of arranging the sale and the legal costs of the party who has the ship under arrest and in whose action the ship was sold.
2. Possessory lienholders, e.g. unpaid ship repairer in possession (however, possessory lienholders' claims are subordinate to all maritime liens which arose prior to the assumption of possession).
3. Maritime liens (including salvor's liens, so-called 'damage' liens and contractual liens in respect of masters' and crews' unpaid wages).
4. Mortgages.
5. Statutory liens, e.g. port and pilotage dues and claims for necessaries.
6. Unsecured claims.

The main maritime liens recognised by English law for which claims are likely to be encountered are (a) damage done by a ship, including collision damage, loss of life or personal injury arising out of the use of a ship, (b) salvage and (c) crews' and masters' wages.

The claims in respect of (a) and (b) should be covered by the hull and machinery insurance and/or entry of the ship in a protection and indemnity association with the result that the principal exposure of the mortgagee is in respect of unpaid wages.

PRACTICAL STEPS

As the lender/mortgagee decides whether or not to enforce its security there are a number of practical steps which it may be advisable to take:

1. Ensure the security documents are properly in order.
2. Check that the terms of the mortgage on the ship give the right to proceed (in particular, check for notice periods in respect of the default relied on and any periods allowed for curing the default).
3. Satisfy all necessary formalities (e.g. service of notice of default and acceleration on the borrower).
4. Ensure that the ship is properly insured.
5. Ensure that the ship remains in class by carrying out repairs recommended by the classification society (if the classification is lost then it will be difficult to sell the ship).
6. Obtain a valuation of the ship as this will enable the mortgagee to decide whether it is worth proceeding against the ship and guides him in his duty to obtain the best price for the ship.

7. Review the ship's trading position to establish whether the ship will be calling at a port where judicial proceedings against it are possible, either by trade creditors to enforce payment of claims or by the mortgagee.
8. Establish whether the ship can be traded profitably under any current charter. Alternatively, the charterer may be willing to get out of or at least renegotiate the charter.

IN REM CLAIMS

An Admiralty action *in rem* is in effect an action against an object or a thing as opposed to an action against a person. The thing or object is usually a ship; however, it may be cargo, freight or an aircraft. In such an action, the court may order that the thing or object, if it is within the jurisdiction, be arrested. If the plaintiff's action is successful then the thing or object will be sold and after the court's costs have been deducted, the proceeds will be used to settle the plaintiff's claim. The mortgagees should gather information about *in rem* claims since in considering whether the mortgagee should lend further money to the owner to enable the owner to continue trading (or whether the mortgagee should take possession and manage the ship itself), the likelihood of the ship being arrested by unpaid suppliers in every port at which it calls will not be attractive. Further, a mortgagee considering a private sale of the ship will find it difficult to sell the ship if there are a number of claimants pursuing it. Under English law, once a person has issued a writ *in rem* against the ship, then the claimant becomes a secured creditor of the ship and can enforce his rights against the ship notwithstanding a subsequent private (as opposed to judicial) sale of the ship.

JUDICIAL SALE

This is a surest way of enforcing a mortgage (although lower prices are usually obtained). On such a sale, all claims against the ship will attach to the sale proceeds which constitute a fund in court. The courts of other countries will normally recognise the effect of such a sale as conferring on a purchaser a clean title, free from all claims and encumbrances. This 'laundering' of the ship's title makes sale through a court the mortgagee's most effective remedy.

1. *Procedure.* The mortgagee must first commence *in rem* proceedings against the ship, arrange for the ship to be arrested and thereafter obtain a court order for the valuation and sale of the ship. In an English Admiralty sale the ship is sold free of all liens, encumbrances and debts whatsoever up to the date of the sale as all claims are transferred to the proceeds of sale, which are then retained in court pending claimants' obtaining judgment and court orders for the determination of priorities and payment out.

2. *Tactics.* It may be advantageous for the mortgagee to purchase the ship. First, this prevents sale at an undervalue and leaves the mortgagee as owner of a ship with a 'clean' title, which can then be disposed of without the price being depressed by the circumstances of a forced sale. Second, it may be possible to persuade the court to accept less than the full 'price' for the ship. If the amount of the other claims with priority to the mortgagee is less than the sale price of the ship, the court may agree to allow the mortgagee to pay in to court only the amount of the other claims ranking in priority to the mortgagee, thus short-circuiting the performance of obtaining a payment out of court as mortgagee what was paid into court as purchaser.
3. *Choice of jurisdiction.* The choice of forum for a court sale is important. The considerations include:
   (a) the local court priority rules regarding the ranking of claimants against the proceeds of sale of a ship (e.g. in certain jurisdictions, local trade creditors rank as maritime liens ahead of mortgagees);
   (b) whether a judicial sale will 'clean' all claims from the ship;
   (c) the speed with which a sale can be concluded (e.g. whether a sale pending judgment would be possible);
   (d) the time it generally takes for a mortgagee to obtain judgment and get an order for the payment out of the proceeds of sale;
   (e) the costs which will be incurred in achieving and maintaining the arrest and effecting the sale, which generally constitute a first claim on the proceeds of sale. If the sale proceeds do not cover these costs the party initiating the sale will generally be responsible for them. Further, it may be necessary for the arresting party to provide security for the costs of the arrest (the definition of which varies from jurisdiction to jurisdiction) and in some cases even the potential losses of the ship owner;
   (f) commercial considerations, notably as to the place where the best price can be obtained (auction procedures may impact on the price). Expert advice on the market should always be sought.
4. *Crew.* On a sale through the courts, the first priority of the mortgagee is to discharge and repatriate the crew as their wages continue to run until this happens and their claim has priority over that of the mortgagee. It may be advisable, in a manner acceptable to the local court, to make all payments necessary regarding the crew if by doing so one will stand in the place of and receive the benefit of the priority enjoyed by the crew members.

Conclusion

This chapter is intended to give a brief insight into the law of ship financing. As we have seen, the overall market looks optimistic. Finance will need to be raised to meet the demands of replacing the world's ageing fleet and for meeting new demands especially in the area of financing oil rigs and platforms. It is likely that ship financing will become more complex. In order to find the best possible structures for the financing banks and borrowers, such structures will have to take into account tax considerations, and the possibility of combining different types of financing within one transaction.

Appendix: UK tax considerations

Capital allowances

There may well be tax advantages available that enable the owner or financier effectively to reduce the quantum of the instalment payments due to it – but based upon the assumption that some tax benefit will arise and be granted to the owner or financier. Normally such assumptions will be set out in some detail in the documentation and the documentation will also deal with the responsibilities of the parties in the event that such tax benefits are not available.

In this context lease transactions have been structured on the basis that the financier (owner) of the ship will be able to obtain capital allowances which can be applied to reduce its tax burden in the United Kingdom or, alternatively, for the benefit of such allowances to be passed around within the same 'group' of companies in order that other members of such group (with taxable profits) can effectively obtain the benefit of the allowances.

The Capital Allowances Act 1990 (the CAA) states in Section 24 that where a person carrying on a trade 'has incurred capital expenditure on the provision of machinery and plant (e.g. a ship) wholly and exclusively for the purposes of the trade, and in consequence . . . the machinery or plant belongs or has belonged to him' he is entitled to a writing-down allowance equal to 25 per cent (or a proportion thereof for part years).

Subject to certain qualifications, the owner may, by written notice within two years from the end of the period for which the allowance arises, elect to postpone the whole or part of any writing-down allowance due to him for that period. This can then be claimed in a later period, albeit that allowances postponed cannot be used in a later year for group relief and certain loss claims.

The availability of such allowances is, needless to say, subject to a number of detailed and complex qualifications. One of these is that the ship must be used for a qualifying purpose as defined by the CAA. Section 39(b) of the CAA provides that

> a ship is also used for a qualifying purpose at any time when it is let on charter in the course of a trade . . . if (a) the person carrying on the trade is resident in the United Kingdom or carries on the trade there and (b) that person is responsible as principal . . . for navigating and managing the ship throughout the period of the charter.

Corporation tax

As mentioned above, especially with regard to lease or equivalent asset financing transactions, the financier (owner) may well be seeking to reduce the rate of corporation tax which it (or another member of its group) is paying on its UK profits. Corporation tax is currently charged at the rate of 35 per cent.

10

The function and capability of forfaiting

D. IAN GUILD
Chief Executive, Banque Indosuez Sogem Aval Ltd

Introduction

The key mechanism which underlies forfaiting, the discounting of bills of exchange, promissory notes or other forms of evidenced debt, has been an integral part of international trade for many centuries. However, the key difference between this function and forfaiting, or the provision of à forfait finance, as the world knows it today, is that the debt instruments are purchased from the beneficiary, the seller of goods or services, on a *non-recourse* basis. This means that, assuming the seller's documentation emerges in the agreed form as the commercial transaction progresses, the forfaiter who buys the debt has no recourse back to the seller, should the latter's client default on payment.

Forfaiting, therefore, is the selling on a non-recourse basis of any acceptable debt instrument which calls for payment at specified time periods in return for the delivery of goods and services. The non-recourse element also applies to any other party who has previously held the instrument, whether or not it is the seller of the goods, assuming, quite naturally, that the documentation is legally in order and the debt instruments are endorsed with the all-important words *without recourse.*

Purchasing the debt instruments in this way means that the forfaiter assumes a considerable amount of risk, associated with collection of the debt when it falls due. However, the forfaiter counteracts this in two ways, the most important of which is, prior to purchasing the debt, the securing of a third party guarantee or aval, which can be claimed against in the event of default. As will be discussed later, this can take various forms, but usually it involves some form of bank guarantee from an institution in the importer's country.

The second way in which the forfaiter can reduce risk is by trading on purchased debt into the secondary forfaiting market (to be discussed in depth later), enabling the forfaiter to reduce exposure in one particular deal and assemble a more varied risk portfolio, both in terms of individual types of importers (perhaps sectorally) and also geographically. It must be remembered that the risk for the forfaiter, as for others involved in international transactions, is both commercial and political: importers may become insolvent, but on the other hand, solvent importers may not be able to pay to schedule if their government suddenly introduces exchange controls.

This, in brief outline, is therefore how forfaiting works and its advantage to exporters is more or less self-explanatory: they receive due payments at agreed times with no recourse back to them in the event of buyer default or political intervention. This confers the advantages of guaranteed and planned cash flow (which, in turn, permit planned and orderly investment in productive capacity) and additionally obviates the need by the exporter to chase up slow payers or legally pursue bad debts.

Moreover, forfaiting possesses two other key characteristics, compared with several other forms of guaranteed international payment mechanisms. Exporters can receive up to 100 per cent of the value of the receivables, less, of course, the discount charged by the forfaiter (see box). And the financing is made available to the exporter at a fixed rate.

Calculating the discount

The discount on a forfaiting transaction is quoted as either *straight discount* or *discount to yield.* A straight discount of 10 per cent on $100,000 is simply $10,000. However, over a year this represents a yield of $10,000/100,000 or 11.11 per cent, with the latter figure then known as the annual *discount to yield.* This is compounded annually. Of the two rates it is the latter which is the more useful, since it gives the all-important yield or interest rate associated with the transaction.

The actual rate paid depends on interest rate conditions for the currency in which the finance will be provided and the forfaiter's margin for perceived risk and administration costs. The actual overall amount paid reflects the discount rate charged and the time-span between payment to the exporter and presentation of the paper on maturity.

Post-war origins

It is always difficult to focus precisely on when any particular type of trade finance technique emerged. Undoubtedly, prior to the Second World War some form of forfaiting activity took place – some discounting arrangements with third party avalisers. However, as with countertrade, it was the period immediately after the Second World War that witnessed the real launch of this technique as a significant trading mechanism.

War-ravaged Eastern European countries needed grain, mainly from the United States, and, starved of foreign exchange, needed some form of extended credit to get their hands on it. Swiss bankers, based mainly in Zurich, seized the opportunity to fund the deals, basically in the manner outlined above – buying US and other suppliers' bills of exchange and promissory notes on a *without recourse* basis, having first assured themselves an acceptable aval, and then presenting the debt for payment on maturity.

As has been finally proven over the last year or so, Eastern Europe, including the Soviet Union, never managed to establish under the communist command economy system the ability to end the need for expensive, high-technology machinery and capital goods equipment. Neither did it significantly develop industries which, themselves, generated hard currency in the West to substantially put its international trade on a multilateral, hard currency basis.

The result, therefore, was over forty years of foreign exchange shortages (alleviated only in the Soviet Union's case by its vast mineral and energy wealth), and the need for a variety of trade and project finance techniques. This need was partly provided by forfaiting, both in its own separate capacity and also, latterly, as an integral part of other complex arrangements involving, for example, various forms of countertrade.

Hence from forfaiting's beginnings as a Zurich-based business concentrating on grain deliveries, its use steadily expanded to include a host of other commodities and, ultimately, the area which became its hallmark: capital goods trading and big ticket project business.

Today, it is still this area with which forfaiting is most associated. However, assuming acceptable arrangements can be made, there has been an increased willingness amongst forfaiters in recent years to fund shorter-term trade deals – some, for instance, have even financed oil deliveries involving payment maturities of as little as a few weeks.

There has been another way in which forfaiting has changed. Over the years, the credit requirements which ushered in its appearance in East–West trade after the Second World War, became an increasing feature of business between the industrialised states and developing countries. As newly independent countries throughout Africa and the Far East, along with Latin American states, rushed to develop their economies, became locked in crises of economic expectations, were periodically buffeted by wildly gyrating raw material prices and, ultimately, experienced the soaring price of oil, their need for credit exploded.

Most tried to handle their problems by borrowing ever-increasing amounts of cash in hard currency and at interest rates that were periodically apt to soar. However, this situation also provided opportunities for exporters willing to utilise forfaiting. For them – and for the forfaiters who organised the funding – this method of financing conferred some advantages over those who sought payment from ballooning mega-borrowing, the purpose of which, in many cases, was never precisely specified beyond being for 'infrastructural requirements' or general 'balance of payments support'.

Forfaiting, however, is inextricably linked with specific trade or project deals and the risks associated with them are, therefore, individually assessed and avalised. This does not mean that an exporter (or funding forfaiter) is free from sovereign risk and that outstanding debts will never be swept into a general debt moratorium or rescheduling. However, the closely specified nature of the trade or project-based deal, combined with the existence of a specific guarantee linked to it, gives the forfaiter that extra lien, should country risk problems, in particular, arise.

In turn, this has meant that in some cases forfaiters have been willing to fund deals to countries that have been off-cover with export credit agencies because the latter have been viewing the importing country's market as a whole, rather than the specific performance of an individual client in particular. All the same, forfaiters stress that they are no soft touch when it comes to funding deals and object to suggestions that forfaiting is *last resort* financing.

The future of forfaiting

Looking to the future use of forfaiting, both in terms of the types of trade forfaiters may be willing to fund and the countries to which they may, in the main, fund it, several major points should be borne in mind. The foreign exchange position in Eastern Europe (and the developing countries) is as bad as ever: indeed during 1990 the Soviet Union even fell behind on short-term trade payments, an unprecedented development. Moreover, industrially the region is in a state of advanced decay, bordering in some cases on collapse. This is doubly unfortunate, given the high consumer expectations and demands which *perestroika* has released throughout these newly democratising states.

Putting these considerations together, it is obvious that Eastern Europe's need for credit will be unprecedented. Direct bilateral and multilateral aid, some of it through the newly constituted European Bank for Reconstruction and Development, will play a major role, but the attitude of the commercial banks could well remain conditioned by the legacy of the Third World debt crisis, which also had strong echoes in Eastern Europe, particularly Poland. Consequently, it seems unlikely that, for its part, the commercial banking community will try to satisfy East European – and, indeed, Third World – credit demands in the loose, undisciplined manner that characterised their policies during the 1970s and from which they are still suffering the effects.

In summary, there will remain a massive demand for trade and project funding, but the banking community could well approach this with considerable caution, even when the International Monetary Fund (IMF) and other multilateral agencies, such as the new insurance organisation, Multinational Investment Guarantee Agency (MIGA), are providing their official blessing and support.

All this, therefore, points to specific funding for specific business backed by specific guarantees. There are several ways in which this can be achieved, including the export credit agencies themselves continuing to develop policies which consider more individual risks in a country than merely the overall risk associated with the country itself. But, increasingly, forfaiting seems set, for all the above reasons, to play a significantly more important role still in funding deals with East European and developing countries.

And as for the forfaiters themselves, they are no longer clustered around Zurich's Bahnhofstrasse. A considerable amount of business is still done from Switzerland, but in more recent years, it seems fair to claim that London has become the forfaiting capital of the world. The market is essentially dominated by three specialist forfaiting companies, though a number of banks located in London can offer forfaiting, in many cases as an ancillary service to their mainstream and, often, more conventional trade finance services. Certain of the major banks have opened New York offices and several US banks now offer this product world-wide.

A closer look at forfaiting

The debt instruments

The debt instruments involved in forfaiting transactions are primarily bills of exchange and promissory notes. The former is drawn on the obligor, the importer, by the beneficiary, the exporter and accepted by the former. The promissory note, a kind of legally dressed-up IOU, is issued by the obligor, the importer, in favour of the beneficiary, the exporter. Forfaiters regard both instruments as equally acceptable as the basis of an à forfait financing deal, provided there is a *clean* obligation by the obligor to pay the forfaiter when the debt matures.

However, there is a potential legal complication regarding bills of exchange which can generate a preference amongst some exporters to utilise promissory notes, rather than the former, in international trade transactions in general and when entering into forfaiting transactions in particular. This stems from a legal provision under Article 9 of the International Convention for Commercial Bills agreed at a Geneva Conference in 1930. This states that the drawer of a bill of exchange guarantees both acceptance and payment. However, 'he may release himself from guaranteeing acceptance, but any stipulation by which he releases himself from the guarantee of payment is deemed to be not written'. This effectively means that an exporter drawing a bill of exchange on an importer may not necessarily be liable as its endorser, but, under the terms of the Convention, will not be able to shake off its legal liability as its drawer.

This condition, however, does not apply to promissory notes. Moreover, the Convention in question specifically confers the advantage that the endorser of a promissory note can legally be freed from any liability by endorsing the promissory note with the words *without recourse.*

Not surprisingly, exporters utilising promissory notes as the basis of forfaiting transactions can have some justification, in theory at least, for feeling more comfortable. On the other hand, those seeking to utilise bills of exchange still have little to be concerned about as the forfaiter taking them will always be willing to give a written undertaking that it will not take any legal action against the exporter in the event of buyer default – an undertaking that the exporter should always remember to ask for, should it not be offered.

As a further comfort, it is useful to know that such an undertaking given by a forfaiter is legally enforceable in many countries, should any problems subsequently develop relating to this legal obligation under the 1930 Convention. And it should always be borne in mind that it is extremely unlikely that a reputable forfaiter will try to extricate himself of herself from such an undertaking to an exporter in those countries where such undertakings are not legally enforceable. Hence the need for the exporter to deal with a respectable forfaiter.

Security

Forfaiters are not merely in the business of purchasing bills of exchange, promissory notes or other forms of evidenced receivables on a non-recourse basis and taking a bet on whether they will be paid when the debts fall due.

They take obvious risks, both commercial and political, in purchasing the instruments, but the key means by which they contain such risks, and hence provide the service they do to exporters, is by securing the paper with an appropriate guarantee. This guarantee can basically take one of three forms: an aval, a formal letter of guarantee or a *burgschaft.*

The *aval* springs from the old *Code Napoleon* and involves the bill of exchange or the promissory note being inscribed with the words *per aval,* and signed and completed in the name of the party on whose behalf the aval is being provided. In law, the avalist assumes the role of the committed party to the promissory note or bill of exchange. In the eyes of the forfaiter, the avalist therefore becomes the debtor.

The aval is, in many respects, a simple form of guarantee for the forfaiter as the aval itself is inseparable from the documentation; indeed, it is an integral part of the documentation, relating to the forfaiting deal. Also for the forfaiter, it represents a commitment by the avaliser to pay regardless of the performance of the underlying trade transaction and therefore does not present problems should the debt instrument be sold on by the forfaiter. In cases where guarantees are issued separately from the principal documentation, problems of transferability may arise.

The concept of the aval is not legally recognised in all countries. It has, for instance, no formal recognition in English law, but as it represents an endorsement of the documentation, it would probably have the same legal standing in the United Kingdom as it would in a country where such an endorsement is known as an aval in law. However, in countries where one or more parties to the transaction feel that the legal status of an aval is insufficient for their purposes, the forfaiter may receive its guarantee by the formulation of additional documentation attached to the promissory note or bill of exchange – in essence a letter of guarantee. Such a letter of guarantee must be, like an aval, a stand-alone commitment by the guarantor, usually a bank, to pay the forfaiter the required amounts should there be a payment default on presentation of the bill of exchange or promissory note on the due date. As with the aval, there must be no reference to the guarantee being conditional on the performance of the trade transaction.

There is no such thing as an internationally standardised letter of guarantee, let alone a general acceptance of such a letter of guarantee in international or national commercial law. However, in order to ensure its value as, indeed, a guarantee it must cover a series of important points. For instance, the guarantee must be assignable and transferable so as to allow the forfaiter to trade the debt in the secondary market if it so wishes. It should, as mentioned, specifically state that it is unconditional. Moreover, it should also be described as divisible, though for all practical purposes this tends not to be the case, regardless of the wording.

Whilst they provide the required security, the administration involved in assembling letters of guarantee is far greater than that required in organising an aval.

The last form of possible security for a forfaiter is an instrument called the *burgschaft*. Its use has been generally limited over the years, primarily mobilised only in the case of forfaiting transactions relating to East Germany. And in the wake of German reunification it seems a strong possibility that the *burgschaft* could steadily disappear from the forfaiting lexicon. The key problem with a *burgschaft* as an instrument of guarantee for a forfaiter is that it carries with it at least an element of conditionality. In essence, the provider of the *burgschaft* will not be made liable for the required indemnity should the importer default until proof has been provided that the underlying transaction involving the à forfait finance has been satisfactorily completed; in other words that the goods involved have been received and accepted in good condition.

Aside from these traditional forms of security for forfaiters, there have also been some limited moves towards export credit agencies providing some form of guarantees to help forfaiting transactions perform. Italy's official export credit insurer, Sezione Speciale per l'Assicurazione del Credito all' Esportazione (SACE) is probably the most advanced in this respect in providing guarantees. By contrast the United Kingdom's ECGD has been debating the possibility of providing a specific policy for some time, though nothing has emerged, whilst in the United States, the Export–Import Bank has considered exploring some form of guarantees for forfaiters, although forfaiting has never been a technique which has significantly caught the imagination of US banks and exporters.

The secondary market

Aside from the formal types of guarantees outlined above, allied with in-depth research by the forfaiter to assess, for example, any transfer risks, the other key means by which forfaiters can limit or disperse risk and, thereby boost the security of their overall operation, is by selling off some of the primary paper they have purchased into the secondary market.

There are basically two forms of forfaiting deals: *primary deals* and *secondary deals.* A primary deal involves a forfaiter setting up an arrangement involving all the various parties, including, most obviously, the exporter, but also the avaliser and the importer. This deal, once constructed and mobilised, then involves the forfaiter purchasing the agreed, avalised paper at the appropriate time from the exporter and presenting it when due on, as stressed, a non-recourse basis to the exporter.

However, the purchased bills are assets which, given their legal characteristics, can usually be sold in their entirety or in broken down clusters to other parties with the attached aval continuing to apply – hence, in part, the bills' saleability. The on-selling of primary paper to other parties is known as a secondary deal and, indeed, this practice, carried out on a considerable scale, fuels a substantial *secondary market* in forfaited debt.

As mentioned, the sale by a forfaiter of primary paper into the secondary market is a way of further reducing residual risk attached to the deal and might result in a better balance of overall risk for the forfaiter whose book may have become overly weighted towards a certain country or group of countries where risk is perceived to be higher. The advantages to the forfaiter flowing from the existence of a secondary market are also in the interests of the exporter.

To begin with, the existence of a market in which a primary forfaiter, having constructed a deal, can partly or even wholly off-load associated bills, can in certain circumstances encourage the former to assemble the arrangement in the first place, not forgetting, of course, that forfaiting also involves the provision of fixed interest rate finance – a further risk which the forfaiter has to take.

Also, aside from off-loading risk, the secondary market can also help keep the forfaiter more liquid. That is to say, it will have more funds in reserve to assemble a deal quickly for an exporter, a point of some significance if the latter is in a highly competitive situation and, itself, can only proceed with the deal if it can gain early access to finance given, perhaps, its own cash flow constraints.

Finally, for the forfaiter, the secondary market is also, frankly, a forum in which the skilful player can make a profit by not only selling on its own primary paper at a premium, but also by actively trading a secondary market portfolio.

The participants in the secondary market are, in addition to the primary forfaiters themselves, primarily banks and financial institutions that wish to invest in à forfait paper as an extension of their overall financial activities. Uncommonly, well-off individuals participate in the market, as an alternative form of investment.

One last point should be noted about the secondary market: there are a small group of countries, one or two of which are located in North Africa, who do not wish to have their trade paper traded on secondary markets. This essentially stems from their desire to know as precisely as possible to whom they owe payments – a policy which may have some bearing on their future borrowing plans. If, for example, a country in mind has a group of banks as possible future financiers, they may not wish to be told on approaching them that, as a result of having purchased millions of dollars worth of à forfait paper, these banks do not have sufficient capacity left for that country's specific requirements.

When a country does not wish to see its trade paper traded, the forfaiter has two choices. The first is simple: it can simply walk away from the deal. The second involves assembling the deal, but based on the written legal understanding that the bills will, indeed, not be sold on, in whole or in part, in the secondary market.

Assembling a forfaiting deal

There is no single, simple way in which a forfaiting deal is initiated and assembled, though certain basic principles come into play so that the deal is finally consummated in the accepted manner.

To begin with, the actual initiator of a forfaiting deal can be one of a variety of parties: an exporter, an importer, a bank active on behalf of one of the principals to a transaction or a consultant or trading house itself trying to assemble a transaction on behalf of an importer or exporter. And then, of course, there are the primary forfaiters themselves, as mentioned located mainly in London, who may proactively seek out opportunities to provide their services. This they may do by approaching exporters known to be bidding for business in difficult markets where the advantages conferred by forfaiting could be especially useful. Alternatively, some primary forfaiters enjoy close relations with certain countries known to require credit for various projects and capital goods imports and are consequently in a position to make proposals directly to the competent authorities.

However, it usually tends to be the case that it is the exporter or the exporter's bank who approaches the forfaiter. This reflects two factors: the responsibility for discounting the bills of exchange or promissory notes, given that they are respectively drawn by the exporter or payable to it, rests with the latter. Secondly, and particularly in today's difficult trading climate, the more aggressive – and successful – exporters seek to accompany their sales bids with competitive financing proposals which enhance the attractiveness of their product to the importer.

Given the second point, it is essential that exporters approach a forfaiter at the earliest possible stage because, in so doing, precise financial proposals can be assembled, including, of course, the all-important cost element, and integrated into the bid price. Alternatively, of course, the forfaiter can explain why its method of funding would not or could not apply and consequently the exporter can rule it out as an option for its proposed deal.

In practice, however, exporters, despite this often-given piece of advice, still tend to come to forfaiters after they have begun negotiations with an importer, perhaps even quoted a price and maybe even signed a contract. They then at this point run the risk of receiving a very unwelcome piece of information: the discount they would have to accept on the trade paper is unacceptable within the margin they have left themselves on the deal and they, therefore, lose out on the advantages that a forfaiting transaction could bring.

Questions the exporter must answer

When an exporter approaches a forfaiter, he or she must have to hand answers to a series of fundamentally important questions:

1. What is the extent of the finance, the currency in which it is to be denominated and the maturity period?
2. What is the name of the importer, its country of location and, if different from the latter, the country to which goods are to be shipped?
3. How familiar is the exporter with the importer and does he or she have any general or specific information on the latter, such as usual bankers and the means by which payment is settled?
4. What form would the forfaited debt take: bills of exchange, promissory notes, etc.?
5. Who is the proposed guarantor, where is the guarantor located and what form of guarantee is proposed?
6. When and in what amounts will the bills of exchange or notes arrive?
7. When are the bills scheduled to mature?
8. What types of goods are involved and when is delivery scheduled?
9. Are there any authorisations or special conditions attached to the goods, such as a specialist licence?
10. Through which bank in what country would the forfaiter receive funds?

Most of these questions have a specific significance. In other words they are not just routine enquiries designed to set the wheels in motion. Indeed, should the answers in some cases turn out to be not what the forfaiter wishes to hear, then the wheels may not begin to turn at all.

For example, take the last question: if it is proposed that the forfaiter, should it purchase the paper, be paid through a bank in a country – not necessarily the importer's country – where there are known to be stiff foreign exchange restrictions and perhaps where foreign funds have even been recently frozen, the forfaiter may decide that the deal is too risky.

Another unwelcome response as far as the forfaiter is concerned is if the proposed form of guarantee, or the guarantor itself, is not acceptable owing to previous difficulties surrounding either.

Assuming, however, that the forfaiter is happy with the answers to the questions, the attempted formulation of an acceptable deal then moves into its next stage. This rests largely with the forfaiter, though it needs to be assisted by the exporter.

The forfaiter must now assess four separate types of risk associated with the proposed deal:

1. The sovereign risk associated with the importer's country. (In other words, primarily, what are the chances of hard currency emanating from the country in question at the required time?)
2. The importer risk.
3. The exporter risk: the detailed risks associated with the guarantor.
4. The type of guarantee (given that, by now, the general risk will have been regarded as acceptable).

In order of action, the forfaiter will probably begin with the assessment of the guarantor: if on closer analysis the forfaiter has doubts about the guarantor's credibility, then he or she will either request another guarantor or merely drop the deal straight away. Given that the guarantors are usually banks or state institutions whose bona fides can quickly be checked out, an assessment can usually be made in a matter of hours, thus putting the forfaiter well on the way towards being able to quote on the deal, if it is so wished. This is especially the case given that the guarantee is unconditional and consequently once the acceptability of the guarantor is established, other risk assessments, whilst still very important, can assume a less crucial nature.

As far as sovereign risk is concerned, a major forfaiting house with its ear to the ground generally should have to do very little out-of-house research to establish possible transfer or other risks. And, ultimately, the risk associated with the underlying trade transaction and the parties to it, depends upon the bills of exchange or promissory notes being in order and avalised. And this risk is contained by the fact that the forfaiter is unlikely to fund the exporter ahead of receipt of documentation, unless it is done 'under reserve'.

This means that should the documentation turn out to be unacceptable, the forfaiter can reclaim funds. Even so, the forfaiter will still make various enquiries about the financial and trading performance of the exporter and importer, given that they may show something that would suggest the trade deal may, perhaps, never be consummated and thus the forfaiter is wasting time continuing to consider it.

Discount indication

Assuming that the forfaiter's risk assessment shows up favourable results, the forfaiter is then in a position to give the exporter an indication of the discount that would be charged to conduct the transaction. At this stage a precise quotation would not be involved and the forfaiter, additionally, would not be giving any commitment to carry out the funding. However, the exporter now has a figure around which he or she can continue to assemble a bid or, if the underlying trade transaction has been agreed, to decide whether or not the discount at which the bills must be sold is acceptable within the financial framework of the deal.

In the latter case, the answer should be forthcoming more or less straight away, given that the exporter is probably in touch with a number of different possible financiers, other forfaiters amongst them. Moreover, there will also be those who are still assembling bids who may know more or less straight away whether the forfaiter's proposed discount can be accommodated within the bid price.

However, for those exporters who believe that the discount can be realistically worked into their bid, they will then request the forfaiter to turn the indication into a specific discount quotation.

Once the exporter has decided to ask for the specific discount quotation, two new aspects of the deal assembly process then come into operation: the option period and the commitment period. After quoting a definite discount, the forfaiter is then running the risk – remembering that a fixed rate is quoted – that the rate may shift in the period between quotation and shipment of goods (assuming that the company's tender is accepted at all).

This risk is best viewed in two sections: the interest rate risk which pertains between the submission of the tender and its acceptance by the buyer. As the exporter's offer is perhaps only one among many there is no guarantee that it will win the bid and require the funding. During this period the forfaiter will usually offer the exporter the option to take up the finance at no cost, provided it does not extend beyond two days or so. After that an option fee is likely to be levied, but, regardless, an option period on the finance is unlikely to last for more than one month; two to three months are exceptional. And then, of course, at times of wildly gyrating interest rates, the option period may be very short. Indeed, it can be known in exceptional conditions for no option period to be granted.

Once the tender, with its associated finance, is accepted by the buyer, another risk then ensues for the forfaiter, bearing in mind that the finance is being provided on a fixed interest basis and that shipment may not take place for perhaps up to a year. At this point, both the exporter and the importer are committed to the commercial and financial transaction and either could be faced with considerable legal consequences should they walk away from it.

In order to cover the risk, the forfaiter during this period will charge a commitment fee. This is simply because, though the funds are scheduled for use, they are not actually being used, and they cannot be committed to another party, which might even be offering a more profitable deal.

Whether the forfaiter grants an option or enters into a commitment, it will have forwarded an offer document – perhaps a telex initially, but later confirmed in writing. This offer document will make reference to a number of items which the forfaiter will need to see before discounting the bills. These may include exchange control permits, import licences and any other authorisations which may be needed, such as proof that any required stamp duty has been paid.

Given that the forfaiter is now committing funds, perhaps for an extended time period, he or she obviously has an interest in the commercial transaction performing: hence the level of information requested in the first place (such as the types of goods, etc., see above) which now has a bearing on the forfaiter. Quite a few of the required documents, such as necessary import authorities can, by their very nature, be acquired before the transaction goes through and the forfaiter will wish to check as much of this as possible before the delivery date.

In order to speed up the discounting operation the exporter should make sure that all the necessary paperwork is to hand at the earliest opportunity. After the exporter has accepted the forfaiter's offer, the preparation of a series of bills of exchange or signed promissory notes, depending on the selected mechanism, must be arranged with the importer. And as a further step the exporter will arrange, probably using his or her own bank, to have the notes avalised or the letter of guarantee prepared. The exporter then endorses them to the forfaiter with the all-important words 'without recourse'.

When all this is in place the forfaiting arrangement is ready for execution and the documentation is usually lodged with a bank, after the forfaiter checks the authenticity of all the relevant signatures.

Finally, when it is available, the exporter takes the shipping documentation to the bank and the relevant dates are added; either the actual day of the bill of lading, or an agreed number of days after the bill of lading, depending on the credit agreement that the exporter has arrived at with the importer. The issue date on the shipping documentation determines the bills' or notes' maturity dates.

With all documentation to hand, checked, endorsed and dated, the exporter can then proceed to the forfaiter who will discount the bills immediately at the originally agreed discount. It could be that the exporter's goods will only have left the quayside twenty-four hours before and the exporter is now in possession of payment, less the discount, and has no further worries about the transaction.

Settlement

To complete the financial transaction the forfaiter now has to present the bills or promissory notes to the guarantor when the first series matures, having perhaps initially written to the guarantor pointing out that the transaction had been concluded. The guarantee is an absolute obligation to pay and should the guarantor refuse to do so then the forfaiter must immediately launch a legal action. Walking away from a guarantee is very rare.

There does obviously remain the question of sovereign risk; simply that the guarantor cannot get the funds out of his country. However – and here once again is one of the advantages of forfaiting transactions in difficult markets – even if a government declares a debt moratorium or sweeps billions of dollars of loans into a rescheduling agreement, there has been a historical tendency for funds associated with forfaiting transactions to be treated separately.

One disadvantage, however, which the forfaiter does face, compared with other lenders, is that should one series of bills be dishonoured, the forfaiter cannot, whilst seeking to get these paid, accelerate payment of those to come, even if it presumes, as is likely, that it will face increasing payment difficulties. The problem is a legal one: given the nature of the funding technique, forfaiting does not allow a forfaiter to call a default ahead of a bill's maturity date.

Advantages and disadvantages for the exporter

The advantages of forfaiting for the exporter have been clearly pointed out above. In essence, they involve the provision, usually on shipment, of up to 100 per cent of the value of the goods shipped with no recourse back to the company, should the foreign buyer default or funds not be made available for some other sovereign risk reason. Moreover, the funding is at a fixed rate throughout: in other words the bills are discounted at the initially agreed rate even though delivery of the goods may take place at some considerable time in the future. The interest and currency rate risks therefore belong to the forfaiter, not the exporter.

Further advantages are that forfaiters work with already existing commercial instruments, promissory notes and bills of exchange, and there is no need to draw up expensive additional paperwork. Moreover, by gaining an option to finance at a fixed rate from a forfaiter, the exporter is able to build this figure into the bid calculations.

Of course, there are some disadvantages to the exporter. The exporter, for example, has to make sure that all the documentation relating to debt instruments and the aval is valid. Consequently, the exporter must take the trouble to know about any rules specially pertaining to, for example, the debt instruments in the buyer's country, though, in fact, much of this work is assumed by the forfaiter.

Documentation aside, the exporter has to try to find a guarantor that is acceptable to the forfaiter. This will be easier in some countries than others. For example, in a developing country likely as not set to reschedule payments, the quality of the guarantor would have to be very good – and perhaps it would even have to be demonstrated that on previous difficult occasions involving fund transfer, the guarantor has always managed to deliver the funds.

Finally the advantages conferred by forfaiting come at a price; the discount on the face value of the receivable, only some of which can be 'lost' in the bid. It is the cost of forfaiting that tends to make some exporters dismiss the technique out of hand: many of those who do so, however, do not fully appreciate what forfaiting can do for their company's export drive, nor (and, in a way, why should they?) the risks borne by the forfaiter.

Aside from the advantages which the exporter can enjoy, the latter is also in a position to enhance the bid because he or she can pass on some of the advantages to the buyer, including the offer of fixed rate finance and the easy documentation process.

On the other hand, the exporter's client may not necessarily welcome the proposed financing technique. For example, the aval which the importer must seek and which must be acceptable to the exporter and the forfaiter will count against the company's credit lines. Moreover, the importer will have to pay a fee to gain the guarantee. There is also the question that the debt instruments involved in a forfaiting transaction are legally regarded as being 'abstract' documents which have to be honoured regardless of the performance of the underlying trade deal. This, therefore, means that those importers who do not, themselves, fully appreciate the concept of forfaiting, may finish up in legal difficulties stemming from the nature of the transaction and then entering into another legal battle with the supplier if there are alleged irregularities with the transaction itself.

Also for the importer, there is the thought that as everything will be so legally sealed up, dealing with an exporter who wishes to have his receivables forfaited would mean that the importer might not be able to fudge by a few days or weeks or longer the payments, as perhaps might be possible if the credit was being supplied in some other way. This, therefore, may have a bearing on whether the importer is prepared to deal with the exporter.

Finally, an importer may also decide not to deal with an exporter forfaiting his or her receivables because of a suspicion that some of the cost of the operation will be handed on to the importer.

Comparisons with forfaiting

Medium and long term

In comparing forfaiting with other forms of trade finance, it is only fair to compare like with like. The cost of forfaiting cannot be compared with an exporter having an order fully funded out of the country's national aid budget, as can happen.

Generally speaking, there are relatively few commercial alternatives, offering such a simple mix of fixed interest funding on a non-recourse basis amounting to 100 per cent of the value of the receivables.

Looking at medium-term finance, there are the export credit guarantee agencies, such as the ECGD, which insure credits against non-payment, and the private insurance market. The latter will only deal in risk stretching out to around three years.

The private market can provide a more flexible form of cover than that offered by the ECAs which, by and large, still tend to look at country risk as a whole, rather than individual risks, though this is changing. ECA cover for more than two years also qualifies for Consensus support; that is to say that the ECA will provide fixed rate finance at the officially agreed minimum rate between members of the OECD, by subsidising the difference between this rate and commercial rates.

However, there are now moves afoot to remove this service: indeed certain countries, the so-called Category 'A' countries, have been removed already, with the result that a country such as the Soviet Union must pay the full commercial rate for finance. Assuming, as seems likely, that the subsidy element will steadily be negotiated away in coming years for all countries, then the ECAs will revert to providing just insurance and guarantee services.

There are other problems, as well, with ECAs. Cover will seldom, if ever, stretch to 100 per cent of the value of the receivables – 85 per cent is much more likely to be the maximum figure. Moreover, ECAs and private export credit schemes are in many respects no different from any other insurance bodies when it comes to paying claims: they take a long time, especially compared with forfaiting where the exporter is guaranteed payment straight away, provided documentation is in order.

Finally, operating with medium-term insurance is not a 'one-stop-shop'. Finance has to be negotiated to be insured and that may take time and considerable effort.

There is, of course, the more novel method of utilising variable rate, commercial medium-term funding, allied with some form of interest rate and currency hedging on one of the burgeoning number of the world's financial futures exchanges. But these can be fickle places in which to seek security and must be constantly watched. Moreover, the commercial finance the exporter is looking to protect from both an exchange rate and interest perspective is still unlikely to cover 100 per cent of the value of the contract and the arrangement still needs some form of repayments guarantee, probably the goods themselves, in the event of a default, unless – and this seems unlikely – the bank is prepared to take a considerable element of the risk on to its own books. And the whole process is further away still from the concept of 'one-stop' trade finance and insurance.

Medium- and long-term finance is also available via the traditional project finance route and the more slightly modified routes, such as build–own–transfer (BOT) and build–own–operate–transfer (BOOT). The principle in all of these cases is the same: that the income stream from the project pays back the finance and the risk is written on the project itself.

There is a long journey between the theory and practice, partly because, particularly in the BOT and BOOT cases, someone has got to put up funds either as loans or equity. There could well be some form of ECA involvement and in the end the whole thing depends on the product stream flowing or, in the case of, say, a power plant, the host power authority agreeing to take the electricity at an agreed price formula for a good many years before the cost of erecting the installation is paid off, let alone the profit margin addressed. In short, the whole process can become a complex, sometimes highly political affair as state guarantees are sought from the host country's government.

Away from the mega-project, leasing can be competitive as a means of obtaining capital goods at financing rates which can be fixed for a considerable time period. However, unlike forfaiting, leasing deals tend to be awash with documentation and for the exporter looking to 'sell' capital goods on a leasing basis, it must access suitable taxable profits to offset against the cost of the assets.

Short term

It was mentioned earlier that, though traditionally associated with medium-term capital goods business, in recent years forfaiting has been mobilised to fund short-term business of perhaps only a few weeks. In this respect, therefore, it can be compared with some of the short-term funding schemes, which, in some cases, are provided by credit insurers. As its name implies, this gave participating banks more or less comprehensive cover which they could pass on to their clients.

A number of specialist schemes have been set up in the United Kingdom by banks and one by a specialist trade finance house, to provide short-term non-recourse finance. To a greater or lesser extent they operate in harness with an ECGD policy or a policy of a private insurer, and to that extent they are subjected to the limitations such insurers impose as outlined above. However, they do offer an element of non-recourse finance.

Then, aside from these specialist schemes, there is international factoring, which without dispute has gained in popularity in recent years. This also leaves, however, a residual risk to the exporter of perhaps 20 per cent of the value of the receivables. Moreover, the practice tends to be associated with a long string of repeat deals, rather than one-off high-value transactions and, arguably, those who complain about forfaiting discounts being high would have similar criticisms about the cost of factoring.

Using forfaiting holistically

Finally, it should be pointed out that forfaiting, whilst being used as a mechanism in itself, has been increasingly used on occasions as part of holistic trade finance arrangements involving other mechanisms. For example, there have been instances where lease payments have been forfaited: in other words, where a leasee or a leasor is seeking credit beyond the contracted lease payment date, the leasor can take payment by a forfaiting route utilising the agreed bills, suitably avalised and these are then presented to the forfaiter at the agreed time for payment.

Also, forfaiting can have a role in countertrade transactions – deals that are struck in the first place because of the lack of foreign exchange. Thus, in say mandatory counterpurchase deals, cash gaps can be bridged by a forfaiter stepping in with forfaiting finance to make the deal function. Then, there are instances where finance may be mixed, involving an element of forfaiting, but also, perhaps, a tranche of lending supported by an ECA. More innovative still, there have also been one or two examples where government aid agencies have been willing to step in partly to guarantee losses from defaults on ineligible notes in the interests of trying to move capital goods into an agreed area.

Lastly, in an attempt to extend the forfaiting service for exporters further, some forfaiters have been offering *with recourse* pre-shipment funding. Given possible long lead-lag times between a company signing a contract and making shipment when it can access normal forfaiting funds, some forfaiting houses have bolted pre-shipment funding on the front end of their service.

At this point they do not have the usual documentation to discount and this can be reflected in variable interest rates and lower than 100 per cent funding. However, the arrangement can give the exporter working capital during the production period and, in order to provide it, the forfaiter can take a specific lien on that stream of output designated for the export deal under a so-called 'Romalpa' clause. This gives the forfaiter a beneficial interest in the goods, regardless of their state of development, and whether or not, for instance, the supplier goes into liquidation.

In summary, forfaiting in the future may move considerably beyond its traditional function in order to help finance trade in a world which does not promise any let up in today's difficult international commercial climate.

11

International aid and how to tap it

ROBIN ROACH
Managing Director, Trade Through Aid Ltd

The aim of this chapter on international aid finance and how to tap it is to provide the reader with an overview of the subject and guidance on how to secure aid-funded business. Extensive recourse is made throughout the chapter to tables and charts to illustrate the text. Primary sources for these exhibits are the *Organisation for Economic Cooperation and Development 1989 Report* and the *World Bank Annual Report 1989*.

The structure of international aid finance

To clarify lending terminology and thereby avoid unnecessary confusion, it is as well to preface any analysis of the make-up of international aid finance with some definitions. The word 'aid' or 'assistance' usually refers to funding flows which qualify as 'official development assistance' (ODA, not to be confused with the United Kingdom's bilateral organisation, the Overseas Development Administration). The characteristics of ODA are that it is undertaken by the official sector with the promotion of economic development and social welfare as its main objective. If ODA contains a loan element, this is usually at a concessional rate. Technical cooperation is included in ODA aid and usually comprises grants and a relatively small volume of loans.

Development Assistance Committee (DAC) members are Australia, Austria, Belgium, Canada, Denmark, Finland, France, Germany, Ireland, Italy, Japan, the Netherlands, New Zealand, Norway, Sweden, Switzerland, the United Kingdom, the United States, and the Commission of the European Communities.

Actual net disbursements of ODA from DAC members to developing countries and multilateral institutions were \$46.5 billion in 1989, compared with \$48.1 billion in 1988 – a decrease of 2 per cent in real terms. Total ODA from all sources in 1989 amounted to \$51.3 billion which was at virtually the same level as 1988.

Official development finance (ODF) is used to measure the inflow of resources to developing countries. It is made up of grants, development lending by multilateral financial institutions such as the World Bank, bilateral ODA, and other official flows for development purposes, but which have too low a grant element to qualify as ODA. Net ODF to developing countries reached an estimated $67 billion in 1989.

Total flows include ODA, but also official and private export credits, long- and short-term private transactions including bank lending and grants from private voluntary agencies. Total resource flows reaching developing countries from all sources are estimated at $109 billion for 1989, against $104 billion in 1988.

Multilateral flows are channelled from donor member countries through international organisations such as the World Bank Group or United Nations Development Programme (UNDP) to developing countries. Bilateral flows are provided directly by the donor country through its own bilateral agency (such as the United Kingdom's Overseas Development Administration) to a developing country on a government-to-government basis.

The breakdown of total net resource flows to developing countries between (a) ODF, (b) export credits and (c) private flows (including banking) for the years 1985–9 is given in Table 11.1.

The present overwhelming importance of ODF (of which ODA forms the major part) in total net resource flows to developing countries, is clearly shown in Figure 11.1, which shows total net resource flows from all sources. Export credits, bank lending and direct investment to developing countries made up over two-thirds of total net resource flows in the early 1980s. By 1988, however, these sources diminished to around 40 per cent of total resource flow. Within the total ODF flow of $67.1 billion in 1989, ODA accounted for $51.3 billion.

In this chapter, we are essentially concerned with ODA. Who are the main contributors?

Aid donors

Aid donor groups are shown in Figure 11.2 for the major regional contributors from 1970 to 1989. In the 1970s, the Arab donors primarily and, to a limited extent, the Central and Eastern European donors, played a significant part in total ODA contributions (e.g. in 1975, at a combined total of $18 billion, they contributed 40 per cent of the ODA total of $45 billion). By 1989, however, with the reduction in Arab contributions, DAC member countries, at around $48 billion, accounted for 94 per cent out of a total ODA of $51.3 billion. DAC member countries are, therefore, currently the primary contributors to the ODA aid programme.

Table 11.1. Total net resource flows to developing countries, excluding Taiwan (US$ billion)

	1985	1986	1987	1988	1989[a]	1985	1989
						Per cent of total	
Official development finance	48.9	56.2	61.6	66.1	67.1	58.0	61.6
1. Official development assistance	37.3	44.4	48.3	51.7	51.3	44.2	47.1
of which: bilateral disbursements	28.8	34.9	38.2	40.3	39.8	34.2	36.5
multilateral disbursements	8.5	9.5	10.1	11.4	11.5	10.1	10.6
2. Other ODF	11.6	11.8	13.3	14.4	15.8	13.8	14.5
of which: bilateral disbursements	3.7	4.0	6.6	7.9	9.0	4.4	8.3
multilateral disbursements	7.9	7.8	6.7	6.5	6.8	9.4	6.2
Total export credits	4.0	−0.7	−2.6	−0.5	1.2	4.7	1.1
1. DAC countries	3.4	−0.9	−2.9	−0.9	1.0	4.0	0.9
of which: short term	3.2	3.0	4.1	2.0	1.0		
2. Other countries	0.6	0.2	0.3	0.4	0.2	0.7	0.2
Private flows	31.4	28.2	34.4	38.7	40.7	37.2	37.3
1. Direct investment (OECD)	6.6	11.3	20.9	23.4	22.0	7.8	20.2
of which: offshore centres	3.7	6.8	13.5	9.9			
2. International bank lending	15.2	7.0	7.0	5.8	8.5	18.0	7.8
of which: short term	12.0	−4.0	5.0	2.0	4.0		
3. Total bond lending	5.4	2.7	0.5	0.4	1.0	6.4	0.9
4. Other private	1.3	3.9	2.5	4.9	5.0	1.5	4.6
5. Grants by non-governmental organisations	2.9	3.3	3.5	4.2	4.2	3.4	3.9
Total net resource flows	84.3	83.7	93.4	104.3	109.0	100.0	100.0

[a]Provisional.
Source: OECD.

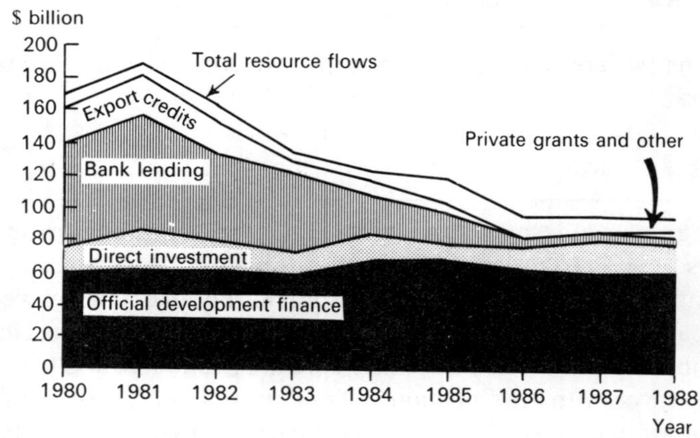

Figure 11.1 Total net resource flows from all sources by type 1980–88 (at 1987 prices and exchange rates) (*Source*: OECD 1989)

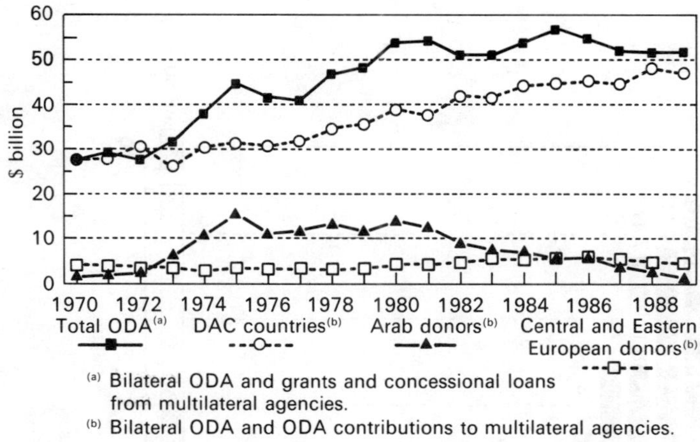

Figure 11.2 Aid by major donor groups (at 1988 prices and exchange rates) (*Source*: OECD 1989)

Development Assistance Committee donor performance

Overall

The ODA performance of DAC countries in 1989 is shown in Figure 11.3. Japan has emerged in 1989 with $8.96 billion actual contributions (or $9.5 billion at 1988 corrected prices) as the single largest donor in volume terms. The United States, at $7.66 billion actual contributions, now takes second place. The decline of the United States from $10.14 in 1988 to $7.66 in 1989 results in part from 1988–9 instalments paid in 1988. All current forecasts, however, confirm that Japan will hold on to and increase its lead as the major contributor. The United Kingdom at $2.59 million is sixth in the league table for total contributions behind Japan, the United States, France, Germany and Italy.

The percentage of national overseas development assistance to gross national product

If the more revealing percentage of national ODA to national GNP is considered, the Scandinavian countries Norway at 1.02 per cent, Denmark 1 per cent and Sweden 0.98 per cent head the table, followed by the Netherlands at 0.94 per cent, France at 0.78 per cent and Finland at 0.63 per cent. The United Kingdom at 0.31 per cent is a moderate performer with a relative decline in recent years from 0.43 per cent in 1976–80. As will be

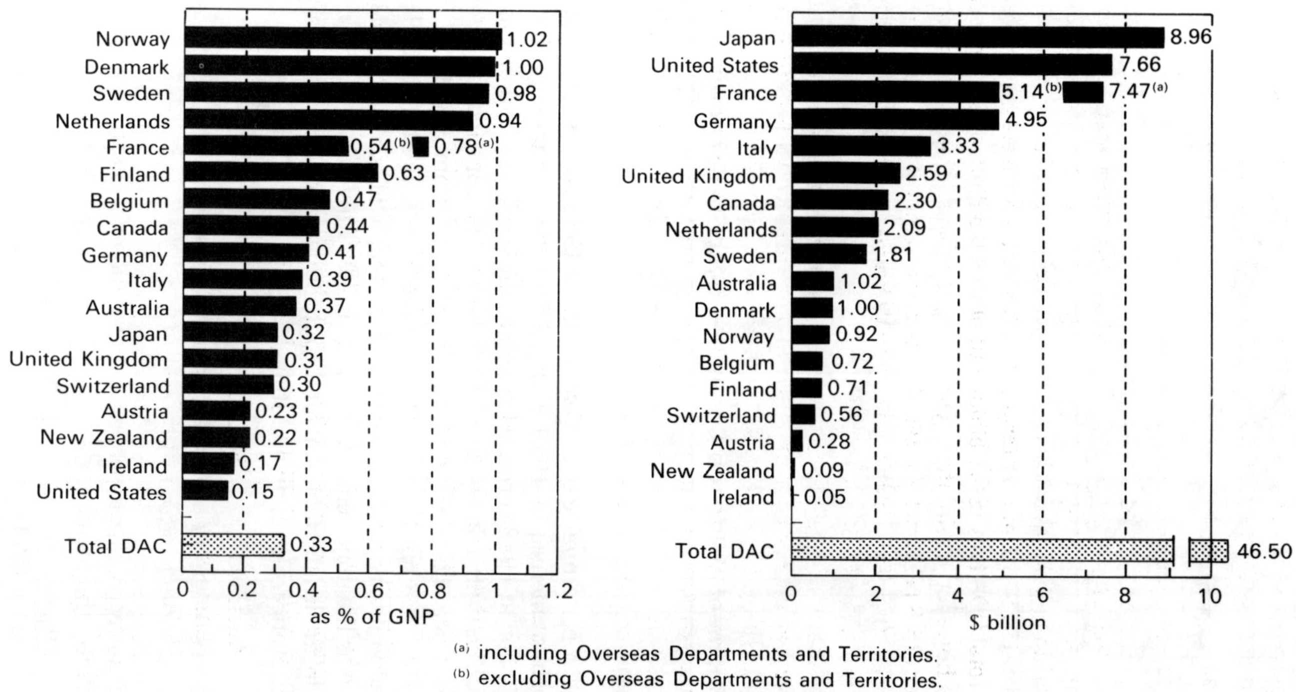

Figure 11.3 Net ODA from DAC countries in 1989 (*Source*: OECD 1989)

emphasised later, the Scandinavian countries' bilateral agencies are, through their government's dedication to overseas development, significant players in the aid scene. There are also worthwhile opportunities for foreign companies to participate in these programmes.

Bilateral and multilateral flows

The ratio of multilateral ODA (routed through the international aid institutions) to bilateral ODA (direct country-to-country assistance) overall and within individual donor country programmes is also significant. For the period of 1975–80, multilateral ODA disbursements were around one-third of the total ODA flow ($6.1 billion out of $18.9 billion, or 32.3 per cent). In 1989, however, multilateral ODA at $12 billion, dropped to nearly one-quarter (25.8 per cent) of total ODA disbursements of $46.5 billion. In DAC countries, therefore, direct bilateral ODA was, on average, nearly three times multilateral ODA in 1989.

The share of UK aid channelled through multilateral institutions, however, at 46 per cent in 1987–8 is at variance with most other DAC countries (Italy 17 per cent, the Netherlands 25 per cent, Japan 30 per cent, Germany 30–33 per cent). The UK ratio of multilateral to bilateral ODA has, for some years, been near 1 : 1 and this low proportion of bilateral and tied ODA assistance, therefore, diminishes UK companies' commercial prospects within international aid-funded business.

Bilateral aid

Given the substantial volume of bilateral aid which, as has been indicated, makes up over three-quarters of ODA lending by DAC member countries, it is worthwhile to examine the degree to which this aid is tied to suppliers of goods and services of the individual donor countries. This so-called 'tying status' is shown in Table 11.2 for DAC members in 1988. Donor countries with significant percentages of untied bilateral aid which is freely available for world-wide procurement are as follows:

Australia	56.3 per cent
Denmark	73.13 per cent
Finland	26.57 per cent
Germany	54.76 per cent
Netherlands	74.35 per cent
Norway	60.0 per cent
Sweden	67.51 per cent

The UK bilateral ODA, as can be seen from Table 11.2, is largely tied with only 17.45 per cent freely available for world-wide procurement. In terms

Table 11.2. Tying status of ODA by individual DAC members, 1988 (US$ million)

Countries	Bilateral ODA								Multilateral ODA				
		Of which:							Excluding EC				
	Untied[a]	'Cash'[b]	Untied technical cooperation	Untied import financing	Partially untied[c]	Of which: Technical cooperation	Tied[d]	Of which: Technical cooperation	Untied	Tied	EC	Total ODA	Associated financing[e]
Australia	508	461	x	16	–	–	395	235	269	36	–	1,208	35
Denmark	441	8	113	324	9	9	162	–	304	35	74	1,025	
Finland	106	58		48	–	–	293		194	32	–	625[f]	17
Germany	2,615	245	1,197	1,051	–	–	2,160	732	876	25	975	6,651	–
Netherlands	739	145	327	221	814	306	255	–	467	48	208	2,532[f]	19
New Zealand	37	16	3	19	9	9	32		10	–	–	88[f]	–
Sweden	665	5	–	66	42	42	320	185	489	–	–	1,516	47
United Kingdom	281	104	7	74	–	–	1,329	636	662	14	580	2,866	331
Total DAC													

[a]Fully and freely available for essentially world-wide procurement.
[b]Amounts not directly financing imports: budget and balance-of-payments support, local cost financing and debt relief.
[c]Contributions available for procurement from donor and substantially all developing countries.
[d]Mainly aid tied to procurement in the donor country, but also includes amounts available for procurement in several countries, but not widely enough to qualify as 'partially untied'.
[e]On a disbursement basis.
[f]Including administrative costs.
Source: OECD 1989.

Table 11.3. Multilateral agency commitments, 1988 (US$ million)

Agency	Concessional	Non-concessional	Total
World Bank Group: IBRD, IDA, IFC	4,352	15,691	20,043
European Commission (EC) and European Investment Bank (EIB)	4,785	615	5,400
UN (all grants)	3,678	–	3,678
Asian Development Bank and Fund	1,094	2,062	3,156
African Development Bank and Fund	763	1,405	2,168
Inter-American Development Bank	120	1,433	1,553
Arab Funds	579	666	1,245
Council of Europe	13	571	584
International Fund for Agricultural Development (IFAD)	250	–	250
Caribbean Development Bank	59	15	74
Total	15,693	22,458	38,151

of the volume of untied bilateral ODA, the most significant contributors, in descending order are:

Germany	$2,615 million
Netherlands	$739 million
Sweden	$665 million
Australia	$508 million
Denmark	$441 million
Norway	$343 million

Multilateral aid

Multilateral agencies

Table 11.3 shows the commitments of concessional (soft loans) and non-concessional flows from the multilaterals in 1988 in descending order in volume of lending. The table illustrates the significance of the multilateral agencies' contributions to economic development in developing countries.

In terms of total volume of lending, the World Bank group (WB) with commitments of $20.04 billion in 1988 is the dominant player. Both in terms of funds committed and also net disbursements, it accounts for over half the total multilateral activity. Also in its world-wide geographical coverage, as opposed to the regional bias of some of the other agencies, and its major involvement in private sector development in developing countries through its IFC affiliate, it is the most significant multilateral

Table 11.4. World Bank cumulative concessional and non-concessional lending to 30 June 1989, by sector (US$ million)

Sector	Non-concessional IBRD	Concessional IDA	Total	Ranking	Percentage of total volume
Agriculture and rural development	34,177.4	19,010.4	53,127.8	1	23.6
Development finance companies	17,674.6	1,489.1	19,163.7	5	8.5
Education	6,051.6	3,562.7	9,614.3	8	4.2
Energy	37,738.2	5,821.1	43,559.3	2	20.2
Industry	12,831.9	1,685.4	14,517.3	6	6.4
Non-project	13,334.4	6,172.9	19,507.3	4	8.6
Population health and nutrition	1,250.6	1,262.7	2,513.3	12	1.1
Small-scale enterprises	4,475.8	424.0	4,899.8	10	2.1
Technical assistance	329.9	832.9	1,162.8	13	0.5
Telecommunications	2,596.3	1,269.8	3,866.1	11	1.7
Transportation	26,235.3	6,878.9	33,114.2	3	14.7
Urban development	7,147.7	2,180.8	9,328.5	9	4.1
Water supply and sewerage	7,698.3	2,109.3	9,807.6	7	4.3
Totals	171,481.9	52,700.0	224,182.0		

Table 11.5. World Bank lending, fiscal years 1987–9, and cumulative ranking by sector to 30 June 1989 (US$ million)

	Total lending 1987–9	Ranking 1987–9	Ranking Cumulative from Table 11.4
Agriculture and rural development	10,914.2	1	1
Development finance companies	6,377.1	4	5
Education	2,176.5	9	8
Energy	9,962.9	2	2
Industry	4,625.5	6	6
Non-project	7,542.6	3	4
Population, health and nutrition	982.0	11	12
Small-scale enterprises	1,519.5	10	10
Technical assistance	374.9	13	13
Telecommunications	879.3	12	11
Transportation	6,219.2	5	3
Urban development	4,373.9	7	9
Water supply and sewerage	2,295.9	8	7
Total	58,243.5		

contributor. In this chapter, therefore, the WB is taken as the model in our brief examination of how multilateral aid funds are deployed sectorally and regionally.

Distribution of multilateral funds by purpose and region

Table 11.4 shows the concessional (International Development Agency (IDA) soft credits) and non-concessional lending (International Bank for Reconstruction and Development (IBRD) loans) for the main lending sectors to June 1989. It should be emphasised that all the figures given are *cumulative*, that is they represent total lending since the WB started operations in 1946.

Historically, this table shows that, as could be expected, agriculture and rural development takes first position with $53.13 billion (23.6 per cent) of lending, closely followed by energy with $43.56 billion (20.2 per cent). Within the energy sector, power provision and distribution (for example, rural electrification) predominate with over 80 per cent of funds allocated. Excluding development finance and non-project lending, other priority sectors are transportation, $33.11 billion (14.7 per cent), and industry, $14.52 billion (6.4 per cent).

More recent lending is shown in Table 11.5, which gives World Bank lending for fiscal years 1987–9. The table shows the totals of lending

Table 11.6. World Bank cumulative lending to 30 June 1989, by region (US$ million)

	Non-concessional loans IBRD	Concessional credits IDA	Total	Percentage	Ranking
Africa	14,217.0	17,102.0	31,319.0	13.97	4
Asia	57,887.8	28,890.2	86,778.0	38.71	1
Europe, M. East, N. Africa (EMENA)	43,760.9	5,475.3	49,236.2	21.96	3
Latin America and the Caribbean (LAC)	55,616.3	1,232.5	56,848.8	25.36	2
Total	171,482.0	52,700.0	224,182.0		

Table 11.7. World Bank project approvals, fiscal year 1989 (US$ million)

	IBRD loans		IDA credits		Totals	
	Number	Amount	Number	Amount	Number	Amount
Africa	12	1,560.6	69	2,364.1	81	3,924.7
Asia	38	5,657.1	24	2,175.4	62	7,832.5
EMENA	31	3,511.8	8	255.7	39	3,767.5
LAC	38	5,703.7	5	138.4	43	5,842.1
Total	119	16,433.2	106	4,933.6	225	21,366.8

volume for the three years as well as ranking by sector in volume of lending. Table 11.6 shows the regional distribution of lending.

The figures show that the WB has been throughout its history primarily a non-concessional lender, with $171.5 billion of IBRD loans (76.5 per cent) as opposed to $52.7 billion of softer IDA credits (23.5 per cent). In regional terms, Asia with $86.78 billion (38.71 per cent) emerges as by far the largest recipient, followed by Latin America and the Caribbean at $56.85 billion (25.36 per cent), Europe, the Middle East and North Africa (EMENA) with $49.24 billion (21.96 per cent) and Africa a poor fourth at $31.32 billion (13.97 per cent). This historical imbalance against Africa has, to some extent, been redressed in recent years as is shown through an examination of IBRD/IDA project approvals for the fiscal year 1989 (see Table 11.7).

Table 11.7 shows that in 1989, Africa has the highest number of project approvals and in terms of volume of lending is no longer fourth at the bottom of the table, as shown in Table 11.6, but third above EMENA.

Japanese aid

Over the last ten years, Japan has emerged as a major donor country, and in 1989, with net ODA disbursements of $8.96 billion, it became the largest contributor. For this reason, a separate section is devoted to how Japanese aid is structured and its accessibility to non-Japanese suppliers of goods and services.

Aid disbursements by Japan are expected to continue to increase given the fourth medium-term expansion plan, which aims at disbursing more than $50 billion during the period 1988–92. Japan's ODA/GNP ratio at present is modest at 0.32 per cent, but will be raised progressively and rapidly to a point much nearer to the DAC countries' average. Multilateral contributions average about 30 per cent of total Japanese ODA (as compared to the UK figure of 46 per cent). Contrary to the popular belief that Japan's ODA is primarily aimed at its own export promotion, about two-thirds of ODA loan commitments by Japan are untied for world-wide procurement, and the remainder is untied for procurement in developing countries. More than half of Japan's Exim Bank loans, which are not counted as ODA because of insufficient concessionality, are also completely untied. Further steps have been taken since 1988, when Japan decided gradually to untie the engineering service components of ODA loans and to allow foreign consultants to participate in Japanese grant-financed development surveys. The share of low-income countries in Japan's ODA is above the DAC average. The major part of bilateral aid for geographical, economic and historical reasons is extended to Asian developing countries. However, a substantial amount of aid is also directed to sub-Saharan Africa, much of it as part of Japan's contribution to international action in support of structural adjustment efforts. In June 1989, Japan also announced the launching of a three-year $600 million untied grant programme in favour of low-income sub-Saharan African countries. This succeeded a previous programme of $500 million; Japan is the top bilateral donor in four African countries: Kenya, Zambia, Malawi and Nigeria.

Japan also announced, at the Western Economic Summit meeting in 1989, a revised recycling plan for its trade surplus. This amounts to $65 billion and will follow the current scheme for $30 billion. At this summit, Japan also announced that it would expand and strengthen its bilateral and multilateral aid for environmental preservation over the next three years with a target of about $2.25 billion aid.

The mechanisms through which Japanese aid is administered are summarised below. Multilateral contributions, which make up 30 per cent of total ODA, are dealt with by the Ministry of Finance in consultation with the multilateral agencies such as the World Bank and the IMF. UN agencies are handled by the Ministry of Foreign Affairs.

Bilateral aid, which constitutes 70 per cent of total ODA is made up of 40 per cent loans and 30 per cent grants. Loans are dealt with by the Overseas Economic Cooperation Fund (OECF) under the supervision of three ministries: Finance, Foreign Affairs, Trade and Industry; and the Economic Planning Agency. Grants are administered through the Japan International Cooperation Agency (JICA) under the supervision of the Ministry of Foreign Affairs. Half of these grants are allocated to technical cooperation and half to project and non-project aid. Project grant aid is used for civil works and equipment procurement. Initial contracts are tied to Japanese consulting engineers or contractors, but the procurement of goods is unrestricted and world-wide.

Non-project grant aid is designed to support the balance of international payments of the recipient country and is usually associated with the implementation of structural adjustment programmes agreed with the WB and IMF. The aid is normally provided on an agreed list of items or commodities for specific countries. The main thrust of Japanese non-project grant-aided programmes is directed at sub-Saharan African countries and, because of their long experience in dealing with these countries, the detailed administration of these programmes has been entrusted to the Crown Agents, United Kingdom, and the UN's Office of Project Services (OPS), New York. Both these organisations have complete freedom in authorising procurements, provided the items concerned fall within the agreed listings. Country allocations within the 1990 $600 million programme take into account the financing gap of individual countries, their debt repayment obligations and other macro-economic factors.

A recent addition to the Japanese non-project grant aid has been the programme of assistance to small-scale organisations in developing countries. This was started in May 1989 and is administered through Japanese diplomatic delegations overseas. The main recipients are non-government organisations (NGOs) in the developing countries. The NGOs request funding for specific projects from the local Embassy which then, in consultation with the Grant Aid Division of the Ministry of Foreign Affairs, decides project viability and funding allocations. The scheme is aimed at non-governmental grass-roots ventures, which can include local government bodies, research institutes and medical facilities.

The Exim Bank has a major role in recycling Japan's trade surplus into overseas investment. It achieves this through four main activities: export credits, import credits, untied direct loans and the untied cofinancing of multilateral agency projects. Export credits make up around 20 per cent of bank lending and usually allow for up to 70 per cent untied procurement on products required to be packaged. Import credits focus on natural resource development and offer especially favourable terms on the import of manufactured goods, such as aircraft, advanced computers, special machinery and road construction machines. Luxury items and food are not eligible. Priority on untied loans overseas is given to officially endorsed projects and procurement is generally untied and subject to international competitive bidding (ICB). Where the ability to manage large procurement programmes is weak in overseas countries, recourse to experienced intermediaries such as the Crown Agents is made. Untied direct loans overseas account for over $3 billion in funding each year. In the case of untied loans disbursed through cofinancing agreements with the major multilateral agencies, an early involvement in project preparation and funding is sought. Cofinanced inputs and share of funding on individual projects may be substantial, and close coordination is maintained with the agencies in finalising the extent and purpose of cofinanced inputs. Procurement is subject to the normal bidding and tender procedures of the agency concerned, which will mean ICB on all major components.

Recent trends in international lending

Although the absolute amount of resources flowing through the international aid system does not vary greatly from year to year, the mix of activity undertaken does vary significantly. Certain trends can often be determined and it is important for providers of goods and technical services to be aware of them and, where necessary, to modify their marketing efforts to take them into account. Structural adjustment or policy-related lending, for example, obliges the borrower to accept stringent conditions regarding management of the economy in general and the sectors involved in particular. In return for this, the borrower can gain access to much-needed foreign exchange, which can be used to support general balance of payments' activity and pay for the importation of a wide range of goods including agricultural inputs, spare parts and raw material for industry. Various schemes have been developed, including sectoral import programmes, commodity loans and credit lines aimed at particular sectors or types of beneficiary organisations.

Emphasis has been placed on the linkages between various economic sectors. There is, for example, little point in building an agro-industrial complex if the raw material for it cannot be reliably delivered at all times, owing to a poor local transport infrastructure. This is particularly true in Eastern Europe and the USSR. Equally, adding new productive capacity in a sector where the existing capacity is badly run down and inefficient is clearly not very helpful. Consequently, much more aid agency lending is now sectorally based, e.g. a sum of money is agreed to cover a variety of activities throughout a sector in areas where the greatest benefit can be obtained for the scarce financial resources available.

It is, therefore, felt necessary that organisations supplying goods and services to aid programmes should themselves investigate sectoral priorities at the planning stage to gain insight into opportunities for their output as they develop. In some cases, it is even possible for a commercial organisation to make suggestions for sub-sectoral activities, provided it can clearly demonstrate them to be of importance.

Various other topical themes in development including the staggering developments in Eastern Europe and the pervasive impact of new thinking on environmental factors are now discussed. Summarising, aid-funded business is not a static entity and it will repay companies wishing to exploit the opportunities created by it to study and apply the knowledge gained by closer examination of these trends.

Eastern Europe

The recent dramatic and fast-moving political events in Eastern Europe have transformed the business climate and are progressively creating new business opportunities for Western suppliers of plant, equipment and services. A massive international aid effort is now gathering momentum to assist Eastern European countries in their painful adjustment to fully democratic institutions and open market economies. Primary recipients of these aid programmes are currently Poland, Hungary and Czechoslovakia, who will be followed by Bulgaria, Romania and, to a limited extent, Eastern Germany. Principal donor institutions include the EC through its PHARE Programme (see below), the World Bank, the US and Japanese governments, the Scandinavian governments and the United Kingdom with its Know-How Funds and other funds such as the Overseas Project Fund and Hands On Training Scheme.

The purpose of this section is, therefore, to summarise the various initiatives in restructuring the East European economies, and indicates some principal areas where foreign suppliers can contribute to these programmes. Emphasis is given to Poland and Hungary who, at this stage, are the prime recipients of aid-funded programmes.

GOVERNMENT ASSISTANCE

Although there are relatively few grants available from international governments for exporting products or setting up new businesses, there are several useful sources of UK financial assistance to exporters in opening up markets in Poland and Hungary. These are as follows:

1. The Hands On Training Scheme (HOTS) for overseas decision-makers.
2. The Overseas Project Fund (OPF).
3. The Know-How Fund (KHF).
4. The Management Training Scheme.
5. Pre-Investment Feasibility Studies (PIFS).
6. The UK/Polish Agricultural Development Fund.

HOTS

A world-wide scheme, which can fund up to 50 per cent of eligible costs such as air fares, accommodation, subsistence and tuition fees for overseas participants in UK company management training schemes, HOTS is an ideal vehicle for the induction of management personnel from potential partners overseas into European management practice and standards. The scheme is essentially intended to supplement and support existing company training programmes.

OPF

The Overseas Project Fund is designed to support bidding, feasibility studies and consultancies for major overseas projects. It is also intended to encourage contractors and consultants to form national consortia rather than compete with each other in going after such work. The scale of project aimed at is large, the target being £50 million or more. Smaller projects can be supported, but they should have the potential to reach £50 million in subsequent contracts. Individual consultancies of over £5 million can also be supported, or less where they can be seen to be leading, potentially at least, to major capital projects for the United Kingdom. Construction, installation, consultancy, design engineering, supply of plant, equipment and materials and operational training are looked for by the fund assessors in evaluating proposals for support.

KHF

The Know-How Fund is designed to provide British expertise to Poland (allocation £50 million) and Hungary (allocation £25 million), in assisting their economic reform programmes. The fund has also been extended to Czechoslovakia. Other East European countries will be included in the fund's coverage when they have demonstrated their full commitment to democratic reform. Initial KHF priorities are as follows:

1. Poland – banking, financial services, industrial restructuring, agriculture, tourism and energy.
2. Hungary – privatisation, financial services, management training and public administration.

Two additional programmes are also being supported by the KHF. These are for the financing of management training for potential East European joint venture partners and also for pre-investment feasibility studies (PIFS), which may lead to long-term investment projects.

Agricultural Development Fund

The agricultural development fund (£15 million) is designed to encourage the setting up of small private UK/Polish food processing businesses in Poland.

EUROPEAN COMMUNITY AID

The main thrust of European Community aid to Eastern Europe is administered by the EC's PHARE unit (Poland, Hungary: Assistance for the Restructuring of their Economies). The programme is coordinated with other Western support through the 'Group of 24' (G24) countries. The main objectives of EC aid are as follows:

1. To meet immediate and short-term needs arising from lack of foreign exchange for essential imports of equipment, spare parts and agricultural goods.
2. To help develop the basis of a modern market-oriented business sector.
3. To assist in the preparation of development plans for the agricultural, industrial and environment sectors.
4. To focus on pump-priming projects and programmes and to act as catalysts for actions and support programmes by non-EC donors.

The sum of 300 million ECU (about $350 million) was made available from the Community's 1990 budget, of which 200 million ECU were allocated to Poland and 100 million ECU to Hungary. Priority sectors will be agriculture, industrial restructuring, training and environmental pollution control.

Proposals by the Polish and Hungarian authorities for priority areas for assistance are as follows:

Hungary	*Poland*
Finance	Food supply and processing
Environment	Agricultural technology
Energy	Environmental protection
Agriculture	Science and technology
Telecommunications	Training
Transport	

Community budget financing is provided as a grant to the recipient which can cover works, supplies, technical cooperation and, where required, local costs. Participation in tenders is open to all EC member states and Hungary and Poland. Goods supplied must originate in these countries.

Other organisations with involvement in the Eastern Europe programmes are the European Investment Bank (1,000 million ECU (1990–92)); the World Bank Group made up of the International Bank for Reconstruction and Development (IBRD) and its private sector affiliate, the International Finance Corporation (IFC); the United Nations Industrial Development Organisation (UNIDO); the International Monetary Fund (IMF) ($16 billion currency stabilisation fund); and the recently formed European Bank for Reconstruction and Development, which is based in London.

Privatisation

The sale of public sector assets to private buyers has been much in vogue over the last decade. This phenomenon has spread to many developing countries, but its realisation has been through processes rather different from those found in the developed world, and the international aid agencies have not been slow to become involved.

First, it has proved necessary to restructure most public sector assets to make them attractive to potential investors. This is not easy and often involves the adoption of painful remedies to correct severe distortions and other structural weaknesses. These include excessive manning levels, heavily subsidised input costs, unrealistic charges for outputs, non-accountable management structures with a tendency towards corruption, inefficient administrative systems, under-utilised and outmoded capital plant and equipment with little incentive to modernise and a workforce lacking in key technical skills and motivation.

International agencies such as the World Bank are becoming more adept at analysing and prescribing the right remedies to meet a particular situation by frequently adopting a 'stick and carrot' approach, aimed at cajoling a sometimes less than enthusiastic public sector enterprise into accepting the actions necessary for change and eventual privatisation. The United Kingdom has particular skills in this area and some well known British merchant banks and accounting firms have been very successful in winning the associated professional advisory contracts.

The preparation process before privatisation generally takes longer in developing countries and, in some cases, has proved very difficult to achieve. However, in most cases, a realistic plan for privatising these assets is arrived at. At this stage, involvement with more private sector oriented international organisations such as the WBG's IFC, which has hitherto been low-key, becomes more developed. The IFC can make loans to newly privatised enterprises or take equity, and its involvement usually secures sufficient interest from potential investors for the process to become complete. A few years on and all being well, it will quietly divest its interest and move on somewhere else.

Adoption of the frequently onerous economic conditions now attached to much of the aid agencies' structural adjustment lending should ensure that the distortion once present in the public sector enterprises (often called parastatals) will be overcome, and their management refocused to operate in a free market environment. The potential benefits to many developing countries of the privatisation process, if pursued enthusiastically and given top-level support, can be enormous. Aid-backed opportunities for supplies of goods and services, especially those related to productive enterprises in readiness for privatisation, are often excellent. The privatisation vogue is probably here to stay for a considerable time, given the sheer volume of moribund parastatals which still exist in many developing countries, to which must now be added the Eastern European countries.

EC structural funds

The EC's financial instruments for structural purposes include the following:

1. The Guidance Section of the European Agricultural Guidance and Guarantee Fund (EAGGF).
2. The European Social Fund (ESF).
3. The European Regional Development Fund (ERDF).
4. The European Coal and Steel Community (ECSC), grants and loans.
5. The European Investment Bank (EIB).
6. The New Community borrowing and lending Instrument (NCI).
7. The Euratom loans.
8. The specific measures for certain sectors (energy, transport, environment, research and innovation).

These instruments cover a range of measures or of aid and loan schemes, each of which has its own particular characteristics and specific purposes. The three major funds (EAGGF Guidance, ESF and ERDF) are the main instruments for different structural policies, i.e. policy for agricultural structures, social and employment policy and regional policy, and are usually referred to as the European Community's Structural Funds. Funding for other major programmes, in particular Integrated Mediterranean Programmes (IMPs) and the Special Programme for Portuguese Industrial Development (PEDIP) is available from the Structural Funds (primarily ERDF), special Community budget lines and from EIB loans.

The budget for the Structural Funds is being doubled in the period 1988–93, reaching a funding level of over $18 billion per annum in 1993 and is expected to continue thereafter at around $10 billion per annum. The bulk of this funding will be devoted to improving the physical and social infrastructure of the less developed European regions in order to reduce the disparities and economic imbalances between more and less prosperous regions and to strengthen the economic and social cohesion of the Community as a whole.

The total size of structural funding, taking into account EC funds, including the EIB, supplemented by national, regional and local contributions from the beneficiary countries is estimated to reach a cumulative total of $200 billion over the period 1988–93.

In accordance with Community policy, this vast increase in structural funding programmes in Europe will be accompanied by changes in procurement procedures to ensure complete transparency, so that local preference cannot be applied. It has been estimated that in the case of Greece and Portugal, approximately one-third of the funds available are used for procurement of goods and services from other EC countries. This business represents sizeable opportunities for companies who have not yet taken full advantage of EC-financed business outside the home market. French and German companies in particular have been forming local joint ventures and associations, setting up subsidiaries or appointing local agents to help them enter or penetrate these markets. However, to do this, a well defined and focused marketing strategy is essential, taking into account the special requirements for gathering effective marketing intelligence for structural funding programmes. This differs in many ways from that required for projects funded by the multilateral agencies and regional banks, or the EC's own EDF programmes for countries assisted under the Lomé convention.

In the latter case, extensive market intelligence can be obtained within the agencies themselves. Much useful preliminary background information on structural funding programmes can be obtained by research within the organisations detailed below.[1] The gathering of detailed market intelligence must, however, be carried out with the government, regional and local authorities in each of the countries assisted by the programme since responsibility for the identification, preparation, approval and implementation of programmes is devolved as far as possible and usually takes place within the regions and municipalities in each of the beneficiary countries. Hence, local market knowledge, contacts and language capability are essential requirements prior to the eventual establishment of a more formal commitment suitable for long-term penetration of the market.

Environment

Environmental issues have assumed increasing importance in aid agencies' lending programmes. Until the early 1980s, the environment was given scant regard in national development priorities. More obvious aspects of environmental degradation, i.e. sewerage and sewage collection and disposal, accidental spillage of polluting material such as crude oil and clear health hazards have always been within the aid-funded remit. But, as the realisation became clearer about the linkages between development, industrialisation and man's increasing exploitation of the global environment, so aid donors are implementing new policies for the environment.

This includes mandatory environmental impact assessments (EIAs) carried out as an integral part of most project preparation exercises where any likelihood of environmental damage could ensue as a result of the project. It is now not uncommon to find up to 5 per cent of a project's cost estimate taken up with environmental components. There has also been a considerable increase in integrated environmental projects in their own right. For example, during fiscal year 1989, the WBG approved two such projects; in 1990 this had increased to eleven. Encouragement is also being given to developing greater awareness amongst aid recipient countries of the need to have national environmental programmes frequently executed through Ministries of the Environment, many of which have been newly created.

This increased activity in the environment has created major new opportunities for consultants and suppliers of environmentally related equipment and systems covering all aspects of environmental measurement, management and control. It has also posed new problems for project and programme designers. Projects deemed to have an unacceptably high environmental risk attached to them are unlikely to be supported unless considerable modifications are made to ameliorate the identified hazards.

Securing aid-funded business

The enormous variety and scope of aid-funded business, encompassing so many developing countries, make opportunity analysis and precise targeting prerequisites for success.

The supplier must, therefore, at the earliest stage, identify what part of his range of products or services may be suitable for aid-funded business. Then, by market research, he must confirm that these selected products or services, or adaptations or extensions of such products or services, can be exploited in such markets. Given the size, diversity and geographical spread of the aid-funded market, it is invariably necessary to target a limited number of funding agencies and countries or regions for this initial investigation.

In many cases, the supplier's products and services may only feature as sub-components of procurement packages within aid projects. In such cases, the best route is through sub-contracting to the main supplier or joint bidding with another firm. The identification of such opportunities requires fundamental in-depth market research.

Having determined the potential demand for specific products or services, the supplier then needs to conduct a fuller investigation into forthcoming projects or technical assistance programmes. This will involve extensive analysis of published information, shortlisting of potential programmes or projects and visits to the agencies for detailed follow-up with agency personnel. These visits will also often enable identification of other opportunities within projects to be made at an early stage in the project cycle.

In addition, aid funds may be available to support potential projects which the firms themselves may have identified in developing countries. Local grants, loans, lines of credit and facilities for equity participation can often be utilised, provided the proposed project satisfies eligibility criteria. Discussions with the relevant country and project desk officer in the agencies and resident in country agency missions will clarify these possibilities, and show how access to such funds can be gained.

Registration is a necessary, but not sufficient, prelude to obtaining technical assistance work within agency-funded programmes. In the case of consultancy firms with more than five full-time professional staff, this registration should be made with the consultancy unit within the funding agency. In the World Bank, this unit is called the Data on Consulting Firms or DACON unit. The registration process will not, in itself, generate bid invitations. DACON is, however, used by the WB to help executing agencies prepare short-lists when required. It is also used by the WB to verify the experience and capability of short-listed firms when these are submitted to the WB by the executing agency. In the case of suppliers of plant and equipment, local dealers or agents/representatives will have to be appointed. It may also be advisable to ensure that the company is registered on overseas governments' approved lists of suppliers and with aid agency-approved procurement agents.

Obtaining business in aid-funded programmes requires total commitment and support from top management, who must recognise that instant success may not be possible, since many projects have a lengthy gestation period. It also takes time for an untried firm to become recognised and established in the aid environment. The most difficult hurdle is securing the first contract, from which others will follow if the firm has fulfilled expectations.

Advertising and promotional material may well need to be adapted to bring it in line with developmental aims and aspirations, and to demonstrate to aid donors and beneficiaries alike that one's firm is alive to developing countries' special circumstances and needs. Some firms have appointed specialists or even dedicated units, to track aid-funded business, whilst others prefer to use external consultants to provide this service for them. But perhaps too many companies still leave this activity to hard-pressed sales and marketing staff, whose other priorities prevent them applying the level of dedicated effort so necessary for aid-funded business success.

External consultants tend to adopt a multi-client approach to aid business marketing, thereby achieving measurable cost savings, and allowing their client firms to defer significant investment until the market's potential is manifest. In any event, firms uncertain of the potential market are advised to commission an initial opportunity analysis, rather than waste time and money on chasing ill-defined and unproven possibilities. The UK Department of Trade and Industry's Marketing Initiative Advisory Scheme (part of the Enterprise Initiative) is invaluable in this respect, enabling the smaller and perhaps more resource-restricted firms to participate in aid business market development with substantial initial help from the Scheme.

Bidding for aid-funded business is not straightforward. Whilst there is a degree of similarity between the agencies, each has its own procurement procedures and preferred methods of doing business. It is important to adhere strictly to tender specifications. Alternative proposals may be offered, provided they are submitted separately from a compliant bid.

There are different procedures for gaining agency-funded business for the two groupings of (a) suppliers/contractors and (b) consultants. With the exception of the minority case of direct agency recruitment of consultants and some UN agencies' direct procurement of goods, it should be emphasised that the evaluation and selection of both groups is entirely the responsibility of the borrower executing agency rather than the lender. In some cases of consultancy work, the agency, as has been noted, may provide guidance to the borrower in drawing up a short-list and in all cases, will need to be satisfied as to the experience and competence of bidders. The final responsibility, however, rests with the borrower, with the lending agency overseeing the validity of the evaluation and selection process.

Suppliers and contractors will normally be required to tender for business for major packages of work, under ICB rules. Such procurement must be advertised in the UN publication *Development Business*, and a major local newspaper in the country in which the project is to be executed. Contracts under ICB must be awarded to the lowest *evaluated* bid. Evaluated is emphasised because no bid is admitted unless all tender requirements for such items as back-up spare parts, training, after-sales service and maintenance are fully complied with. Price alone is not, therefore, the sole determining factor. ICB is the usual procurement method adopted by the agencies. It may not, however, for smaller specialised packages, or off the shelf items, be the only method used. Where relevant, bidding by invitation only (limited international bidding), local competitive bidding, international or local shopping will be used, because such techniques are more cost-effective.

Local project directors or, in the case of the EC, local country delegates may often have substantial budget allocations and discretion for direct procurement of specialised equipment up to varying financial ceilings for individual orders. Through exploiting local knowledge and awareness of detailed project component requirements, suppliers can obtain significant short-term business.

With large complex projects containing major components, a prequalification exercise is carried out for the main contractors. This enables the local executing agency to analyse and assess the company's experience, performance and financial status. Invitations to prequalify are issued in the same way as invitations to bid, a process which has already been described. It is of the utmost importance that prequalification submissions should be geared *fully* to the local requirements of the project to be carried out. Any company which satisfies prequalification requirements is entitled to bid.

Consultants, unlike suppliers and contractors, are not usually subject to a bidding process. The borrower normally draws up a short-list of between three and six consultants. These will be drawn from a broad spectrum of agency member countries with no more than two firms from any one country and, wherever possible, at least one firm from the borrowing country. It follows, therefore, that if a consultancy organisation can identify a particular country as a major source of potential business for its services, then a local association or joint venture with a local firm may be of great benefit. This may also, in lower-income countries, qualify the joint venture for a significant local preference in bid evaluation. The evaluation, ranking and selection of consultancy bids by the borrower are primarily done on the basis of experience and competence, and price considerations, unless a wide variation is evident, are secondary.

It is also fundamentally important that consultants and contractors should, before preparing and submitting proposals, brief themselves fully on project requirements with the aid agency officials who have helped to identify, prepare and appraise the project. They should also be prepared to visit the executing agency in the developing country (a) to obtain first-hand knowledge of local preferences, requirements and evaluation criteria, and (b) to establish credibility with key executing agency personnel and, in particular, with nominated members of the evaluation committee. Where the scale of the project warrants it, at least two visits to the executing agency should be made. The first visit should be designed to achieve (a) and (b) and the second should be after submission of bids and immediately before and during the final evaluation and selection process. In many cases, there are final queries to be answered and, although this should not strictly occur, final adjustments to the bid may be made.

Reverting to the funding agencies, the consultant, contractor or supplier may, through orders obtained or analysis of potential business opportunities, be able to identify a large market potential for his product or services within a particular agency or agencies, especially where a technical edge or innovation is involved. In this case, serious consideration should be given by the company to giving technical marketing presentation/seminar within the agency. Such events require very careful preparation and presentation, and particular care is needed in identifying key agency personnel, ensuring their attendance, and in following them up after the event. They cannot be used to 'hard sell' a particular organisation, but should demonstrate clear knowledge of novel techniques and their application to development, or deal with new approaches to topical subjects, such as the environment.

Cofinancing

Cofinancing is the cooperative financing of a project or programme by a number of donors. This may involve a combination of multilateral and/or bilateral donors and can also include participation by private sector banks.

There are two main forms of cofinancing: joint financing where donors contribute a share of the total cost of the project, which will have a common list of goods and services to be provided; and parallel financing where a project is broken down into distinct, separate parts, each of which is financed by a donor in accordance with its own rules and practices. Hence, some differences in procurement regulations can result from the way in which a project is cofinanced.

Many multilateral agency projects, notably those for the World Bank and the Asian Development Bank, are cofinanced. Sources of cofinance can include other multilateral agencies, government bilateral funds, commercial bank and national export credit agencies. In the case of the World Bank, over half its projects involve additional funding from such sources. The United Kingdom has cofinancing agreements with the multilateral agencies. Where, for example, ODA or ECGD are participants as cofinanciers of defined project components, then these UK-financed components represent a major opportunity for UK companies, since procurement for these components is invariably tied to UK goods and services.

The Projects and Export Policy (PEP) department of the UK Department of Trade and Industry and the Overseas Development Administration (ODA) identify and monitor projects throughout the year, which appear to provide good tied cofinancing opportunities. Regular discussions are held with the agencies to agree which of these opportunities will be cofinanced. A priority, therefore, for exporters is to brief themselves regularly on project components which (a) have been cofinanced and (b) are being considered for cofinancing. This can be done with the World Aid Section of the UK Department of Trade and Industry, which maintains a register of such opportunities. Other such offices exist in the trade departments of all major trading nations.

Note

1. Research should be carried out within the following organisations:
   (a) the overseas trade delegations, chambers of commerce and embassies of the beneficiary country (i.e. Portugal or Greece);
   (b) Government trade departments (i.e. Department of Trade and Industry, London);
   (c) the relevant EC directorates in Brussels.

12

Currency management for protection and profit

FRANCESCA TAYLOR
Associate Director, Mayflower Brokers Ltd

Introduction

Managing currency and interest rate risk has become increasingly difficult in the last few years and with the onset of the Single European Market, deregulation, globalisation and Hong Kong/China 1997, things do not appear to be getting any simpler.

Companies often fall into the trap of deciding, on the basis of little or no information, that they will not use financial instruments to hedge a risky position – this is sometimes not only naive but also irresponsible. The vast array of financial techniques provides for the construction of very simple through to very complex hedges which in some cases carry no up-front costs. This bewildering choice of alternative methods can lead some managers to give up and manage 'the same way as we have done it for fifteen years', i.e. not to manage it at all. The next few sections will bring some of these financial instruments within reach of the commercial manager and provide a refresher course for those involved in day-to-day foreign trade. Whereas currency fluctuations are probably the most visible form of risk, recent interest rate rises have equally caused a number of trade finance contracts to be re-examined, and this risk should also be carefully managed.

Foreign exchange risk management

The most important thing to remember about foreign exchange is that it is dangerous. It should never be treated lightly and certainly never ignored. It is probably the most important variable you will need to consider when planning a tender or managing cash flows after contract award. The foreign exchange (FX) market has its own procedures and practices and whilst most companies transact at arm's length from the market, the ability to obtain the best prices depends upon a thorough understanding of how the market operates.

Background to the foreign exchange market

The period of 1980–88 has generally been accepted as one where there were two major trends for the dollar/sterling rate. The first trend where the dollar strengthened against sterling led to an exchange rate of $1.03 that many UK exporters fondly recall. This trend had taken a number of years to form and although there were day-to-day fluctuations, an exporter was basically safe if he followed this trend. The second trend went in the opposite direction with the dollar losing ground against both sterling and major trading partners in the rest of Europe and the Middle East.

During the first period, a UK exporter could arrange to receive dollars as a future payment and do nothing until actual receipt, when he or she converted them into sterling. This way the exporter rode the trend and made windfall profits. The second trend meant this style of hedging, or lack of it, was completely inappropriate since forward cover on the exchanges would give a better sterling out-turn. These are extremes of hedging, i.e. do nothing and sell forward, and will be discussed later in the chapter.

Since 1988, the market has been very volatile, with changing scenarios and no clear obvious trends, therefore currency management has had to evolve into an active, rather than a passive, discipline.

Techniques relating to foreign exchange

When the Bretton Woods agreement for fixing foreign exchange rates broke down in 1972 the various currencies started to 'float' against each other. Therefore, it was never possible to predict accurately how many US dollars, for example, a contract would bring in, when based on sterling prices and vice versa. In principle, there are two very simple techniques available: spot and forward foreign exchange. Both of these have been around for many years and were the original 'building blocks' for the very sophisticated methods that followed. It would therefore seem logical to start at the beginning with these two simple methods and illustrate them by way of examples.

Spot foreign exchange

If the exporter telephones his bank today and asks for a rate to convert US dollars into sterling, he would be quoted an exchange rate. This would be a spot rate and would be fixed on the telephone for value two business days later. As mentioned earlier the FX market has its own procedure and practices, and this is one. It has arisen because the movement of currency around the world is not always instantaneous, owing to time delays and the different time zones, so two business days gives a safe margin. If the exporter requires his sterling sooner he can make a special request to the bank for either 'same day value' or 'value tomorrow'. They will make an adjustment to the rate which is normally against him.

1656	BARCLAYS BANK PLC LONDON			283 0909 TX 887841 BAST		
	SPOT	1 MTH	2 MTHS	3 MTHS	6 MTHS	12 MTHS
STG	1 6903/13	94/92	190/187	271/268	515/510	922/912
DMK	2 7852/82	162/155	324/314	459/448	858/841	1486/1463
SFR	2 3723/55	124/115	252/240	363/348	699/675	1326/1280
HFL	3 1329/66	173/165	349/338	496/482	932/911	1661/1627
FFR	9 3727/868	418/397	840/810	1192/1159	2242/2182	4018/3885
YEN	257 22/56	169/161	340/329	484/474	927/812	1730/1633
LIT	2045 2/8 2	40/23	90/68	137/108	268/228	453/392
FBC	57 52/64	29/17	58/43	79/61	153/118	285/218
HKS	13 158/69	63/58	128/118	176/167	334/321	650/570
RAN	4 4454/32	72/103	163/197	263/297	587/642	923/1025
	ADJUSTING RATES NOW					

Figure 12.1 Sample Reuters' foreign exchange page

Example: A company has received notice from its bank that US$725,000 has just arrived for its account. The company decides that the sterling equivalent is required and phones the bank for the exchange rate. It is quoted $1.6913; therefore the $725,000 will yield £428,664.34 ($725,000/$1.6913 = £428,664.34). The deal is struck on the telephone and the bank will expect the US dollars to be delivered to them in two business days' time; on the same day they in turn will deliver the sterling to the company.

As currencies continue to move against each other, it is important to keep up to date with their relative values. Reuters is a screen-based information network, see Figure 12.1. The page shown details the major currencies against sterling and is compiled by Barclays Bank PLC. The spot rate for dollar/sterling is shown as $1.6903/13; this means $1.6903–1.6913. If you sell dollars for sterling you are on the right at $1.6913; if you buy dollars with sterling you are on the left at $1.6903.

In fact, if you sell any of the foreign currencies shown against sterling, you will be on the right, and if you buy any of the currencies with sterling, you will be on the left, e.g. selling Swiss francs at Sfr 2.3755, buying Hong Kong dollars at HK$13.158. However, not all companies trade in sterling. A US$-based organisation would approach things in much the same way by selling the currency against US dollars using the exchange rate on the right-hand side, e.g. selling Deutschmarks at 1.4869. However, any US company selling English pounds would need to sell on the *left* as sterling is always quoted the opposite way round. Figure 12.2 shows a Reuters' page compiled by Chemical Bank, London, based on US dollars. In addition to Reuters, there are other screen-based systems such as Knight Ridder, Telerate and Unicom.

All major and some minor currencies can be converted at spot, although some exchange rates for exotic currencies may be hard to find. Most

1359 CHEMICAL BANK	LONDON	TEL 071-240 5801	TELEX 266742 CHFX	
	STG	DM	YEN	SF	FF
SPOT	1.9664–69	1.4864–69	130.71–76	1.2667–72	5.0210–25
1M	83 81	4 6	7 6	1 3	36 41
2M	169 167	15 17	7 5	6 10	112 119
3M	240 237	25 27	7 5	13 17	192 202
6M	430 425	69 72	0 3	29 36	445 455
1Y	748 738	169 174	2 7	50 65	1025 1055
2Y	1300 1250	280 360	125 25		1950 2200
3Y	1800 1650	200 400	450 250		2650 3100
4Y	2200 2000	100 400	700 450		
5Y	2600 2350	50 350	925 675		

Figure 12.2

international banks contribute to an electronic information system giving current exchange rates. They are continuously updated.

The Exchange Rate Mechanism

In October 1990 sterling entered the exchange rate mechanism (ERM). The UK authorities now 'protect' sterling by monitoring the currency's position relative to permitted cross-rates against other member currencies. The parity grid is given in Table 12.1. Should a key cross-rate be reached, the two central banks concerned will intervene in 'unlimited amounts' on the foreign exchanges to bring the rate back into line. The most recent entrants into the ERM, sterling and the Spanish peseta, both operate in a ± 6 per cent band around their central key rate. All the other currencies are contained within $\pm 2\frac{1}{4}$ per cent.

Companies have been calling for exchange rate stability for years. Whilst the ERM goes some way to help, it is by no means a panacea. First, a 6 per cent band may not really help as in theory a 12 per cent loss on the currency is still possible because a company could buy a currency at the top of the band which then falls to the bottom of the band. Second, the existence of the ERM could also delude some companies into not hedging their foreign exchange exposure, thus causing losses. Finally, a vast amount of trade is carried out in US dollars or dollar-based currencies where the EMS/ERM will have little or no impact.

In fact should sterling within the ERM become volatile and require central bank intervention then interest rate policy in turn will need to become more flexible to add the additional support to the currency (i.e. when the currency is weak it may be necessary to move base rates up 1–2 per cent). Thus a foreign exchange mechanism to enhance stability for importers, exporters and investment overseas may actually hinder companies, whilst focus is shifted away from commercial departments to the interest rate management of the whole company.

Table 12.1. European Monetary System: bilateral central rates and intervention points. The table shows the amount of the currency in the top row against the currency in the left-hand column. In each cell the central rate and the upper and lower limits are given. Thus, for example, the central rate between the French and Belgian francs is 16.2608 FFr per 100 BFr (or, alternatively, 614.977 BFr per 100 FFr)

		BFC/LFC	FFC	LIT	DFL	DM	DKR	IRL	SPTA	UK£
100 BFC/LFC	+2.25%		16.6310	3,710.20	5.58700	4.95900	18.9143	1.85100	334.619	1.74510
Belgium/	central rate		16.2608	3,627.64	5.46286	4.84837	18.4938	1.80981	315.143	1.64352
Luxembourg	−2.25%		15.8990	3,546.90	5.34150	4.74000	18.0831	1.76950	296.802	1.54790
100 FFC	+2.25%	628.970		22,817.0	34.3600	30.4950	116.320	11.3830	2,057.80	10.7320
France	central rate	614.977		22,309.1	33.5953	29.8164	113.732	11.1299	1,938.06	10.1073
	−2.25%	601.295		21,813.0	32.8475	29.1500	111.200	10.8825	1,825.30	9.5190
1,000 LT	+2.25%	28.1930	4.58450		1.54000	1.36700	5.21400	0.510246	92.2400	0.481050
Italy	central rate	27.5661	4.48247		1.60590	1.33651	5.09803	0.498895	86.8726	0.453059
	−2.25%	26.9530	4.38300		1.47250	1.30650	4.98500	0.487799	81.8200	0.426690
100 DLF	+2.25%	1,872.15	304.440	67,912.0		90.7700	346.240	33.8868	6,125.30	31.9450
Netherlands	central rate	1,830.54	297.661	66,405.3		88.7526	338.537	33.1293	5,768.83	30.0859
	−2.25%	1,789.85	291.040	64,928.0		86.7800	331.020	32.3939	5,433.10	28.3340
100 DM	+2.25%	2,109.50	343.050	76,540.0	115.235		390.160	38.1825	6,901.70	35.9970
Germany	central rate	2,062.55	335.386	74,821.7	112.673		381.443	37.3281	6,500.00	33.8984
	−2.25%	2,016.55	327.920	73,157.0	110.1675		373.000	36.4964	6,121.70	31.9280
100 DKR	+2.25%	553.000	89.9250	20,062.0	30.2100	26.8100		10.00870	1,809.40	9.43610
Denmark	central rate	540.723	87.9257	19,615.4	29.5389	26.2162		9.78604	1,704.05	8.88687
	−2.25%	528.700	85.9700	19,179.0	28.8825	25.6300		9.56830	1,604.90	8.36970
1 IRL	+2.25%	56.5115	9.18900	2,050.03	3.08700	2.74000	10.4511		184.892	0.964240
Ireland	central rate	55.2545	8.98480	2,004.43	3.01848	2.67894	10.2186		174.131	0.908116
	−2.25%	54.0250	8.78500	1,959.84	2.95100	2.61900	9.9913		163.997	0.855260
100 SPTA	+6%	33.6930	5.47850	1,222.30	1.84050	1.63300	6.23100	0.609772		0.553740
Spain	central rate	31.7316	5.15981	1,151.11	1.73345	1.53847	5.86837	0.574281		0.521514
	−6%	29.8850	4.85950	1,084.10	1.63250	1.44900	5.52600	0.540858		0.491160
1£	+6%	64.6050	10.50550	2,343.62	3.52950	3.13200	11.9479	1.16920	203.600	
UK	central rate	60.8451	9.89389	2,207.25	3.32389	2.95000	11.2526	1.10116	191.750	
	−6%	57.3035	9.31800	2,078.79	3.13050	2.77300	10.5976	1.03710	180.590	

Source: Bank of England.

Classification of spot currencies

At present the vast array of foreign currencies world-wide can be generally sub-divided into the following:

1. Major currencies – freely available spot and forward markets.
2. Minor currencies – freely available although the spot market may lack liquidity. There are often restrictions on the forward market regarding the maturity, e.g. not longer than six months.
3. Exotics – spot rates are available, but very restricted with regard to amounts and government intervention. Forward market often lacking or very intermittent, or very expensive.

Although the list is subject to change, you can find below indications of currencies in each section:

1. Major – US dollar, DMK, Swiss franc, yen, sterling, guilder, French franc, lire, Belgian franc, Hong Kong dollar, ECU, Scandinavian currencies, Australian dollar, Canadian dollar, etc.
2. Minor – peseta, New Zealand dollar, Singapore dollar, drachma, Austrian schilling, Irish punt, South African rand, Middle East currencies.
3. Exotic – Indian rupee, Indonesian rupiah, Thai baht, Malaysian ringitt, Chinese renminbi, most African currencies, Russian rouble.

Proxy currencies

Most 'exotic' and some minor currencies have a proxy currency which trades in a similar fashion. It is often necessary to go back to the trade flows of a country to establish which is the current proxy currency. Some of the main trade currencies are listed in Figure 12.3, but this is not a definitive list, so checks should be made with your advisers. The proxy could be linked officially or unofficially to the exotic currency in question but this will be more normally by the impetus of market association.

As Figure 12.3 shows, there are no currencies linked to sterling. This is correct, although various African currencies used to be tied to the pound. Consequently, most currencies need to be converted to sterling either through the US dollar or the Deutschmark. For example:

Saudi rial → US dollar → sterling (not Saudi rial/£)
yen → Deutschmark → sterling (not yen/£)

Forward foreign exchange

The forward foreign exchange rate is the rate that the bank will quote to you if you wish to sell your currency receivables forward to a specific date. So,

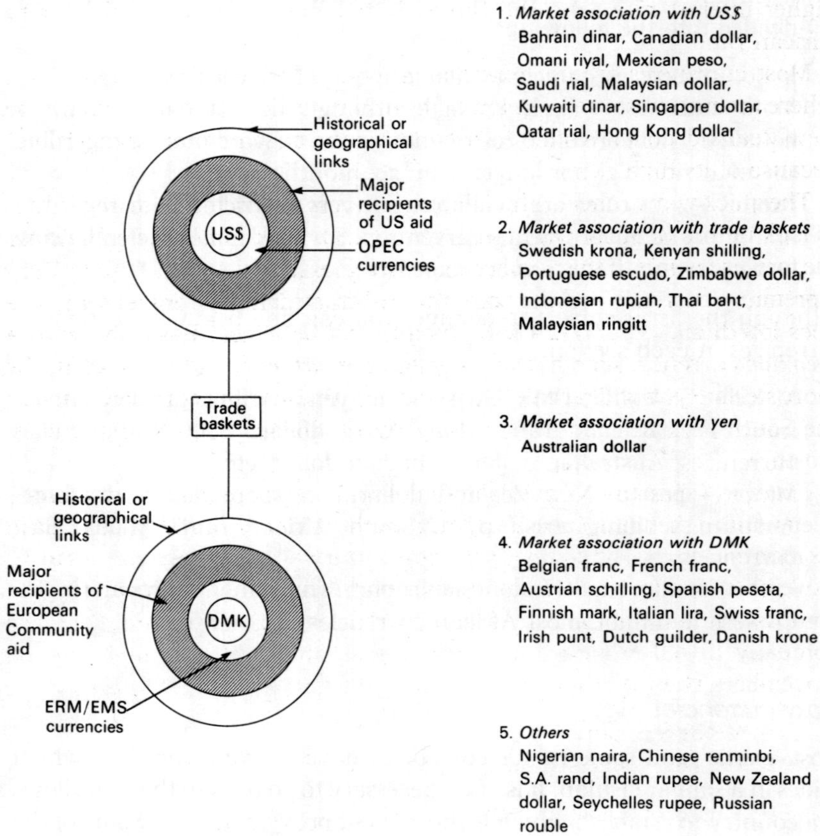

Figure 12.3 Currency links

for example, if you were exporting to the Middle East and were being paid in dollars in three months' time, you might want to sell those dollars forward to the date of receipt.

The bank would quote you an exchange rate which would take into account the spot rate and a forward adjustment, i.e. for dollars into sterling:

spot	$1.6913	
forward adjustment	0.0268	
(See Figure 12.1)	$1.6645	outright forward rate

The amount of the adjustment will vary depending on the maturity of the transaction. Where the foreign currency has a domestic interest rate lower than that in the United Kingdom, the forward adjustment is subtracted from spot. It will be added to the spot rate only when the foreign currency has a higher interest rate than the United Kingdom's, for example the South African rand.

Most currencies are, for example, now at a 'premium' to sterling, i.e. where their interest rates are lower than those of the United Kingdom. The New Zealand dollar is known as a 'discount currency' or high yielder, because of its high rates.

The quick way to check whether a currency is at a premium or discount is to look up the Reuters' page (see Figure 12.1). Look under the column for the forward points: if the number sequence goes high/low, i.e. 190/187 it is a premium currency and the points are subtracted; if the number sequence goes low/high, i.e. 207/242, the points will be added. Basically, with a *premium* currency, such as the US dollar, the *further forward* you sell it, the more sterling you will receive. Conversely, with a *discount* currency, such as the South African rand, the *further forward* you sell it, the *less* it will be worth.

Example: Company XZ has been successfully exporting to France and has been notified that one particularly large payment is due on 10 November (in six months' time). The company wish to sell forward the French francs to 10 November as they wish to be certain of the rate they will achieve. The company would call the bank and request an outright forward rate for the company to sell French francs and buy sterling, with a value date 10 November. The rate they achieve should be very close to 9.1688.

9.3868	spot
0.2182	forward adjustment
9.1688	outright forward rate

In this example, should the company have a dollar-based balance sheet, the forward calculation would be effected in much the same way as the company would sell French francs and buy US dollars at 5.0680:

5.0225	spot
0.0455	forward adjustment
5.0680	outright forward rate

All company XZ has to do is to ensure the bank will receive the French franc's *value* 10 November, in order to receive sterling (or dollars) on the same day. It is normal practice for the bank to telephone the company two business days before (8 November) and confirm the payment instructions on both sides, i.e. where does the bank want its French francs and where does company XZ want its sterling (or dollars). It can take two days to move currency, so the payment of francs will have to be generated on the 8 November.

Payment instructions

It is worth mentioning that it is impossible to hold dollars anywhere other than the United States or French francs anywhere but France. Foreign currency accounts can be held anywhere, but the physical money transmission must go through the respective domestic country. The instructions could all be given from London but the currency must be correctly routed: for example a yen account could be opened for the company by Midland Bank PLC, but any yen payments into it would have to go to

Bank of Tokyo, Tokyo
Account Midland Bank London
A/C Company XZ
No. 246221

A typical payment instruction from the bank for the delivery of dollars will be along these lines:

Pay: Citibank New York
A/C Citibank London
Re: foreign exchange – Company XZ

The exporter in turn will have payment instructions for the sterling:

Pay: Lloyds Bank
42 High Street
Putney

Sort Code 12-34-56

A/C Company A
Account No. 62611223

Re: foreign exchange

As companies undertake more foreign exchange transactions, so the fine tuning on the payment instructions will grow to include contract references, identity of sender and a number of sub-accounts, e.g. company A Number 2 Account, A/C No. 62611224. For any currency hedging to begin to be effective you must be able to identify all your payment flows and be able to act immediately.

Identification of the exposure

The key question for anyone involved in trade finance is 'what constitutes a foreign exchange risk?' The same problems and answers apply to virtually all domestic economies which export. The disciplines are the same. For a UK-based company with a sterling balance sheet, the answer is, any level of the business that is involved in a currency other than sterling, e.g. a company exporting to the United States and receiving US dollars in payment, or a company selling goods in the United Kingdom but where a fundamental piece of machinery has to be imported from Germany; alternatively, a UK importer of fine wines from elsewhere in Europe where the payment for each shipment is in, say, French francs or lire. Another related risk would involve a Belgian subsidiary of a UK company where all manufacturing costs were in Belgian francs but where the goods were sold in the United Kingdom and France. In addition, how would the Belgian company be valued in sterling terms on the parent company balance sheet? Collectively these types of risks can be categorised into three main areas.

Transaction exposures: receivables or payables in foreign currency

For example, a UK exporter sells machinery to the United States which is priced in US dollars. The contract was awarded when the exchange rate was $1.60; however, the actual cash was received ninety days later (as per contract) when the exchange rate was $1.6950. If we assume the notional value of the contract was $250,000, the exporter needed to recover £156,250, i.e. $250,000 divided by $1.60. However, owing to events beyond their control, the company only received £147,492.63, i.e. $250,000 divided by $1.6950. In this case a foreign exchange loss would be suffered. Transaction exposures can also arise on cash movements including dividends and interest, and can also markedly affect the profitability of trade. In the extreme, contracts with very low profit margins can become loss makers owing to an unforeseen FX swing. This could wipe out any profit. However, it should be mentioned that unforeseen foreign exchange profits can also sometimes be made. Any other European or US exporter could also experience a shortfall in currency proceeds in the same way, or indeed a windfall profit.

Translation exposures: balance sheet transactions

A UK or US company with a Belgian subsidiary will need to value the subsidiary at year end for the financial accounts, but what exchange rate should be used? There is no real movement of currency between the two countries; however, there will be a year-to-year difference in the valuation as FX rates move. Balance sheet transactions do not involve movements of cash.

Economic exposures: competitive positions against foreign manufacturers

One frequently quoted example is that of both Jaguar and Porsche/BMW, both of whom compete for the same luxury market customers in the United States. Each company will be exposed against the US dollar: for Porsche the risk would be US$/DMK and for Jaguar the risk would be US$/sterling. However, in addition there is also an exposure to sterling/DMK, because as the respective home currencies fluctuate against each other the relative manufacturing costs in each company will alter, thus creating a competitive advantage to one side or the other.

Following on from this, the non balance sheet transactions can be further categorised into existing transactions, future transactions and contingent transactions. These can also be linked to existing exposures, exposures on firm commitments and exposures on transactions which may take place (tenders, 'call off' contracts, etc.).

To complicate matters further the export finance manager needs to establish the following:

1. When will he receive payment (do allowances have to be made for banking delays, or late payment from customer)?
2. How much will he be paid (will foreign or local banks deduct any charges)?
3. What will be the currency of payment?
4. Is the currency convertible?

With the best will in the world it is nearly impossible to have complete information, so decisions necessarily have to be taken on a 'best efforts' basis. The important thing is to be aware of which factors or estimates are unknown and which are firm, and act accordingly.

Treatment of the exposure

The basic assumption possible is that once an exposure has been identified most companies want either to restrict their losses to predetermined amounts or to profit from market movements in exchange rates – or both. Indeed most treasurers are especially defensive when managing currency risk, whilst most commercial managers or export finance managers are actively trying to gain market shares and meet deadlines, sometimes therefore creating a further currency risk. In a company where there are two distinct departments, one managing FX risk and one effectively creating it (export department) it is vital that a regular dialogue takes place. It is all too easy for the treasurer to assume that the commercial department is aware of the possible devaluation of UAE dirham, and for the commercial department to assume the treasurer has intimate knowledge of the very latest option derivatives. Both departments have to juggle their time, and need to have their attention focused on important matters before any opportunity becomes a threat. Daily or weekly discussions about market movements and impending contracts will assist both departments and the long-term well-being of the company.

Pre- and post-contract exposure

It is important when designing a currency hedge to be completely specific about the risk. For most export contracts there will be two distinct phases:

1. Tender to contract phase – contingent liability.
2. Post-adjudication – actual liability. Contract awarded.

Both phases need to be managed separately. There is no point worrying about a future cash flow, because if the contract is lost, it will not materialise. However, when pricing a tender and deciding upon an exchange rate a number of variables need to be considered, including the cash flow characteristics.

Tender to contract phase

Which currency to choose

If the exporter is responding to a call for tenders, the currency of the bid will be predetermined, along with a number of other variables such as the level of contract bonding, amount of downpayment and contract specifications, etc. In this case compliance with the contract is crucial; however, there is nothing to stop a second bid being presented in a different currency.

If you are in the position to choose the currency of the bid there are a number of points to consider.

YOUR DOMESTIC CURRENCY

The first and most important factor is, why bid in currency at all? Would a sterling or dollar price be acceptable if you are in the United Kingdom or United States? In this case, there would be a very much reduced risk for the exporter. The FX risk is transferred from the exporter to the buyer who now has to sell his local currency to buy your currency and pass it on under the terms of the contract. For taking on this risk, most buyers would expect a price reduction; however, it could still be worth while, and should be investigated.

FOREIGN CURRENCY

It can be beneficial in some markets to price the contracts in the buyer's local currency. This will enable prices to be compared without the added FX risks. However, there has to be an effective and freely transferable market in that currency.

It can also be profitable. For example as we saw earlier, some currencies are at a premium to, for example, sterling, meaning that if you sold them forward through your bank you would get more sterling than if you sold them spot.

Example: a UK exporter is bidding into Germany for a contract worth DMK25m with delivery and payment in six months. The main competition is also German. By bidding in DMKs not only would the buyer be able to compare prices but the exporter would also be in a position to offer discounts (up to the amount of the gain on the forward contract). Note that the spot rate is £/DM 2.90, the forward rate is £/DM 2.80.

The German competitor would submit a bid for DMK25m in his local currency (DMK). The UK company would (or could) submit a bid for DMK24.14m, because if we assume the price of DMK25m is identical between the companies, then if the UK company were awarded the business and sold the DMK25m at today's spot rate of £/DM 2.90, the sterling yield would be £8,620,689.

However, if the same DMK25m is sold forward for six months at the rate of £/DM 2.80 then there would be an increased total yield of £8,928,571 – a gain of £307,882.

The base sterling price is assumed to be the original level of £8,620,689. But by selling the currency forward, the company can make a foreign exchange profit and this gain of £307,882 is available for discounts.

Alternatively, a lower bid price can be submitted as follows: taking the core price of £8,620,689 and multiplying by the forward rate of £/DM 2.80 a German price of DMK24,137,929 is achieved.

Note that this ignores the bid/offer spreads charged by the banks.

A note of caution though: this is not a new trick! Sophisticated buyers have seen this sort of currency 'play' for years and could choose to make allowances for this during contract adjudication.

Considerations when dealing in currency contracts

When deciding which currency to choose the following points should be addressed very carefully:

1. Can the currency be repatriated?
2. Can it be converted into your currency?
3. Is there a spot or forward market (if so, how far forward)?
4. If there is no spot or forward market, the currency is 'soft' and further payment ideas should be investigated, e.g. barter counter trade – see Chapter 13.

If any of the answers to the first three points is no, think again and take professional advice.

When dealing with currencies with limited convertibility it is worth looking for an associated or proxy currency, see pages 179–80.

Compiling a foreign currency tender

A company considering submitting a tender in foreign currency will have a number of variables to consider – only one of which is currency. Let us make the basic assumption that the goods have already been priced in sterling, the buyer does not require finance and all that remains is to convert the sterling cost and profit into, say, a US dollar amount. It is then necessary to establish how that rate will be protected, should the contract be won.

1. *Contract specifications*:
   (a) bid currency: US dollars;
   (b) contract adjudication: six months;
   (c) payment profile:
      (i) 20 per cent advance payment, due one month after adjudication;
      (ii) 60 per cent spread equally over two years, commencing six months after adjudication;
      (iii) 20 per cent retention payment, at end of contract, say, two and a half years.
2. *Hedging alternatives*:
   (a) Do nothing until contract award then sell contract receipts forward (or panic) – dangerous;
   (b) Using the forward market. The currency cannot be physically sold forward as the contract has not yet been awarded. However, it is possible to use the forward market to construct a notional foreign exchange rate for conversion; see Table 12.2, which would give an indication rate of $1.54646.
   (c) Currency options. If profit margins allow, options are an excellent way to protect the exchange rate, and can be allowed to lapse if the contract is either lost or rates have moved favourably.

Hedging alternatives

DO NOTHING

Doing nothing can be very dangerous, especially if you are wrong: you could win the contract at a suicidal exchange rate and lose money on everything delivered.

USING THE FORWARD MARKET

Construct a table assuming *today* is the date of contract award, and compile a list of outright forward rates with the aim of arriving at a weighted average rate (see Table 12.2). Here you can see the weighted forward rate is

Table 12.2. Tender to contract hedging

	A Month of payment	B Number of months forward	C Percentage of contract		D Outright forward rate to date of anticipated receipt	E Column C × Column D
Advance payment	June	1	20%	×	1.6821	0.33642
Cash flow	November	6	10%	×	1.6403	0.16403
	March	10	10%	×	1.6135	0.16135
	July	14	10%	×	1.5787	0.15787
	November	18	10%	×	1.5359	0.15359
	March	22	10%	×	1.4931	0.14931
	July	26	10%	×	1.4463	0.14463
Final payment	May	30	20%	×	1.3963	0.27926
			Weighted outright forward		US$1.54646	

Note: Two-year forward points 2,300–2,200, three-year forward points 3,800–3,700, pro rata between the periods on a straight line basis.

$1.5465. However, the date of contract award is not today but in six months' time, so an allowance for market movement needs to be factored in. In a typical three-month period a rate can move approximately nowhere or be ± 5 per cent. In a typical six-month period the rate could likewise move ± 8 per cent. The extent of the allowance for the market movement must be at the discretion of the treasury and commercial departments.

If the company in our example wishes to be conservative it can use 7 per cent:

$$\begin{aligned} \$1.5465 - 7\% &= \$1.4382 \\ +7\% &= 1.6548 \end{aligned}$$

If the rate went to $1.4382 the company would be very happy, but this would not be so if the rate increased to $1.6548, so that second rate is the worst case, and should be used when submitting the bid. However, the commercial department must bear in mind that a 7 per cent margin could lose them the contract. There is no easy answer. For non sterling-based companies the same desk exercise could be conducted using the appropriate FX rate in column D, from Table 12.2.

USING CURRENCY OPTIONS

Assume that the company wishes to protect today's spot rate of $1.6913, and that the original contract value was £22.5 million giving $38,054,250. As contract award is in six months' time, the 'option' period is six months.

The company would purchase from their bank a European-style option for $38,054,250 (or $38m), struck at spot, maturity in six months, to sell US dollars and buy sterling. The cost will vary from day to day, but to give an indication let us assume it is 2 per cent, giving a premium due $761,085 (2 per cent of the US dollar amount payable up-front and non-returnable). The option will guarantee for the exporter a rate of $1.6913 if needed and if the contract is lost it can be abandoned for no charge.

On contract award we could have the following scenarios (see Figure 12.4):

1. Contract won: exchange rate at, say, $1.80. The option is valuable – you need to protect the $1.6913 in the tender. The option will be sold

	Exchange rate $1.80	Exchange rate $1.60
Contract won	Sell back	Abandon
Contract lost	Sell back	Abandon

Figure 12.4

back to the bank for residual value – in this case $1.80 – 1.6913 payable in sterling up-front to the exporter.

2. Contract lost: exchange rate at, say, $1.80. The option is still valuable, the *bank will buy back* the option for residual value – as shown in the example above.
3. Contract won: exchange rate at, say, $1.60. The option is valueless, but the new spot rate is excellent news for the exporter; all his contract receipts will attract a better forward foreign exchange rate.
4. Contract lost: exchange rate at, say, $1.60. No problem. No commitment to the bank.

The company can choose any FX rate they like within reason, say ± 5 cents from spot, and will be charged accordingly; they can even choose a rate to give themselves a competitive advantage. But options are not free and the premium will normally need to be passed on in the costs of the tender.

One element of option cover that can confuse companies relates to how the option rate is used once the contract has been won and the tender period finished. Let us explain. The value of the contract in this example is $38.054m, but this will not be paid until the contract is completed, or it will be received in stage payments. Therefore dollars cannot be delivered to the bank when the contract is awarded as you have not received (or earned) them yet. The way round it is to take out the European option as normal. Then, if we assume you win the contract, instead of exercising the option where you have to deliver the dollars to the bank, you sell them back for the residual value. You will be paid a lump sum up-front which will go to subsidise the forward contracts or the currency options you set up to cover the resultant contract cash flow.

Post-contract exposure

How do you manage the cash flows once you have won the contract? In this section, assume the currency is convertible into sterling, or your home currency, or you are using a 'proxy' currency. There are a number of hedging alternatives available, as follows:

1. Do nothing (i.e. transact at spot).
2. Sell forward/buy forward.
3. Currency option.
4. Collar option.

Do nothing

This is a serious alternative to many companies and a very common form of hedging. Not only is this highly speculative but also highly dangerous; it will ultimately result in a spot foreign exchange transaction as the company seeks to convert into its home currency.

If the export finance department have not done their homework properly and agreed to take payment in, say, Libyan pounds, they will have a further problem in trying to convert the currency back into the parent company, or indeed remit it anywhere.

With a convertible currency, we can assume that no one knows in which direction the currency will move, and also that we will see (a) deviation of currency values from their anticipated trend paths based on economic and financial data, and (b) continuing extreme short-term volatility due as much to political as to economic factors.

In simple terms no one can forecast with 100 per cent accuracy whether tomorrow the US dollar will go up or down. A company may have a view, but unless it has divine influence it will be unable to direct the FX markets. Consequently there is a 50 per cent chance the dollar will go up and a 50 per cent chance it will go down. To follow the argument logically therefore: (a) the company which hedges everything in the forward market will get it wrong 50 per cent of the time, and (b) the company which hedges nothing will get it right 50 per cent of the time. That is why it is important that all FX hedging is undertaken intelligently. The right choice today in terms of financial technique could be the wrong choice tomorrow.

Sell forward/buy forward

See pages 179–80 for details of this.

Currency options

Options are a form of insurance. Once the premium has been paid there is no way a loss can be suffered – because once the exchange rate has been agreed on the option, the cover is there if the importer or exporter requires it, and it will lapse if no longer needed. A little theory is required to introduce the option concept and help make some of the terms more familiar (for further information see the glossary in the appendix to this chapter).

DEFINITION

A currency option gives the buyer the *right* but not the *obligation* to buy or sell a specific amount of currency at a specific exchange rate, on or before a specific future date.

The flexibility of the currency option gives the buyer three alternatives – *when* to exercise the option, *whether* to exercise the option and *how much* of the option should be exercised:

1. *When?* The normal currency option (American-style) allows the exporter or importer to exercise on any business day until maturity.

2. *If?* The currency option is only exercised if it is profitable for the exporter to do so. If the spot exchange rate remains more favourable than the strike price of the option, the exporter should transact in the cash markets, i.e. sell or buy the currency at spot.
3. *How much?* The currency option provides cover for a specific amount of currency. So if the contract amount falls short, it is not a problem since only the part of the option that is required need be exercised.

Example: A company expect to receive DMK3m in three months' time, but owing to a technical hitch on the contract only DMK2m is received. The spot rate has moved against the company so they need to exercise the option. It is therefore exercised for DMK2m, and the remainder of the option – DMK1m – is sold back to the bank for residual value.

MAIN CHARACTERISTICS OF A CURRENCY OPTION

Insurance protection

The exporter or importer pays a premium to insure against foreign exchange risk. The bank in return guarantees a fixed rate of exchange if and when required.

Profitability

The option eliminates the downside risk whilst giving the company the ability to profit from favourable foreign exchange movements.

Sell back

The option can be sold back for its residual if no longer required either in whole or in part.

Example: suppose the characteristics of a particular transaction were these:

1. Transaction period: ninety days.
2. Amount to be received: £5 million.
3. Exchange rate or strike: spot rate, say $1.5500.

An option can be used to cover the transaction in the following way.

The company could purchase an American-style option (this allows the option to be exercised on any business day) to sell £5m and buy dollars at spot, for expiry in ninety days' time. The cost of the option, say, would be 2.0 per cent of the dollar amount.

The option could then be put in a drawer for three months. In a perfect world all the payments arrive on time, so in ninety days we check the spot rate with the bank, then compare the option strike rate with the spot rate. If the exchange rate has moved to, say, $1.50 the option will be exercised and the exporter will deliver his sterling to the bank for conversion at $1.5500.

Table 12.3. Comparisons of currency options and forward exchange contracts

Currency option	Forward contract
Right to buy or sell	Obligation to buy or sell
No obligations to deliver currency	Must deliver on or before maturity
No loss possible (excluding option premium)	Unlimited opportunity loss possible
Eliminates downside risk and retains unlimited upside potential	Eliminates downside risk but no upside potential
Perfect hedge for variable exposures	Imperfect hedge for variable exposures

Should the rate have been $1.65, the option rate would have been worse and it would have been abandoned in favour of a spot transaction. The FX transaction need not be with the same bank as the option.

As mentioned before a currency option requires (usually) a payment of premium. This can in some cases be deferred or offset against another option (see p. 195 on collar options).

To make the best use of options they should be taken out when you believe the underlying currency is going to move in your favour. You would therefore gain an exchange rate movement and recover the premium. If you believe the currency will weaken, it is important to take out a forward contract to protect the sterling value of the receipt.

Decision guidelines for hedging

In deciding which course of action to take the exporter should assess where and how he or she believes the exchange rate will move during the period of the transaction. On this basis the following guidelines can be applied, which will help in choosing the appropriate hedge (see also Table 12.3):

1. Expect foreign currency to move in favour of underlying position: use option.
2. Uncertain about currency direction underlying position: use option.
3. Expect foreign currency to move against underlying position: use forward.
4. Expect no change throughout the life of the transaction: use forward.

Foreign exchange collar options

A foreign exchange collar option provides a cheaper hedge than a standard option and involves a combination of two currency options, one bought by the exporter and one sold by the exporter. The two transactions are simultaneous and can be made to fit the risk profile exactly.

The main difference here is that a standard option for which you pay a premium allows you to take 100 per cent of any exchange rate gain. The collar allows you to take 100 per cent of this move, but only for, say, 6 or 7 per cent. Beyond this, wherever the rate is, no further gain can be achieved.

DEFINITION

A collar option gives the client the opportunity to reduce the premium payable on the purchase of an option by simultaneously writing an option to the bank. The different strike rates will affect the return to the client.

MAIN CHARACTERISTICS

The following are the main characteristics:

1. It provides a cheaper hedge than a standard option.
2. The exporter selects the degree of risk he or she is prepared to take and therefore the degree of profit that he or she is prepared to give up by adjusting the exchange rates on the collar.
3. A collar option can provide a 'stand-alone' hedge, or be used in conjunction with conventional forward foreign exchange contracts.

Example: A UK exporter is due to receive $10 million in three months' time, and wishes to use an option to protect his profit potential in case the dollar decreases in value. The current spot rate is $1.70 and the exporter wishes to hedge his budget rate of $1.75. The premium to buy a standard currency option with a strike price of $1.75 is 1.05 per cent which the exporter considers too expensive.

If the exporter agrees to give up some of his profit potential in return for a lower up-front premium, collar options are a possible solution.

Strategy

The customer *buys* an 'out of the money' option for three months to sell dollars (buy sterling) at $1.75. Simultaneously the customer *sells* an 'out of the money' option to the bank for three months to sell it dollars (receive sterling) at a strike price determined by the size of premium he wishes to pay.

Costs

Figure 12.5 gives the collar option prices.

Customer buys option with strike at	Premium payable (%)	Customer sells option with strike at	Premium earned (%)	Net/ cost/benefit (%)	
$1.75	1.05	$1.55	0.17	Customer pays	0.88
$1.75	1.05	$1.60	0.60	Customer pays	0.45
$1.75	1.05	$1.63	1.05	Zero cost	–
$1.75	1.05	$1.65	1.47	Customer earns	0.42

Figure 12.5 Collar option prices (indication levels)

The exporter has insured against an adverse currency movement for a limited or nil cost and has simultaneously retained the opportunity for limited profit if the currency moves favourably.

Zero cost collar option

The zero cost solution is arrived at where the exporter buys an option at $1.75 and sells an option at $1.63. The nett premium would be zero. In principle the exporter would never achieve a better rate than $1.63 or a worse rate than $1.75 (see Figure 12.6).

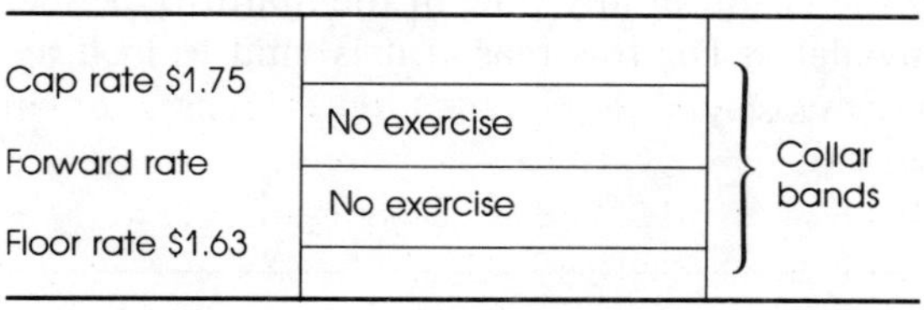

Figure 12.6 Zero cost collar option

The possible outcomes are as follows:

1. No exercise takes place if the spot exchange remains within the collar band (between $1.75 and $1.63).
2. If the exchange rate falls below the floor rate (i.e. to $1.62 or below) the bank exercises its option with the client.
3. If the exchange rate rises above the cap rate, i.e. to $1.76 or above, the exporter exercises his or her option.

The attraction of a zero cost collar means nothing needs to be paid up-front and you will achieve 100 per cent of the gain up to $1.63 in this example. This may be more than enough for your purposes.

The collar transaction should only be used for completely firm transactions, not those where there is an element of doubt. The main risk is that should the currency move in your favour it will also move towards the level where the bank will exercise its option on you. In the example above the bank has the right to buy your dollars at $1.63. What if they do not arrive? You then have to buy them from the FX market and deliver them to the bank under the terms of the option at the market rate on the day. This can be costly. But if the dollars do arrive on time you could convert at any level from $1.75 to $1.63, all of which will increase your currency out-turn of the dollar on the transaction.

The most effective collar options are as follows:

1. When the exporter chooses a strike price 'out of the money' compared to the outright forward for the option he buys from the bank.
2. When both the option sold to the exporter and bought from the exporter are European-style options (i.e. can only be exercised on the expiry date).
3. When the client is hedging receipt of a currency which is at a premium in the forward market (e.g. US dollars) or hedging payables in a currency at a forward discount (e.g. New Zealand dollars).

If the exporter decides to sell an American option to the bank (instead of European) he will need to have a continuous inflow and outflow of US dollars. This is necessary because the bank may choose to exercise the option written by the client, at any time in the maturity period, and the dollars must be available. For this reason it is vital to look at seasonal income streams very closely.

Conclusion

Managing post-contract cash flows is vital since foreign exchange rates are always volatile, so monitoring of positions should be undertaken regularly to avoid any contracts becoming loss-making purely because of adverse movements in exchange rates.

Foreign exchange risk is manageable but not always at zero cost. Economic conditions change and strong currencies become weak currencies, etc. It is important to keep in touch with the treasury department and, finally, to remember that the best way to manage currency exposures is to avoid incurring them in the first place.

Appendix: terminology for currency options

Call option – The right (but not the obligation) to buy foreign currency.

Put option – The right (but not the obligation) to sell foreign currency. Care is needed where it is not clear which is the foreign currency (e.g. German mark against French franc).

Exercise – Conversion of option into the underlying foreign exchange contract on receipt of instructions from the customer.

Strike price – Exchange rate chosen by the customer at which the option may be exercised. Strike prices can be described as at the money (ATM), in the money (ITM) or out of the money (OTM).

Expiry date – Last date on which the option may be exercised up to 3.00 p.m. London time or 10.00 a.m. New York time. Two business days before the value date.

Value date – Last date on which currency may be delivered.

American option – An option which can be exercised on any day up to and including 3.00 p.m. London time or 10.00 a.m. New York time on the expiry date.

European option – An option which can be exercised on the expiry date *only* (up to 3.00 p.m. London time or 10.00 a.m. New York time).

Premium – Price of the option. The bank's cost of hedging the option position in the market.

Intrinsic value – Difference between the strike price and the current market exchange rate.

Time value – Difference between the option premium and the intrinsic value, including the value of the time left until expiry, volatility, forward points and market expectations.

Fair value – Combination of intrinsic value and time value, literally the value of the option to the customer, as calculated by the option pricing model.

Volatility – Normalised annualised standard deviation on the daily spot rate movements for the exchange rate concerned.

13

Countertrading

CLIVE BATESON
Director, London Chamber of Commerce and Industry Examinations Board

Owing to frequent references to barter, countertrade, compensation and counterpurchase without a clear definition of what precisely is involved, it is necessary to take a little time to define clearly the field to be covered. Later on I will attempt the even more difficult task of assessing the size and importance of this market.

Background

To listen to some of today's practitioners of the art of countertrade, a newcomer could be forgiven if he believed that countertrading techniques were developed largely in Vienna after 1945. The need was to resolve many of the problems facing Eastern bloc countries endeavouring to trade with the West whilst hampered by non-convertible currencies. This need was satisfied by a limited number of talented, largely Viennese traders who utilised barter, counterpurchased, evidence accounts and switch techniques to overcome these problems.

Countertrade or compensation as it is known elsewhere in Europe has become the catch all for many different types of transaction which avoid the normal 'goods of country A for currency, either of country B, which receives the goods, or convertible currency of a third nation'. Such alternative transactions take many forms. Those mainly in use today include the following:

1. *Barter*, the oldest form, dates back to pre-money transactions but is still occasionally used today. It is relatively inflexible because of the need to decide, for example, a specific number of sheep for a given quantity of oil. Once structured, price changes in either commodity cannot easily be accommodated. For this reason commercial organisations only rarely get involved and such deals are normally on a government to government basis.
2. *Counterpurchase* also has a long history and was used extensively in

Europe in the early part of this century by UK, French and especially German chemical companies which would purchase feedstocks from European countries with less sophisticated chemical industries in exchange for finished pharmaceuticals and fertilisers. In this case, of course, monetary values can be placed on both sides of the transaction and price changes can be accommodated. It is therefore more 'user friendly' than barter because it is more flexible.

3. *Clearing or evidence accounts* became increasingly popular during the 1960s and 1970s when a solution was needed to accommodate the mismatch of timing that frequently occurred in major transactions between states. A commodity such as sugar, coffee or tobacco is not conveniently available at all times to meet a flow of oil or engineering products produced in factories throughout a year. Thus evidence accounts came into use, initially controlled by central or foreign exchange banks of the countries involved but later also operated by the large international banks. The intention was, of course, that over time, ideally a year but possibly as long as two or three years, the amounts credited to the account by each side would achieve equilibrium. In many instances this system worked well enough but chronic imbalances did develop in a significant number of cases.

   In response to this particular problem the countertraders of Vienna came up with yet another solution, yet another product and yet another source of income!
4. *Switch transactions* arose out of these increasing imbalances in bilateral trading agreements mainly involving Eastern European countries.

Another example best illustrates the origin and nature of these transactions. The techniques described in the previous paragraph were utilised by many Eastern European countries which established bilateral trade agreements with Third World countries to ensure supplies of key commodities. Cuban sugar for oil; South American coffee for machinery. It frequently became clear that the Soviet need for coffee was stronger than the Colombian need for Soviet machinery. Thus a balance in favour of the Third World country would build up in the special clearing account used to record these transactions. Over time this balance became significant and the switch operator came along to arrange for a third country that could use the currency in the clearly account, in the case of the USSR usually roubles, to purchase some product that this third country did need from the USSR.

Of the four broad types of countertrade described above, both counterpurchase and switch can have variants from the classical forms described and the more important of these will be discussed later in this chapter. It is enough at this stage to say that all transactions fall into the above four broad categories which can be described simply as follows:

1. Barter – unpriced goods for goods.
2. Counterpurchase – priced goods for priced goods.

3. Evidence accounts – bilateral trade flows monitored by recording such flows in an account denominated in a mutually agreed currency.
4. Switch transactions – the unlocking of blocked funds arising out of bilateral trade agreements.

Countertrade grew slowly but steadily as Eastern bloc countries increasingly realised that this was a workable route enabling them to acquire the Western goods that they needed to sustain their economies. By the 1970s, Third World countries experiencing sluggish demand for their commodities and less sophisticated manufactured goods began to utilise countertrade to find new outlets for their products. The Third World, from being the hunting ground for the East European manufacturers, themselves became hunters.

After independence has been gained, certain symbols of the nation state must be achieved. A credible defence force is needed, if not to frighten your neighbour at least to keep your own people in order. A national airline and, if you are an oil producer, your own refinery are also priorities. Suddenly we are beginning to look at big numbers.

It takes a great deal of sugar to pay for an airport. At the same time as those needs were emerging, OPEC was beginning to agree quotas for their member states which were simultaneously turning towards establishing government-agreed official selling prices which were mandatory on their parastatal oil-producing companies. Here we had the type of need and the sort of controls that were well recognised in Vienna.

Such was the value of oil, especially after the second oil shock of 1979, that the cargo was now worth significantly more than the ships that carried it. Many oil producers wished to sell rather more oil than their quota permitted and countertrade transactions enabled them to blur both the quantity of oil shipped and the real price it was achieving.

Thus arrived the high point of countertrading volumes and profits. The first five years of the 1980s were undoubtedly the richest in terms of the value of transactions and the profits they generated. Probably the high ground was reached with the Boeing 747 deal for Saudi oil and sustained until perhaps the last really big one, which is still running, another Saudi deal for Tornados from British Aerospace.

Since the mid 1980s oil pricing has become more transparent and quotas have either been accepted by most OPEC nations or ignored with impunity by others (such as Abu Dhabi and Kuwait until very recently). At the same time there has been a significant reduction in demand for the larger projects. These changes, on both the supply and demand side have had a significant impact on the value of countertrade deals being agreed. Oil countertrade has gone into a decline; a decline not entirely regretted by the large trading houses which had seen in Voest-Alpine the extent of the downside risk involved should transactions not be completed as planned. A large Austrian supplier of steel, Voest had become a major player in the supply of high-value products to Iran. But delays in oil shipments, as well as pricing problems, caused such severe losses that the Austrian state had to step in to cover them.

However, today countertrade in all its forms is still alive and well, although as can be seen from some of the above examples it no longer lives exclusively in Vienna. London and New York can both now offer skilled protagonists and the Japanese trading houses also frequently use variants of the four main techniques described earlier.

Assessing the need for countertrading

It is obvious that a Third World country with low foreign exchange earnings or a company in a country subject to exchange control constraints does need to find a way around such problems. The questions to be answered by the potential exporter are as follows:

1. How badly do I need this business?
2. How will I manage the countertrade transaction?
3. What will it cost?

In answering the first question I can do no better than refer to Chapter 1, written by my colleague David Senior. All the factors he outlines in his first section apply with equal or greater force to the decision to embark on a countertrading route to generate or sustain exports. The cost aspects in particular must be considered because the costs of countertrading are significantly higher than those when one is paid by orthodox means. Costs are not only obviously financial such as the fee to the counterpurchase expert or of establishing your own facility, but also include such additional costs as the following:

1. A lengthened lead time because of a longer negotiation period.
2. The danger of new legislation in any of the countries involved. Changed legislation can undermine the structure of the transaction, leading to failure to complete.
3. The higher cost of, or inability to obtain, insurance cover.
4. Changes in the market price of the commodity involved leading to renegotiation or possible cessation of shipments.

If the answer to the first question is a definite yes, I do need this essential business, then one needs to answer the next two questions. Answering the question 'How will the countertrade transaction be operated?' leads inevitably to a solution that can be costed, and therefore both this question and the 'How much will it cost?' question will be addressed in this section.

In-house or outside assistance?

There are two main routes to follow: to utilise either in-house or specialist outside assistance.

In-house

If it is decided to adopt the in-house solution then it is necessary to decide whether the in-house activity is to cover the transaction completely or only partially. If a complete in-house countertrade capability is to be established then it is unlikely to be effective unless the corporation is prepared to face a minimum annual cost in excess of one million dollars to run this facility. This would be the minimum cost for a small but credible operation. It would cover the annual cost of supporting a senior countertrader with two or three support staff plus their office accommodation, large telephone bills (traders live on the phone) and heavy travel costs.

An alternative would be to eschew completely the idea of handling the transaction oneself and to appoint an experienced countertrader to act as a bridge between your needs and an outside trading house. Such experts, and few exist, are expensive but the cost could probably be reduced to about $350,000. The advantage of this solution would be that, once structured, you would not be exposed to a commodity risk since that would become the responsibility of the chosen trading house partner.

The cost of this approach is the absolute minimum if in-house expertise is to be established. Furthermore, its success will depend heavily on the degree of support at all levels within the company. This can be a problem because at least two of the staff in the unit will need to be experienced traders. Remuneration packages may well need to be more generous than those of your existing salaried staff. A bonus element will probably need to be included and this can lead to problems between this new team and your existing staff. This could become critical if it undermines the support of your existing team for the new unit. Not only is the full commitment of the head of the countertrade unit essential but he or she must also be accepted as a credible professional by the international trading companies with whom he or she will be expected to deal.

Using outside help

If the in-house solution is considered too expensive then there are many types of outside assistance available.

BANKS

Major banks in New York, London and Frankfurt have large and experienced countertrade departments, now included with their trade finance activities. However, it must be borne in mind that very few banks now accept the transaction risk; the vast majority are only interested in supplying financial support for the transaction. The commodity risk will remain yours or else will have to be accepted by a commodity trader.

TRADERS

Trading houses such as MB Trading, Conti Grain and André et Cie of Lausanne will usually be interested in accepting commodities. For manufactured products it will be more difficult to find a partner but it is essential that one is found before you are committed to the transaction.

CONSULTANTS

Consultants are legion and most have at one time worked in a countertrade department of a bank, corporation or trading company. They can be useful in identifying a partner but they of course cannot themselves help in taking any of the risk off your shoulders since they do not have the balance sheet strength to support such a commitment.

Some variants of the four main techniques

A number of alternatives exist to the four basic techniques described above. Their usefulness depends rather on the nature of your own company's activities. Certainly the most productive of variations is the counterpurchase sector. A few examples can perhaps best illustrate this.

Frequently a marketing advantage can be achieved by offering a potential customer some help with sales of a product that is causing them concern. An example here can be drawn from the experience of Massey-Ferguson in 1984–5 when they were vying with Fiat for second place in the tractor market behind the local producer in Austria, Steyr. Vineyard tractors represented a large part of the market and the Austrians were suffering a wine glut. There was no way that Massey-Ferguson could dispose of enough wine to finance completely the sales of tractors. However, they were able to devise, in conjunction with their Austrian distributor, a method whereby the farmer could pay for 10–15 per cent of the tractor with wine – some relief at least for the farmer and a distinct marketing plus for Massey-Ferguson.

Japanese motor manufacturers have adopted similar techniques, taking parts and sometimes sub-assemblies from countries where they enjoy high sales of their vehicles but which have foreign exchange problems. Indonesia has developed a significant export of automobile parts as a result, initially, of counterpurchase agreements with Japanese car manufacturers.

Offset is in reality an unusually innovative form of counterpurchase. The British Aerospace contract of Tornados for oil has alread been referred to as a counterpurchase transaction, i.e. priced goods for priced goods. As normally understood this involves movement of oil from country A to country B to pay for the aircraft purchased from country B. In the case of offset there can be an element of either local manufacture or service support which in effect helps to cover the purchase price of the aircraft. This alternative is particularly attractive when the country purchasing high-technology products seeks to upgrade its own manufacturing capability.

In the above cases there is a direct link between the exporter and the importer. However, other opportunities do exist. For example, many countries with foreign exchange problems have emerging tourist industries. There have been a few cases where package holidays have been offered in payment for goods. With the present reduction in tourist activity world-wide, now is perhaps not the time to enter the package tour business. However, a limited scheme similar to the Massey-Ferguson wine in part payment for tractors could be considered.

Switch transactions also lend themselves to variations on the classical triangular transaction. Switch dealers take additional pride in bringing a fourth country into the transaction where a straightforward switch of an obligation from country A to country B cannot be made to work. However, from the user's viewpoint there has to be caution since an additional link in the chain can complicate, delay and even abort the transaction.

The size of the market

In 1983–4 there were studies by the OECD and other intergovernmental agencies that estimated that something like 8 per cent by value of world trade was conducted on the basis of countertrade transactions. At the same time there were a number of traders protesting that the correct figure was around 30 per cent. Most members of this group were closely associated with defence industry transactions and I believe were heavily influenced by the higher level of countertrade deals in this sector. At the time I felt comfortable with an estimate of 8–9 per cent; today I believe the figure has probably slipped to below 5 per cent.

Such a figure may not seem significant but given the situation in your industry it might still be the only way to enable you to penetrate certain key markets. It therefore is essential not only to understand the basic techniques, know who does it, what it costs and how they do it but also to have some view of the future possibilities.

The future of countertrade

The high point of countertrade activity, of expectations for its future growth and, it must be confessed, gross overselling of its possibilities was from 1983 to 1986. During that period many international banks boasted their countertrade unit, department or even separate corporate entity. Some even established trading divisions that took title to goods rather than merely providing the necessary financial support services to other traders. Those enthusiasts are long gone. This is not to say that countertrade does not have its place. In certain markets it will be the only way in for some years to come. There are battle-scarred combatants out there willing to try again and again. Either on behalf of their trading house or if you too have the commitment and determination to persevere, as your in-house expert. There was a famous trader in those heady days of the middle 1980s, who claimed *'La compensation c'est moi'*.

Unfortunately it was not. But for those content to work on practical, perhaps initially small-scale transactions, countertrade in one of its many forms may be the key to unlocking one or two hitherto impenetrable markets.

14

International factoring

JOHN BEANEY AND PETER ROFF

Manager of Griffin Factors' International Division and Marketing Manager, Griffin Factors

Introduction

The reader of this article contemplating using the services of a factor is quite probably suffering feelings of guilt and embarrassment.

Such a business person is probably successful as measured by growing sales and a profitable balance sheet. But there are problems, mostly caused by shortage of cash. Cash flow pressures, as they are called, mean keeping suppliers waiting and maybe as a consequence having to think twice before taking new orders or suffering delays in fulfilling existing orders because of parts unavailability. Visiting the bank manager becomes more than a once a year courtesy call and begins to take more time than canvassing for new business. Facing this paradox you look for a way out and perhaps factoring is recommended; but you harbour suspicions. The fact that you turn to an article on factoring and it begins by addressing concerns like this perhaps further reinforces your misgivings. You perceive that factoring is bad for your image, will upset customers and increase your costs – so you fight shy.

This article is written from inside the factoring industry and it is intended to address honestly the pros and cons of factoring with specific reference to its use in international business. It is intended to be a users' guide.

The article is structured to answer the following key questions:

1. What are the needs factoring satisfies?
2. How is this achieved?
3. At what cost?
4. How can the advantages be realised?

What are the needs factoring satisfies?

Credit assessment

Whether you are selling at home or abroad, whenever credit is given there is risk of non-payment by the buyer. As the giving of credit is necessary to allow buyers time to take goods into stock and sell them on it is fundamental to the sale and without it the total volume of sales would be lower. Seen in this light assessment of buyer creditworthiness is essential to the success of a business. Businesses are started by people with unique qualities but not necessarily skills in credit assessment.

Factors are, however, expert at assessing buyer creditworthiness. This expertise is built up from the factor handling millions of transactions to many hundreds of thousands of buyers. The factor as the recipient of payments gets the most accurate current indication of a buyer's liquidity through handling collections on behalf of his or her clients. This information is stored and pooled for the benefit of all other clients.

The factor supplements this with access to a wide range of reference material, including financial statements where these are published and references from lending institutions and other creditors as well as the assessment of a wide range of specialist agencies.

Bringing this together is the expertise of the credit assessment personnel who are totally dedicated to this important function. The credit assessment team will assess creditworthiness of prospective buyers in relation to the level of expected sales and the period of credit proposed. When a decision has been made it will be constantly monitored to ensure that changes in the circumstances of buyers are picked up and communicated rapidly to the client.

Credit protection

Using the credit assessment skills and their own financial resources, backed usually by major banking institutions, factors also extend credit protection guarantees to their clients. Where approval for a customer is given, the client will be protected against the financial inability of the buyer to pay. In the United Kingdom this point is marked by the insolvency of the buyer and internationally it is non-payment ninety days after due date.

Credit protection from the factor means that the sale is complete after successful dispatch (of goods) or performance (of a service). There is no lingering uncertainty waiting for settlement.

Collections

Open account trade brings with it the need for buyers to make positive steps to effect payments. This is the price to be paid for the flexibility that open account gives both buyer and seller as compared to a letter of credit.

From the responsibility to initiate payment comes the temptation to defer payment beyond agreed credit terms. Delay can be caused by administrative inefficiency. It can be the consequence of a dispute or query, or a deliberate attempt to extract more credit and thus reduce the cost of purchase. Most worrying of course is the situation in which payment is put off because of financial inability to pay. To manage the credit given requires credit control effort. Such activity must be very dedicated because only persistence pays and it must also be conducted in a highly professional manner. Payments are an extremely sensitive area and customer relations are easily damaged where demands are made in error or with a lack of sensitivity. Equally, too, sensitive treatment which is not effective carries an unacceptable cost.

The factor can provide specialist support in this area. Having dedicated professional collectors, the factor can give an assured level of service continuously through the year to match peaks and troughs of activity in an efficient manner. This activity is dedicated and therefore not diverted by other demands such as can occur in a small office with conflicting priorities, sales or collections.

Some people like to use the factor's collection service because they can blame the factor for any aggressive collection. It is worth recalling, however, that the factor will tailor-make the collection activity to reflect the individual preferences of clients, balancing the need for hard or soft collection activity. Our own company's preference is for the factor to reflect the clearly articulated collection philosophy of the client; that is, if the client wants an aggressive collection procedure that must start with very clear statements of terms at the time of order with reminders all through the sale and purchase negotiation and supported at the after-sales activity by prompt resolution of queries. Each part of a business should be consistent to achieve the best results.

Sales ledger administration

The factor operates sophisticated sales ledger systems. They are backed by large and elaborate computer systems with dedicated personnel.

The factor runs a complete sales ledger package, which enables the client to keep accurate records of credit transactions. The whole process from booking invoices to allocating payments is handled by the factor, offering considerable savings on administrative staff and overheads to clients. In addition, most factors provide an on-line computer access to clients to keep them in touch with the position on their ledgers.

The buyer benefits from these services, resulting in more effective collection. Buyers receive monthly statements from the factor in a format they most readily accept, setting out clearly details of the payments that are expected. This feature is particularly helpful in obtaining prompt settlement from large organisations.

In addition, the factor can administer multi-currency ledgers giving full accounting for currency transactions including gains and losses on exchange.

Finance

Meeting the service needs of clients is a vital function of factors and it is noticeable that most long-term users of factoring are those who are fully attuned to the benefits of the service. Nevertheless, obtaining the financial benefits of factoring is often perceived as the single most important aspect of a factor's services.

Where a business sells on credit terms, it needs cash to finance stocks and pay for supplies, materials or labour. It is rare that the credit period available on such supplies exceeds credit given to customers. In such circumstances the need for what is called 'working capital' expands with the level of sales.

Financing the expanding requirement for working capital has been the traditional role of bank overdrafts. Bank overdrafts are usually provided against tangible security. Tangible security includes assets such as company property, directors' private homes and, to an extent, stock and debtors.

As the proportion a bank will advance against debtors is usually less than the cost of sale, there is a potential cash flow shortfall unless additional security is available in the absence of accumulated reserves. There is, of course, no reason why a company should have such assets or that the value of those assets should equal the working capital needs.

Many older, established companies, because of the rate of property asset appreciation, are coincidentally able to support the borrowings by charges on property. However, for a new company or one where property assets bear no benefit in the running of the business, such securities are unavailable to the bank. An expanding business will therefore face the grotesque irony of having a profitable business with orders pending but no cash with which to secure supplies.

The factor's financial facility is geared to the level of sales to creditworthy people. So long as these continue to expand, immediate cash of up to 80 per cent of the invoice value will be payable to the client on fulfilment of the order. Once the factor is assured that sales are valid and collectable, no further security is normally required and no equity in the business need be given away to secure the support.

User profile: who can benefit from the factor's services?

The previous section dealt with the needs that a factor satisfies. This section focuses on describing the type of business with those needs that could best take advantage of the factor's services.

Industry type

A factor's services are suited to businesses producing goods or services which are complete at the point of invoicing. Examples include furniture manufacture, provision of temporary staff, manufacture of printed circuit boards, steel stockholding, printing or distribution of garments.

The reason for this is that goods or services for which further performance is expected after invoicing represent a security risk to the factor and this affects his or her ability to finance the client exporter. In addition, the factor's collection services are geared to collection of accounts receivable where questions primarily relate to issues of ability to pay rather than willingness due to non-performance.

Where the goods or services have been delivered or completed at the time of invoicing, a debt exists which cannot normally be disputed. The factor can therefore finance the invoice without needing to make large reserves against the potential need to recourse the debt to the client in the event of non-payment due to dispute. This makes factoring a truly non-recourse finance facility where a valid sale takes place. Recourse would be inconvenient for the client, who has already used the funds to meet planned expenditure such as paying creditors, and future cash flow would adversely be affected.

Factoring gives smooth, assured cash flow. Safe in the knowledge that the invoice he or she is financing represents a valid sale, the factor can advance a high proportion of its value to the client without additional security such as a charge on assets.

Spread of customers

The factor does require that a client sells to several different customers. If any one customer represents more than between 20 to 30 per cent of the outstanding receivables, a factor will reserve the right to restrict additional funding.

This arises because concentrations, as they are called, represent a dangerous change in the balance of power between buyer and seller. Where a client is overly dependent upon one particular buyer, that buyer is in the position to make continued orders dependent upon sometimes unreasonable performance criteria. The client is also dangerously dependent upon the continuation of business and would be imperilled if the orders were to dry up.

By setting a concentration indicator of 20 to 30 per cent factors know that both they and their client are less vulnerable to disputes and thus better able to develop a growing business.

The factor normally advances 80 per cent of the invoice value, leaving 20 per cent to be paid out to the client upon collection or the insolvency of approved undisputed invoices. The 20 per cent less charges represents a cushion against deductions or queries which hold up payment in the normal course of events. Were it not for this cushion, the factor might have to recover finance previously advanced to a client, which would be disruptive to the cash flow of the client and mitigate against proper financial planning.

Factors have arrived at the 80 per cent over many years of experience and know that it normally provides an adequate cushion. Thus even in the event of the client's insolvency, the factor can normally recover all funds advanced and often realise a surplus. This is reassuring to the client company, its principals and creditors.

Conflicts in factoring

The factor needs clear title to the invoices that he or she finances. Prior claimants, which can include a bank with a floating charge, suppliers under reservation of title or purchases under ban of assignment, represent a conflict with the factor's rights. Where such conflicts are identified, the factor will normally require a waiver to ensure unencumbered title. Such waivers are in the interest of the client because they ensure the factoring finance facility remains non-recourse.

Administration

The factor provides a high level of support to the client – specifically in the areas of credit assessment, collection and the processing of invoices and payments. The factor is, however, dependent upon a basic level of administrative support by the client. Essential, obviously, is the fulfilment of orders, so the accurate taking of orders, processing and fulfilment is key; but in addition the client must have the capability to deal with after-sales queries where they relate to terms or performance.

Turnover criteria

Factoring services can benefit companies at any level of turnover and at any stage in growth cycle. Nevertheless, the economies factoring offers are most beneficial with a turnover either projected or actual of at least £100,000 per annum. For export accounts the criteria is somewhat higher at a quarter of a million pounds and for invoice discounting higher still at £2 million.

Another financial criterion is for profitable trading. This is because in the absence of profits or at least the prospect of profits, the services factoring offers will only put off the evil day. In the case of a loss-making business, the underlying causes must be first addressed, although factoring can be part of a package of measures designed to restore profitability. Factoring provides the essential liquidity to realise the profit potential in a business.

Whilst many companies enjoying the benefits of a factoring service have substantial capital resources, it is not an essential ingredient except where factoring is provided on a recourse basis. In such circumstances the wealth of the business must be at least equal to the potential for recourse in the

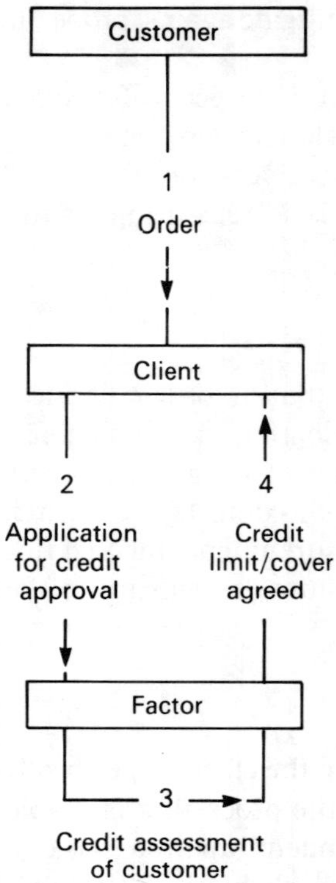

Figure 14.1 How factoring works: application for credit approval

event of buyer insolvency. For here the factor is not providing a guarantee against insolvency of the buyer. In addition, specifically for invoice discounting, a minimum net asset value of £100,000 is most commonly required.

How factoring works

Factoring does not describe one single service; rather, a portfolio of complementary financial services. Companies can avail themselves of some or all of these according to their individual needs.

The services vary in degrees of cost and complexity and come under many different confusing names. Fundamentally, however, they fall into three closely related categories: sales ledger administration, credit management and finance tied directly to the level of a company's sales. These categories mirror the needs as identified above under the categories credit

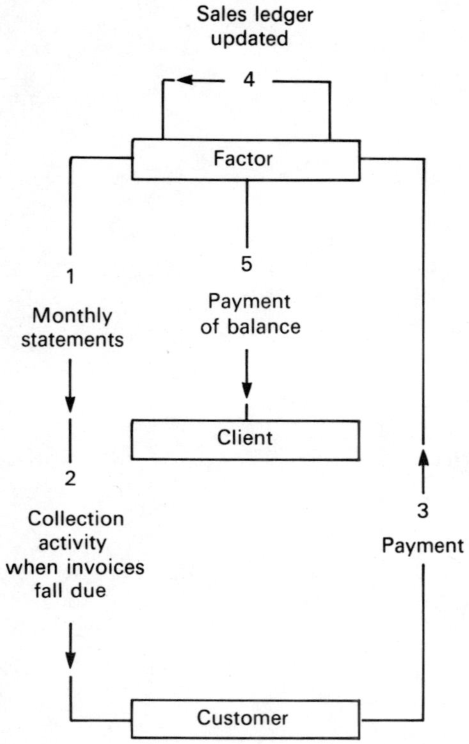

Figure 14.2 How factoring works: delivery of goods and invoice

assessment, credit protection, collection, sales ledger administration and finance.

The most common factoring package is known in the trade as the 'full service'. Companies using this enter into a relationship with a factor under which he or she takes full administrative control of the company's sales ledger and undertakes to buy most of the company's debts as they arise during the normal course of business. The company thus contracts out responsibility for managing and controlling its sales ledger, and no longer needs to chase its customer's overdue invoices.

The mechanics are simple. As soon as goods are delivered or services completed, the factoring user raises an invoice which is sent to the customer with a copy to the factor.

From that point on, the factor assumes financial and administrative responsibility for the invoice including credit cover against customer

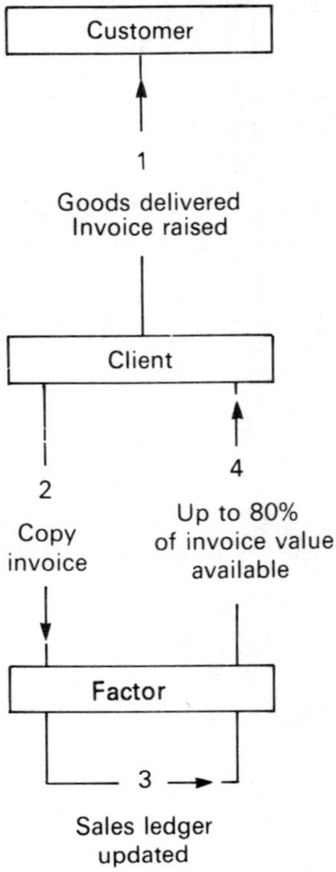

Figure 14.3 How factoring works: payment collection

insolvency. Added to this up to 80 per cent of the face value is immediately available to the client company. Taking the finance this way is completely optional – the client can draw as much or as little of the cash as is available.

The balance is payable either a fixed number of days after the invoice date or when the customer makes the payment. The user thus gets immediate access to cash that would otherwise lie in the coffers for two, three or even more months under normal circumstances.

Credit management

Complementary to the cash is credit management. The factor undertakes to assess the creditworthiness of existing or potential customers and offers up to 100 per cent credit protection on agreed credit limits. Thus under these circumstances it is the factor who bears the costs of a customer collapse rather than the company itself. Factors are skilled in the art of exacting cash from recalcitrant payers and are prepared to be diplomatic under most circumstances but litigious under others.

The advantage of taking the administrative services is that the company saves the costs of maintaining its own department. Managers need not embroil themselves in the day-to-day task of supervising the sales accounts or chasing slow-paying customers; furthermore, the sales relationships are not damaged by management and sales staff pestering customers for payment.

The advantage of taking the financial services include the following:

1. The company gets access to finance linked to current levels of business. By contrast, the amount of money available under a traditional overdraft arrangement is based on historic balance sheet ratios. When a company is up against its overdraft limit and yet confident of its sales prospects, factoring can finance a higher level of sales.
2. The company is in a position to improve its relationship with its suppliers through prompt payments, and to extract the optimum terms for making its purchases, for example through bulk purchase discounts or simply cash payments.
3. Optimum stock levels can be maintained and peaks and troughs in the pattern of demand smoothed out.
4. The service furnishes finance for growth, without requiring any additional injection of new equity from external sources or any additional guarantees from management.
5. It introduces a note of certainty into the vexed question of cash flow management, further supported by the inclusion of credit protection.

The service is not a last resort for companies in financial trouble; rather it is a financial tool by which the working capital tied up in customer credit is liberated to the advantage of the business.

Invoice discounting

Invoice discounting has emerged as the real volume growth area of the factoring industry. Over the last five years the annual increase in volume has risen by an average of more than 25 per cent per annum in the United Kingdom and is rising even more quickly in other markets.

Under an invoice discounting arrangement, the factor provides a financial facility against sales invoices but without any of the credit management services. This service best suits those companies with an efficient accounting system, accounts administration and low bad debt risks. The popularity of the service is the result of the following:

1. High demand for working capital from growth-orientated companies in expanding economies.

2. The fact that the service is confidential; customers of any company using invoice discounting need never know of the factor's existence.
3. When coupled with credit protection it is a source of off-balance sheet finance. Under current accounting conventions there is no obligation to disclose the extent to which the company uses a factor's finance facility; thus gearing, and other key balance sheet ratios, will be enhanced.
4. More companies are paying closer attention to managing the sales ledger asset. Micro-computer systems enhance efficiency of this area of business and thus with the availability of appropriate staff the credit management services of the factor may not be needed.

Credit protection

The option of credit protection is available with invoice discounting. This guarantees the client against customer collapse and indeed protects the factor from the risk that the client may not be able to meet the liability to the factor if the customer goes under.

Invoice discounting clients receive regular visits from the factor's personnel. Sales accounting entries are verified at the client's premises and in addition the payment of preferential and key creditors can be scrutinised closely. All this is designed to monitor security constantly and protect both client and factor from the danger of over-trading.

Otherwise, the company just sends the factor a regular summary of invoices and credit notes (with an aged debtor analysis at the end of each month). The factor will then make up to 80 per cent of the value of the invoices available to the company as and when it is required. Sales ledger and cash collection procedures remain with the client.

Export factoring

Increasing numbers of companies are turning to overseas markets. Markets are larger, customers more numerous and opportunities greater. For the United Kingdom it is also a national imperative in redressing the balance of trade and an improved economic climate.

Although the business person is becoming a creature of the global village and although the business world is contracting with the time it takes to get from one continent to another, it is simply not the same thing to sell goods to a customer in Birmingham, Alabama as it is to one in Birmingham, West Midlands.

The fact is that the international market is fragmented, riven by variations in trade customs, currency systems, laws and languages. This is as true of Europe, despite all the rhetoric about trade harmonisation in 1992, as it is of Asia or Australia.

More and more overseas buyers of Western-produced goods are insisting on open account terms from exporters. They demand the same terms of trade as they would get from domestic suppliers and see no reason to tolerate the inconvenience of bills of exchange or letters of credit.

International factoring provides the means by which exporters can overcome these hurdles. Factors who offer an export service either have their own offices overseas or are part of a network of independent factoring organisations. The largest network of correspondent factors is Factors Chain International (FCI). Through this network exporting companies are able to compete in overseas markets on the same terms as local suppliers.

FCI, founded in 1968, consists of over ninety member companies in thirty-five of the world's main commercial centres. It provides support to exporters who need to sell on open account terms overseas without exposing themselves to undue risks.

HOW EXPORT FACTORING WORKS

As far as a client company is concerned, export factoring works in exactly the same way as its domestic counterpart. The client only deals with the local factor. Details of foreign customers are given to the local factor, who then selects the best correspondent factor to handle the client's business in the country of import. The overseas factor assesses the customers and offers up to 100 per cent protection within agreed credit limits.

The client delivers goods and raises an invoice with a copy sent to the local factor. This triggers the whole procedure. Finance is available from the local factor and the sales ledger (held by both factors) is updated. On the due date the foreign factor collects payments.

Finally, the foreign factor remits funds to the exporting company via the local factor in the quickest possible way, usually using SWIFT (Society for Worldwide Inter-Bank Financial Telecommunications). Delays in the cross-border transfer of funds are thus kept to a minimum.

Buyers are approached in their own local language, in their own country and in the locally accepted way. They make their payments in the local currency and are chased up in the locally accepted way if payments are overdue. Distance and other cultural barriers cease to be a problem. Furthermore the import factor is able to furnish 100 per cent credit protection against customer default. The factor is in the best possible position to make assessments of creditworthiness and keep close to developments which affect the buyer.

Who uses factoring?

Factoring is not a panacea. Certain companies by their very size and circumstances or the industry in which they operate will not be ideal candidates for the factor's services.

On strictly financial criteria, companies with an annual turnover of

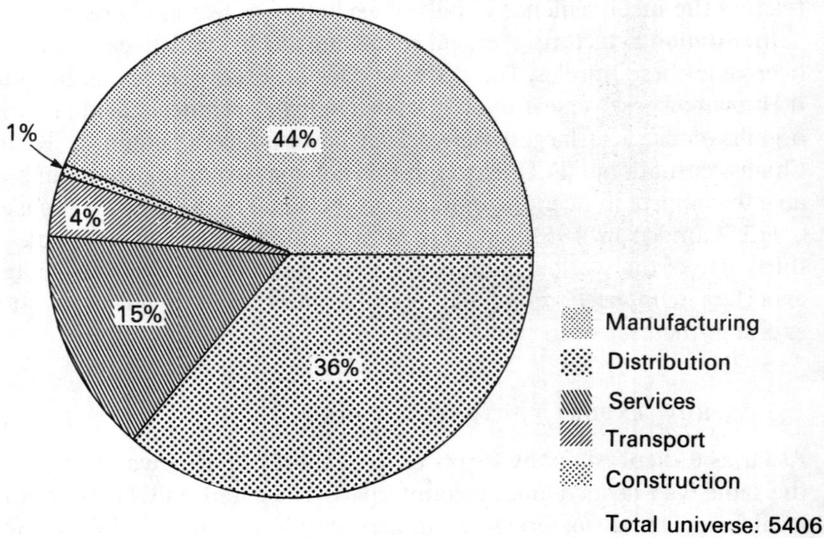

Figure 14.4 Analysis of factoring clients by type of main UK industry

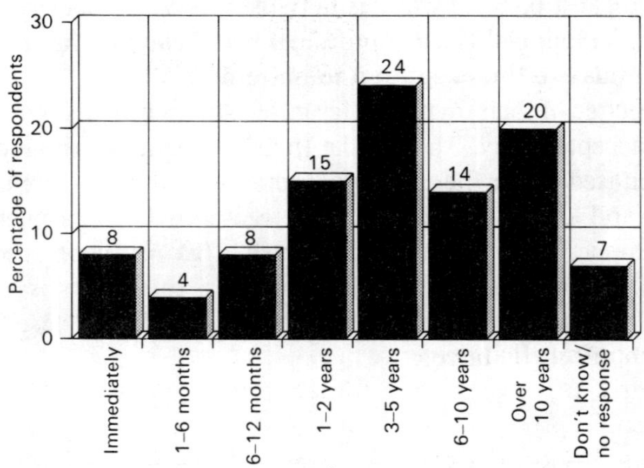

Figure 14.5 Length of time in business before using factoring (*Source*: Business Marketing Services Ltd, 1988; research among users of factoring in the United Kingdom)

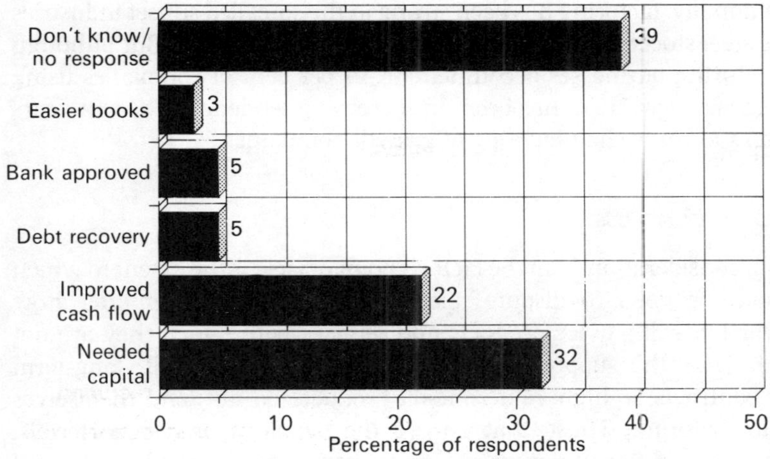

Figure 14.6 Reasons for using factoring (*Source*: Business Marketing Services Ltd, 1988; research among users of factoring in the United Kingdom)

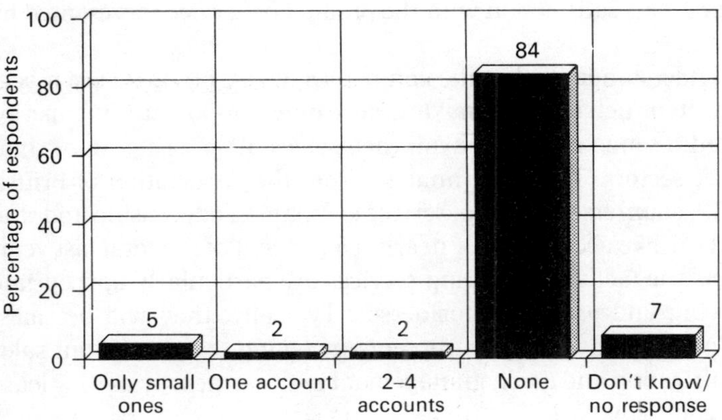

Figure 14.7 Business lost after introducing factoring. (Will factoring adversely affect relations with customers?) (*Source*: Business Marketing Services Ltd, 1988; research among users of factoring)

between £350,000 and £5 million will be best suited to the full service. However, there is an overlap. Larger companies with turnover of £2 million or more are frequently attracted to invoice discounting, where they have the option to take credit protection as well.

Statistics from the Association of British Factors and Discounters, for example, show that the vast majority of UK companies using factoring last year had turnovers of less than £5 million. Nearly 1,500 small companies, with turnovers of £250,000 or less made up the largest category overall.

Traditionally, factoring has been strong in the so-called sunset industries such as steel stockholding, timber, engineering and textiles. But although manufacturing businesses accounted for 44 per cent of companies using factoring last year, there has been an increasing tendency in recent years for factors to serve the new type of growth companies.

Factorable businesses

A crucial consideration from the factor's point of view is the extent to which an invoice is open to dispute. Clearly no customer, no matter how creditworthy, will pay for products and services with which they are not satisfied. Thus the supply of complex parts and equipment, long-term service contracts or high-value one-off products do not lend themselves easily to factoring. Those that do are the suppliers of raw materials, components and consumer goods. Such items can be made, sold and subsequently forgotten by the supplier. Those invoices arising from such sales are less likely to be contentious, are not subject to after-sales service and can be collected by the factor independently for the supplier. The factor can also judge the likelihood of a customer refusing to meet an invoice on the basis of previous satisfaction with the product or service represented by that document.

It is thus understandable that the companies whose products are made, sold and forgotten such as those making electronic components or paper or those distributing machine tools avail themselves of factoring more than those in other sectors. The latest analysis from the Association of British Factors and Discounters shows that service companies, advertising and staff agencies and the like accounted for nearly 15 per cent of the total last year.

This reflects the fact that factoring services are particularly appropriate for fast-growing and profitable businesses. Typically, they will be sales-driven enterprises managed by entrepreneurs willing to contract out sales ledger administration and credit management in the same way as they lease premises or company cars.

The entrepreneur v. the bank manager

The common financial characteristics of the companies described above are high borrowing requirements and a concentration of assets in stock and debtors. The entrepreneur and the bank manager do not always see eye to eye under such circumstances. The banker is often unwilling to lend further cash on the basis of already stretched balance sheet ratios. The entrepreneur, close to his or her customers, can see only an opportunity: more cash means more stock to fuel more sales. At best the result can be frustration; at worst it can be insolvency brought about by over-trading.

At this point, factoring becomes a valuable alternative to the traditional

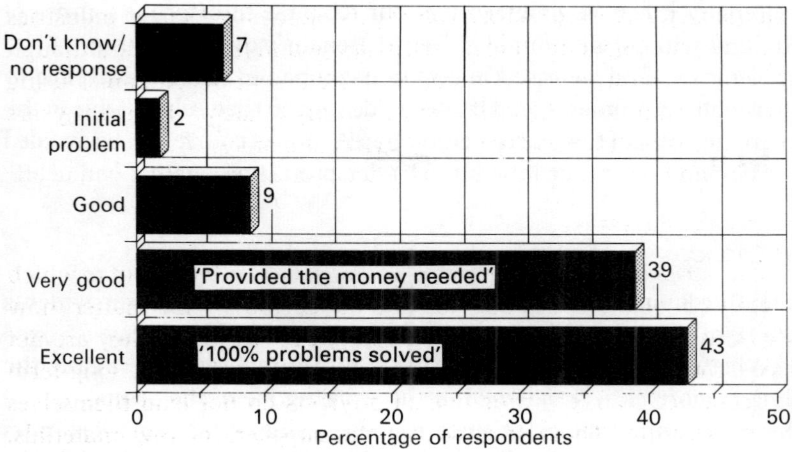

Figure 14.8 Results of using present factoring company (*Source*: Business Marketing Services Ltd, 1988; research among users of factoring in the United Kingdom)

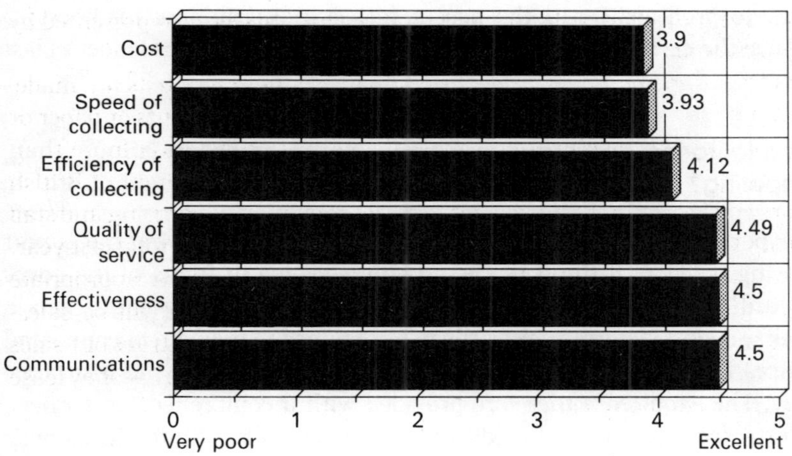

Figure 14.9 Performance ratings of factoring companies (*Source*: Business Marketing Services Ltd, 1988; research among users of factoring)

overdraft. By securing up to 80 per cent of the value of outstanding invoices now, the liquidity is restored and the assets represented by debtors liberated to provide further finance, without formal limits. If carefully controlled, factoring can be the catalyst that transforms a very small company.

Furthermore, the use of factoring can release the entrepreneur owner from the unpalatable necessity of raising money secured on his or her own personal property. It can mean that at a crucial phase in the development of the company it can be financed without recourse to external sources of capital and without dilution of the entrepreneur's own equity.

Problems can and do arise. On occasion companies take the cash tied to one particular customer, spend it and suddenly find themselves liable to the factor in the event of that customer's collapse. This of course can be avoided if the company pays that little bit extra for protection against bad debt.

Asset finance

In matching finance to assets, companies should use factoring prepayments for the right purposes, that is to provide working capital. Finance for fixed assets is better achieved through leasing or hire purchase. In these cases the funding is more closely matched to the working life of the assets.

This is an important point since the true value of factoring lies in its ability to provide immediate finance for keeping businesses working rather than for investment in high-cost fixed assets.

There is a temptation for companies in financial difficulties to turn to the factor as a last ditch source of finance. Today the factor is only likely to oblige if he or she is satisfied that the provision of the service would assist a return to profitability. In the past a rather indiscriminate readiness to advance the cash helped win for the factor the poor image as lender of last resort.

Export factoring and credit insurance: complementary or competing?

For exporters already operating a credit insurance policy, what has export factoring to offer? If the policy is proving effective in terms of the cover provided and the administrative requirements are being met, then a recourse export factoring contract can be obtained to provide collection and finance. The credit protection would thus be provided by the insurance policy. The exporter is therefore provided with a comprehensive service.

Most export factors and credit insurers, such as the United Kingdom's ECGD, have established working procedures to enable their products to work in harmony. In the case of factoring and the ECGD, this takes the form of a special suite of endorsements to the insurance policy which facilitate assignment of its benefits to the factor. This enables prepayments (finance) to be made available to the exporter with the factor being entitled to the proceeds of any successful ECGD claim in the event of buyer non-payment. The exporter enjoys protection against rejection of any claim by the insurer through failure to chase the debt effectively as this becomes the factor's responsibility.

If the insurance policy is proving an administrative burden or the level of credit cover is inadequate, export factoring including credit protection is an

Table 14.1. Comparison of export factoring and credit insurance

Service	Export factoring	Credit insurance
Level of credit protection:		
insolvency	100%	80–90%
political risk	0%	90%
Credit request response time:		
United Kingdom	Within 1 week	Within 1 week
world-wide	Within 2 weeks	Within 1 week
Approval of disputed debts	Not covered	Not covered
Payment to client	On collection or 90 days after due date	On insolvency or six months after due date
Collection	Integral, including legal costs	Responsibility of the client, although recommendations for overdue debts must be followed and a contribution to cost of recovery may be made by the insurer
Terms of sale	Especially beneficial for open account. Factors will handle documentary collections in conjunction with their parent banks	Any subject to insurer's approval
Country coverage	Where open account or DA is an appropriate and accepted term of trade, i.e. Europe, North America and most parts of Asia	World-wide but appetite restricted especially where there is a political risk
Administration	Copy invoice only normally required in respect of a completed sale	Returns on sales and overdue debts required regularly. Full documentation of debt and collection attempts required when pursuing claim
Price	Normal range 1–3% of invoice value. This includes full ledger administration and collection	0.3–1.5% for OECD. 1% typical starting price. Lower rates for established exporters with good claims record

alternative. In circumstances where the insured is not happy with the policy, perhaps through poor claims experience, or when the exporter has not already got an insurance policy, why choose export factoring in preference?

Table 14.1 highlights the comparative benefits of export factoring and credit insurance. Factoring clearly does more for the client, to reflect the generally higher level of fees. When the exporter has no established expertise, or could better employ staff resources, the higher level of service provided through factoring is most beneficial.

It is apparent that factoring provides a higher level of credit protection, 100 per cent compared with 80 or 90 per cent. Normally, however, factors take longer to decide on an application for credit approval on a new customer. The reasons for this are instructive in determining which service is the most appropriate. Credit insurers have developed credit insurance techniques that rely more on the record of the exporter in selecting good risks than positively checking out each individual prospective buyer. They can check records for adverse information and rely more on their spread of risk and knowledge of country and industry rather than the specifics of the individual buyer's financial circumstances. By contrast, the factoring chains have collectively much larger data banks of payment experience and financial information which they supplement with access to locally available information in the individual markets and direct liaison with the buyer.

For the exporter new to a particular market, or without the benefit of first-hand experience with the potential buyer, the positive vetting approach of the factor has distinct advantages. It will validate the correctness of the buyer's legal constitution, ensuring that the correct buyer is invoiced and the ability to pay is properly tested. As a consequence, exporters using factoring do not face elaborate and difficult claims procedures, where their claim can be rejected on an apparent technicality. Under a factoring contract, it is the factor who undertakes the buyer creditworthiness evaluation and is responsible for collection, and so, unless there was a fundamental failure to perform by the seller, the factor cannot avoid payment of the approved invoices.

In summary, credit protection through an export factor is particularly appropriate to the less experienced exporter or one building up a customer base in markets where open account trading is appropriate. For exporters with a good record of choosing reliable buyers, and a strong administrative and collection capability, then low price and broad geographical coverage make credit insurance good value for credit protection alone.

Alternatives to export factoring not involving two factors

Most factors offering an export factoring service do so using local factors in the buyer's market. The advantage of this system is the combination of a single point of communication for the exporter, together with local expertise. This includes the ability to talk to the buyer and access to the most comprehensive and up-to-date credit information. Using two factors, problems caused by language, time zones and cultural differences can be overcome.

Where two or more factors are involved, there is an issue of costs and communication between the factors. To provide international factoring factors join 'chains'. These are similar in concept to associations of correspondent bankers and they facilitate effective communication and high standards between factors.

Within a chain such as Factors Chain International, communication is enhanced by electronic communication links through satellite and education and training opportunities to ensure effective working between the factoring staff in different countries.

The statistics on the growth of international factoring suggest that the chains are succeeding in providing clients with the level of service required at a competitive price. Nevertheless, some factors offer their services without the benefit of representation in the country of the exporter. The potential user of such a service must ask whether they truly have the capability of delivering an effective collection service, especially where problems emerge with, say, a complex dispute. If they claim to have staff conversant in languages, does this capability extend to every market and is cover provided effectively throughout the year, even during holidays?

Negotiating the most cost-effective factoring contract

The most important step is to articulate your needs to the factor clearly, ensure that these are understood and that the service level required can and will be delivered.

As with many purchases, a prospective user must be careful to compare like with like, so look at the small print of factoring contracts. Specifically, there may be additional charges for services, whether money transmission costs, fees for credit enquiries or, in the case of recourse factoring, fees for continuing collection of the debt after perhaps as little as forty-five days after the due date.

It is equally as important to understand whether collection needs to be undertaken through computer-generated dunning or whether you require the close personal attention of a Credit Controller or Collection Clerk. Both sorts of service are available, both are applicable to different circumstances and of course the cost can vary.

In determining whether a factor can deliver, references from other users are valuable and so too is a visit to the factor's premises. Meeting the people you will deal with has to be one of the most effective ways of ensuring good cooperation.

The costs

It is glib but true that factoring costs as little and as much as the client wants, or will allow. Naturally the client will also usually pay for what is received. The client wanting and needing BMW performance should not be fooled by Lada prices.

How then to understand the real cost of factoring? The first step is to understand the structure of the factor's pricing. There are basically two charges: an administration charge covering the services rendered and a discounting charge (or financing interest cost).

The administration charge

The administration charge is usually calculated as a set percentage of factored sales. The percentage is agreed in advance and usually reviewed on an annual basis. The fee covers the main service elements in the factoring package, including credit assessment, credit protection, collection and sales ledger administration. The first determinant for the scale of factor's charge will be the number of service elements within the package and the extent to which each is provided.

The discounting charge

The discounting charge is usually expressed as a margin over a clearing bank base rate. The margin is determined by reference to the anticipated volume of funds utilised, financial circumstances of the client and the relative negotiating strength. The discounting charge is applied (usually monthly) against the value of invoices prepaid based on the daily outstanding balance.

A common misconception

The common criticism of factoring is that it is 'expensive'. Research shows that users of factoring do not share this attitude, so it is important to understand how the misconception arises. It is a common misunderstanding to take the administration fee and the discounting fee, add the two together and express the total as the cost of finance. This would be correct where it is only finance that the factor provides. As has been demonstrated above, it is the total service package that the factor is providing. For the client who needs those benefits, the administration fee is not an expensive cost and certainly not a cost attributable to finance.

The legal basis of factoring

This is an outline of some of the legal bases of factoring. First, there is the relationship between the factor and the client. There are three types of factoring agreement:

1. Offer and acceptance.
2. Faculative type.
3. Whole turnover assignment.

In all three, the relationship between the client and the factor is the same, being based on a full outright sale by the client of his trade debts and they are purchased by the factor. The main apparent difference between the three types is one of timing in relation to the vesting of the debts in the factor.

In the first type, offer and acceptance, the client offers his debts to the factor, title passing on the factor's formal acceptance. An offer is normally made in writing when copy invoices are sent to the factor and the factor then signifies his agreement in writing (if the debt is acceptable).

In the second type, faculative, there is no formal acceptance of the debt when purchased by the factor. If the factor does not reject a debt offered by the client, acceptance is deemed to have taken place and the debt vests in the factor, it being credited to the client's account.

The third type, whole turnover, operates on the basis that all debts vest in the factor when they arise, without further formality, although they are usually later notified to the factor by the client.

It should be emphasised that factoring is not lending. The basic differences are as follows:

1. With lending, the debt is not purchased by the party lending money to the client. The lender normally secures his position by registering a fixed and/or floating charge over the client's book debts.
2. With factoring, the debt is purchased in full by the factor, the factor not needing, therefore, to register a charge to secure his position. Payments from the factor to the client are monies paid on account of the purchase price of the debt. The factor recovers his money from the debtors and not the client.

   Persons considering establishing a factoring business would be well advised to consider the wording of factoring contracts and any associated literature carefully to ensure that it is clear that debts are being purchased. In a recent case in the United Kingdom involving Exfinco (the export finance company), an agreement based on what purported to be goods purchased has been challenged. The basis of the challenge is that the documentation did not prove goods purchased but rather a lending agreement whose priority was not established through lack of a registered charge. This is a complex area and time does not allow detailed study but persons interested would be advised to read *Tolley's Factoring*, by F. R. Salinger, which comprehensively explores the legal base of factoring.

The accountancy profession is currently formulating guidelines on the treatment of factoring. They will hopefully reach a conclusion which can be incorporated in future editions of this book.

Trends in international factoring

Factoring is one of the fastest growing financial services in the world. In most of the so-called developed world, factoring is growing between 20 and

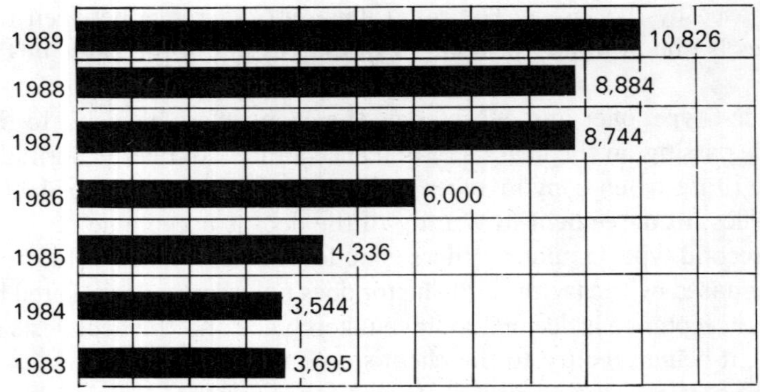

Figure 14.10 World-wide international factoring volumes 1983–9 (figures in US$ million)

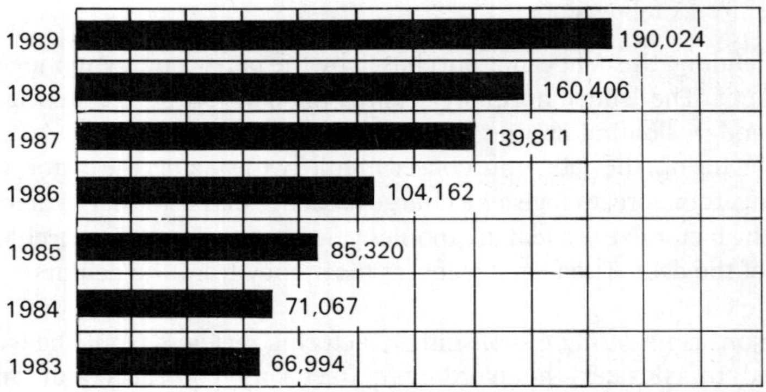

Figure 14.11 World-wide domestic and international factoring combined 1983–9 (figures in US$ million)

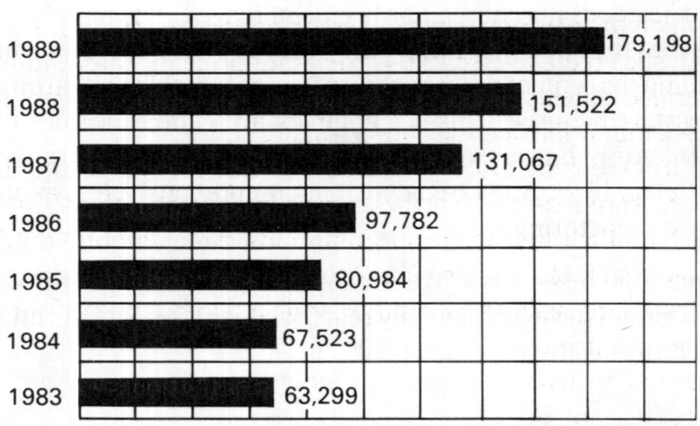

Figure 14.12 World-wide domestic factoring volumes 1983–9 (figures in US$ million)

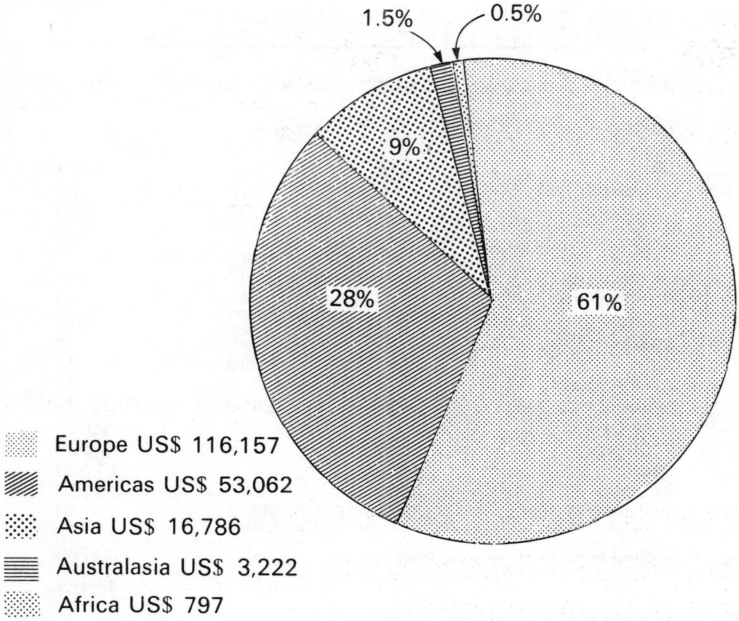

Figure 14.13 World-wide factoring turnover by continent as at December 1989

30 per cent per year. In Italy, growth rates in excess of 40 per cent are regularly being achieved.

Domestic factoring represents the largest element in this US $190 billion industry but cross-border factoring is gaining prominence. Utilisation of factoring services has been encouraged by world-wide inflation and high interest rates, which make management of credit periods so important, and the granting of trade credit so essential to facilitate trade. In international factoring, the service benefits allow exporters to control the risks presented by the growing demand for open account trading terms.

It is apparent from looking at the trends in international factoring, that the main flows are from Asia and North America into Europe, from Europe to North America and within the European nations. An emerging trend is for use of international factoring for intra-Asian trade. These flows and the relative growth rates are explained by the growing acceptability and indeed demand for open account trade.

Where traditional instruments such as letters of credit are rendered inappropriate because of the short delivery times or the need to offer competitive terms, with a minimum of cost and inconvenience to the buyer, how does the exporter control the risk? Going completely to open account

Table 14.2. Factoring turnover by country in 1989 (US$ million)

Number of companies[a]	Area	Domestic	International	Total
	Europe			
3	Austria	1,245	140	1,385
7	Belgium	1,818	605	2,423
1	Czechoslovakia	0	122	122
7	Denmark	650	220	870
10	Finland	4,920	253	5,173
14	France	10,037	741	10,778
14	Germany	5,671	2,147	7,818
3	Hungary	0	40	40
1	Ireland	200	10	210
1	Israel	0	6	6
80	Italy	50,150	1,030	51,180
2	Luxembourg	38	2	40
6	Netherlands	4,450	2,450	6,900
12	Norway	2,505	105	2,610
5	Portugal	520	15	535
16	Spain	1,349	171	1,520
6	Sweden	3,500	210	3,710
2	Switzerland	23	17	40
2	Turkey	2	15	17
32	United Kingdom	19,800	980	20,780
224		106,878	9,279	116,157
	Americas			
9	Canada	1,897	175	2,072
17	United States	46,217	530	46,747
35	Mexico	4,000	6	4,006
1	Dominican Republic	2	0	2
30	Brazil	200	0	200
1	Chile	20	0	20
2	Ecuador	15	0	15
95		52,351	711	53,062
	Africa			
1	Morocco	0	3	3
6	South Africa	770	24	794
7		770	27	797
	Asia			
3	Hong Kong	35	100	135
1	Indonesia	3	0	3
43	Japan	12,090	297	12,387
15	Malaysia	335	2	337
5	Philippines	50	1	51
20	Singapore	1,026	181	1,207
13	South Korea	2,500	100	2,600
1	Taiwan	0	21	21
3	Thailand	40	5	45
104		16,079	707	16,786
	Australasia			
20	Australia	3,100	100	3,200
4	New Zealand	20	2	22
24		3,120	102	3,222
454	Total world factoring volumes	179,198	10,826	190,024

[a]Estimated as at 31 December 1989.

Table 14.3. Accumulative turnover figures for all FCI members compared to world-wide factoring turnover (US$ million)

	1985	1986	1987	1988	1989	Increase 89/88 (%)
Invoice discount	1,623	2,706	4,957	6,328	9,690	53
Recourse factor	11,690	13,930	18,852	21,207	25,745	21
Non-recourse factor	12,555	16,722	24,607	28,310	36,884	30
Collections	796	1,456	2,736	3,237	2,792	−14
Total domestic factoring FCI	26,664	34,814	51,152	59,082	75,111	27
FCI export factor	531	669	903	1,030	1,281	24
FCI import factor	531	669	903	1,030	1,281	24
Non-FCI export	451	748	1,238	1,462	1,946	33
Non-FCI import	409	342	672	669	877	31
Total international factoring FCI	1,922	2,428	3,716	4,191	5,385	28
Grand total FCI	28,586	37,242	54,868	63,273	80,496	27
World domestic factoring	80,984	97,782	131,067	151,522	179,198	18
World international factoring	4,336	6,000	8,744	8,884	10,826	22
World total	85,320	103,782	139,811	160,406	190,024	18

gives all the flexibility but with enormous increase in risk. Factoring offers an intermediate path. It offers positive credit assessment, a hands-on approach to collections and assured payment.

Factoring is not a panacea but an appropriate package of services to meet real needs. It does not offer pre-shipment finance or protection for terms in excess of 180 days and so is most appropriate for consumer goods and services rather than capital goods.

To the UK- or US-based exporter, it is perhaps appropriate to remember the volume of import factoring to either country outstrips the volume of export factoring. Clearly, overseas-based exporters have awoken to the opportunities provided by international factoring to a much greater extent. They recognise that with international factoring they can better compete on terms acceptable to the buyer whilst maintaining the level of assurance and finance necessary to make their endeavours viable and rewarding.

For the company contemplating starting to export or increasing export effort, international factoring offers a unique combination of benefits singularly appropriate to assist market entry. The very fast-growing businesses that have benefited so much from domestic factoring during the 1980s can use this service to capitalise on the opportunities. Publicity about the European Single Market has emphasised the barriers being removed, but does one really believe that the specific issues being addressed through the legislation are indeed the real barriers?

Differences of language and culture will remain after the Single European Market whenever the hurdle of recognising the potential has been overcome. International factoring offers a high level of service support to enable the exporter to focus on the key areas that make that business unique and capable of competing effectively overseas. The exporter can address the market from a position of strength if cash flow is assured – as it is with international factoring.

15

Organisation and choosing a bank

KEITH JOHNSON
Export Finance Manager, Siemens Plessey Radar Ltd

The key to successful exporting is good company organisation. The purpose of this chapter is to give some indication of how to be organised and how to approach and handle the banks to optimise your cash flow.

Organisation

The structure of the organisation is heavily dependent on the size of the company and the ratio between exports and home customers. It is important from the outset to have one director dedicated to and responsible for the export finance activity. If possible, this director should be the Commercial Director or the director directly responsible for the day-to-day bidding and contracting activity. This director will require the overall view of the potential sale through to the contract. Certain points negotiated in a contract can have a profound effect on when payment is received and which method of payment is employed.

For instance, there is no point in securing payment through a confirmed irrevocable letter of credit if it is up to the customer to specify which ship or aircraft will be used to transport the goods. Without the customer's call forward instructions, the goods could wait a considerable time before the correct shipping documents are issued, by which time the rest of the documents are stale and would have all the inherent difficulties of delayed payment whilst sending the documents 'on collection' through the banking system to the customer.

Similarly, if customer acceptance certificates are required, a slow down, deliberate or not, can jeopardise your claim under the letter of credit. These subtleties only come out when reviewing the bid documentation and will continue to change right through to contract signature, and beyond!

Having decided which director is responsible, it is then absolutely vital that a manager is appointed to handle the day-to-day activity. This appointment for the sake of clarity is often referred to as the Export Finance

Manager. This manager must be able to track various activities to ensure that, whilst not being able to be considered as a complete expert on every subject, he or she is at least capable of understanding the problem and finding someone trustworthy who will give reliable information and support to solve it.

The areas that require considerable understanding and contacts are as follows.

The Export Credits Guarantee Department (ECGD)

The ECGD is the UK government insurance organisation set up specifically to support exporters. Following publication of the Kemp Report and a decision from ministers, the ECGD is to be split between credit insurance business and project financing business (see Chapter 3).

Information will regularly be required by the Export Finance Manager for latest developments, possible premium changes, level of cover available in specific markets and the possibility of change in others. With the privatisation of the Insurance Services Group and the reorganisation of the Project Group, it will be vital to understand *both* organisations, particularly the latest developments and indications of support as soon as possible.

Official trade agencies

Major trading nations have government departments dedicated to trade support, for example the Department of Trade and Industry in the United Kingdom and the Department of Commerce in the United States. Most have desk officers responsible for understanding the trading rules and regulations world-wide. Through their Projects and Export Policy Group, the DTI is available to assist the exporter with attempts at applying for support for financing, aid, etc.

It is important to understand the workings of the department and contact the appropriate desk officers in order to obtain an up-to-date view of trading with a particular territory, forthcoming trade missions and, particularly important, to obtain information regarding any relevant ministerial visits to territory. The most effective exporters learn to use their government's machinery to good effect. This varies according to local structure and procedure but one of the most open systems, although not necessarily the most effective, is in London.

The Foreign and Commonwealth Office

The FCO is a vital link in the export chain. All communication with overseas Embassies and High Commissions is conducted through the FCO and the various desk officers are able to give an up-to-date view of a territory and from a political point of view can advise on Ambassador/High Commissioner and Commercial Attaché postings.

If possible a visit to the local Embassy or diplomatic/commercial representative, particularly if one is seeking government support for a particular sale, and a pre-briefing with the FCO can be of considerable benefit.

The Defence Export Services Organisation

Again, desk officers are available to give advice and help for the sale of defence equipment and are able to advise on the latest support available and the various Defence Attaché appointments overseas and at home.

Overseas Development Administration

Whilst the ODA would normally only wish to involve itself on a project by project basis through the Project and Export Policy Division (PEP) at the DTI, one can receive information relating to the eligible territories for aid and the rules and method of application.

The private insurance market

The private insurance market is an ever-increasingly important source of cover. It is important to use the right broker for the kind of risk sought since political risk-broking is a niche market only successfully operated by a small number of brokers.

It may be appropriate to use different specialist brokers for areas such as general insurance, surety bonding, political risk, ECGD, marine insurance, etc., as you then have the best possible expertise and service. A good political risk broker, for instance, will always be prepared to innovate and, in particular, to choose the right underwriter in the private insurance market capable of leading a difficult risk and being able to use that lead to provide full cover.

Other activities requiring up-to-the-minute information are as follows:

1. Foreign exchange activity.
2. Countertrade/offset.
3. Country risk takers – short and medium term.
4. Financing methods.
5. Bonds and guarantees.

Whilst the majority of the above information comes from banks it should be remembered that there are many specialist agencies, consultancies and information organisations that give practical and accurate advice. Often a specialist trader might find a market niche and be able to exploit it exclusively for one company to the exclusion of its competitors, whilst, in other instances, personal contacts could well be the key to solving local difficulties.

In a significant number of instances the banks have experts, or can contact experts, or local representation, which can be a very useful source of information.

It is therefore important that trust and understanding is built up between the company and its bankers, the selection of which is dealt with later in this chapter.

It is absolutely vital that the Export Finance Manager is kept abreast of the bidding situation across the company in order that he has in mind a portfolio of activities so that when opportunities present themselves a ready course of action is at hand. Such a manager should be as much as practicably possible 'office-based'. The salesperson and, when applicable, the contract negotiators must use this individual as an 'information exchange' in order to facilitate effective home-based support whilst they are overseas and remote from any other source of assistance.

Whenever possible, the salesperson should be involved in meetings with the various government departments and banking institutions. Advice and a presentation of the in-territory picture from the salesperson's perspective can be invaluable and will often motivate a quicker and more positive response from the various institutions.

Regular bid review meetings should be held in order to update the Export Finance Manager on the passage and developments of the bid, as well to inform other members of the team as to the latest developments within the export finance community.

An important aspect to successful exporting is the 'team approach' which must be built upon professionalism, communication and mutual trust. During long and drawn out bids the motivation 'sag points' are the times when the astute competitor will take advantage, and the team approach goes a long way to counteracting this syndrome.

Large-value bids often take time to adjudicate and questions will be asked and responses required to be given by the company, sometimes without reference to the supporting financial institutions. It is therefore helpful to set up regular update meetings with the bank, brokers and government departments to ensure a continued interchange of information and ideas.

Once the contract is signed and effective it is important to keep the salesperson informed about its progress. Early warning of a problem will invariably lead to a more pragmatic and sensible discussion with the customer and the possibility of, for example, agreed rescheduling of delivery or payment before liquidated damages or other penalties begin to bite.

If the bid is lost, a Lost Bid meeting should be held and attended by all members of the bid team to ensure that the reasons for the loss are understood and used effectively in subsequent bids.

Choosing a bank

Regardless of the size of the company concerned the one rule that should always apply to an exporter is never bank with just one banker. Notwithstanding their proud boasts, no one bank is effectively able to offer you the complete support required to export to a varied selection of markets.

Whilst there are specialist banks and institutions that are able and prepared to advise and guide their clients through a complicated financing procedure, these institutions, by their very nature, are specialists in a very specific field.

In the more general exporting world it is important to ensure that the home banking situation is irrevocably linked to the exporting scene. There is little point offering the risk free, fee-earning job of paying the salaries and routine banking if the same bank is unable to support your exporting ambitions effectively. The banks should be presented with a portfolio or range of risks and earnings which can be assessed by the bank to ensure that from a relationship point of view the export risks are balanced with a continuity of earnings.

These days banks have many areas of activity, and balance can be achieved by using them in diverse fields such as a travel agency, car leasing, organising a pension fund through the bank's agency, information technology, cheque clearance, salary administration, bonds and guarantees, letters of credit administration, etc. These all add up to a good spread of fee-earning risk. This is why the choice of banks should be a joint decision by the company's export finance, sales, commercial and finance teams; each will have their own requirements of the banking industry.

The following is a list of some of the considerations when choosing a bank, deliberately not placed in order of importance as a bank's particular strength will depend upon, among other things, the type of company, product and target market place:

1. Prime banker:
   (a) locality of local branch/branches;
   (b) locality of international branch;
   (c) general efficiency;
   (d) real time banking;
   (e) consolidation of accounts.
2. Borrowing facilities:
   (a) flexibility;
   (b) availability.
3. Letters of credit administration:
   (a) locality of document checkers;
   (b) efficiency;
   (c) speed of response;
   (d) ability to help solve difficulties in documentation;
   (e) cost.

4. Bonding lines: flexibility, cost and availability.
5. Overseas representation.
6. Export finance services:
   (a) the people;
   (b) accessibility.
7. Risk-taking ability:
   (a) size;
   (b) nationality and alignment.
8. Syndication: position in market.
9. Administrative efficiency.
10. Understanding the workings of government departments.
11. Collation of overseas information: branch/correspondent network.
12. Marketing: bank mandates.

Let us take the points one by one. It is important to obtain a balanced view as to what is best for the particular business, and soundings can be taken with members of trade associations and Chambers of Commerce as to which bank is more capable than others in certain areas.

Prime banker

1. Locality of local branch/branches. It is important to have a local branch close at hand. The particular branch will be made responsible for the day-to-day administration of the accounts, and regular monthly meetings allow for no shocks, particularly on salary payment day, when perhaps a major customer has not paid.
2. Locality of international branch. If processing large numbers of overseas claims through perhaps letters of credit or payments against documents, i.e. collections, it saves time and money to have an international branch close at hand.
3. General efficiency. Do you feel the branch deals with queries speedily and efficiently? Does the management understand your type of business and appear enthusiastic about its future? Do you feel personally looked after, or is your company just another bank balance?
4. Real time banking. Is it vital to have an up-to-the-minute view of utilisable cash or will end of the day or end of the week balances be sufficient for the purpose?
5. Consolidation of accounts. If a group of companies is located in different parts of the country with different bank accounts, the consolidation of accounts can be a very efficient way of reducing overdraft costs.

Borrowing facilities

More often than not the overseas contract has a more volatile cash flow, with an advance payment and payment on delivery. The borrowing facilities, therefore, should remain flexible to reflect the nature of payments. A second lower-priced tier of charging can be negotiated if the payment of a particular contract is to come from a letter of credit. This is based on the fact that if payment terms are secure and the ability of the company to supply the goods is confident, then the bank should charge a lower rate of borrowing.

Letters of credit administration

1. Locality of document checkers and efficiency. The speed at which documents can be delivered to the checking department is all-important. There is no point using the local branch as a post-box if nothing administratively or from a cash flow point of view is gained. Often banks will charge an extra advisory fee for just handling the documents without liability to themselves.
2. Speed of response is vital. Often using the properly regulated local branch of an overseas bank as the advising bank and having it credit the proceeds directly into the company account will speed up cash flow considerably. 'Tenor' letters of credit will, in the right circumstances, be discounted at a cheaper rate by the local branch of the overseas bank. Local banks will also be prepared to accept this sort of risk, but capital adequacy rules might well affect the pricing.

   One has to be sure of the payment risk dimension within a letter of credit and if in any doubt one should seek recourse to credit insurance or confirmation which will relieve the concerns relating to transfer risk.
3. Ability to help solve difficulties in documentation. If difficulties do arise it is helpful for the bank to be able to put pressure on the opening bank. The pressure can more effectively be applied if the letter of credit is routed from the overseas opener to its local correspondent and that particular correspondent is the company's banker.

   It is in circumstances where documents are wrong or stale where a combined approach through both the banking system and the company's contractual and sales route can help speed up in-territory decision-making considerably.

Bonding lines

More and more overseas buyers are demanding guarantees or bonds as 'a good faith of the contractor to fulfil his obligations'. These bond requests have, over the years, become more sophisticated, to such an extent that in the United Kingdom the Bank of England has now ruled on the capital adequacy for such bonds and has generally become the arbiter of such requirements.

This, naturally, has put pressure on banks to earn a realistic return on the bonds and pricing has gone up. Some banks have tried to take advantage of this situation, which should be resisted. Banks are prepared to open up 'stand alone' bonding lines at competitive prices as most believe that it at least gives them a good picture of the kind of territories in which the company is doing business. It is also a good springboard to market other banking services directly linked to exports and, in other cases, unconnected to exports!

Often an 'on demand' type bond will be requested from the buyer. Exporters can now be in a situation where being non-compliant with the bond wording will rule one non-compliant in the bid or actual contract. Banks are prepared to issue these types of bonds on the strict understanding that tightly worded counter indemnities are signed and, where applicable, extra security taken.

It is sometimes the case that the bank is unable to issue a bond on behalf of a company with a weak balance sheet, but a government department's bond support scheme if available can alleviate this difficulty.

Additionally, in the United Kingdom the ECGD or the Lloyd's Private Market are prepared to insure on demand bonds against an unfair call. The banks might well wish it to be recognised within the company that the insurance is specific to their bond, again in the circumstances where, although a successful exporter, the company has a weakened balance sheet.

One typical drawback to official cover is that, unless the underlying contract is insurable by them, they are unwilling to insure the bonds. In the case of bid bonds, this can create difficulties and the Lloyd's Private Market has a stand-alone policy which allows you to insure your on demand bonds, whilst not having an insurable interest in the underlying contract.

Of course, the usual checks are carried out as to the company's ability to perform but, at least, this policy allows a company to bid and then negotiate a contract minimising the potential risks to such an extent that credit insurance is not required.

Overseas buyers will occasionally not accept a bond issued direct from the exporting country. They will sometimes require a local bank (sometimes of indigenous origin) to issue the bond. In these circumstances it is advantageous to use the exporter's bank with a representative branch in the country concerned. The advantages are twofold. First, one can obtain a very much more competitively priced bond as the pricing for indigenous banks to issue bonds is higher and not as easily negotiated as in the exporter's market. Second, the administration of the bond is more manageable. If reductions are required or bonds require cancellation and/or return, the exporter's bank's branch will be more disposed to help. This can be of particular advantage when exporting to a territory of ever-changing political dimensions.

Overseas representation

When putting together an involved financing package, or a bid requiring complicated letters of credit arrangements, or bidding in a local currency, it is helpful to have a local representative of your supporting bank in the territory. Apart from the obvious sense of support one receives, it is sometimes important for the buyer, particularly a government buyer, to see the local banking community being used. Costs can be held down and security is obviously tighter.

As previously described, the issuance of bonds through the local branch can also have great advantages even over those banks having 'strong correspondent relationships'.

Export finance services

When exporting on a regular basis, relationships are built up with bankers who are capable and trustworthy, and a particular organisation could have many weaknesses except for that one individual. If this is the case, it is important to view the selection with one eye on the possibility that the particular individual might leave, putting the exporter in a tricky situation.

On the other hand, using a large organisation, particularly for a small deal, can mean you may not be given the kind of attention you believe you deserve. This is why a balance has to be struck and this balance can only be judged by someone specifically made responsible for the day-to-day difficulties and frustrations of dealing with the banks and the banking system. Good and successful exporting comes from establishing a workable banking solution with trusted people.

Risk-taking ability

The Third World debt crisis has made risk-taking much more difficult, but this does not mean that difficult territories are off limits. For example, every bank in the City of London will be delighted to support an exporter for five years' financing with the benefit of a 100 per cent government guarantee as issued by the ECGD. The difficulty arises when one requests the financing of the front end advance payment at a realistic rate or the confirmation of a letter of credit.

The private insurance market produces another layer of risk sharers, and now that Lloyd's of London underwriters are able to issue political risk policies direct to banks the opportunity to use such covers to assist the finance of export contracts is greatly enhanced.

Syndication

Where, for instance, financing in a risk-shared market (the UK ECGD reduces the amount of credit support available from typically 85 to 70 per cent or less) or a large letter of credit requires confirmation, syndication of the risk may be called for. The syndication exercise should be carried out under the strict supervision of the exporter and not left to one bank to arrange its own package.

Whilst the exporter will need to select a lead bank carefully, he or she should also be closely involved in the selection of banks forming the syndicate. The advantages are twofold. First, business can be offered to the banks the exporter knows and wishes to do business with; the exporter will have an insight as to which of the banks are really dedicated and supportive. Second, the banks much prefer direct exposure to the exporter and this assists them in their marketing of other products to the exporter as and when the opportunity arises.

The first syndication exercise undertaken by an exporter can be extremely time-consuming but once one successful syndication exercise has been completed and the particular risk-taking venture has been successful, there exists for the exporter a built-in syndicate for future projects.

The banks are given a good exposure to the company and future work can then be spread across the various banks, keeping contacts up and confidence high. A further advantage is that the pricing of such a risk can be more closely controlled by the company and the level of risk taken by each bank monitored so that future business can be spread in similar ratios.

Administrative efficiency

Exporting, in particular, requires efficient administration and no more so than when using banking facilities.

It is important when selecting banks to visit the relevant departments. If the company is a particularly high user of letters of credit or documentary collections, it is vital to know whether the system of checking or the issuing of payment instructions is halted by the absence of one or two key individuals.

The use of computers should now be extensive, particularly on documentary collections. Automated reminders, sent in the language of the recipient, can save days in collection times. Direct crediting of bank accounts or extensive use of the international 'SWIFT' system can again enhance profits by the early receipt of cash through administrative efficiency. The level of charges raised by the banks for these clearing systems must, however, be monitored closely as they can be costly for smaller accounts.

Understanding the workings of government departments

Depending upon the type of export concerned, it is more often than not that a government department will be involved. It is useful to be able to use your bank as a sounding board and for extra help when dealing with a particular problem. If financing is required, the bank simply must have an understanding of the government departments. If aid is part of the package, unless your banker has a good idea of the workings of and a good relationship with of the relevant overseas development administration, delays and difficulties will occur.

If a case is particularly difficult, it is important for the bank to be able to write briefings in a way which is acceptable and usable by government agencies. In certain cases they can ensure that the Embassy or representation in territory is adequately briefed and, in the majority of cases, understand what is achievable within the government circles and what is not.

Collation of overseas information

It is important for an exporter to use the banks more widely in respect of their undoubtedly excellent contacts in territory. Overseas branches should be in touch with local politics and the economic situation, and the collation and disbursement of that information can be vital in winning overseas business. This, however, is a 'two way street'. The company must be focused in the territories it wishes to address and then brief the bank extensively in the products and the types of opportunities that it wishes to aim for.

In summary, the bank to choose is the one which has a good overseas network: correspondents or branches and takes on the task enthusiastically. Again, when visiting the specific territory, a visit to the local bank staff to reinforce the briefing can often mean a contract won that would have otherwise gone to the competition.

Marketing: bank mandates

It is important for a bank relationship to remain fresh and enthusiastic. More so than any other part of commerce, banking understands competitive bidding. Honesty goes a long way to keeping the relationship firm whilst giving the various banks an insight in the workings of the exporter.

If one requires a competitive bid from various bankers, it is vital that they all receive the same information at the same time. There is nothing worse than for a bank to call foul after a mandate has been awarded, as a bad reputation is quickly gained. The banks need to be kept informed as to developments in various product lines and territories, and they will also need to keep in regular contact offering advice and guidance. The banks that neglect their customers, or those that overprice a particular product, deserve to lose out to the more astute competitor.

These are the areas requiring close consideration when choosing a bank. Personal preferences as to working practices will also enter into the formula, which in the end should give a balanced and clear view of the bank's capabilities.

Conclusion

Having decided the method of approach and the type of response being sought, it only remains for the exporter to decide precisely which banks and how many are required for the foreseeable future.

There should be a nucleus of institutions which can be turned to for advice and guidance. This advice and guidance will be freely available to the exporter, particularly if he or she knows there is a strong chance of competing for and winning mandates for projects as they occur. In my experience no more than eight to ten banks are required to support and cover the majority of day-to-day exporting activity throughout the world.

Each bank will have its strengths and weaknesses and to obtain the best advantage it is possible, in certain circumstances, to combine, say, two banks – one with international strength and one with a strong export finance team in the exporting country – to produce the most effective financial package. It is important for the relationship with these banks to be reviewed regularly, say annually, to ensure that there still remains a good understanding on both sides, of products, aspirations and capabilities.

There are certain headings under which the review should be conducted. These include the following:

1. Speed of response to general enquiries and queries.
2. Quality of response – were the questions really answered effectively? Do they sound committed to supporting you, or was the response half-hearted? Did you have to wait until Mr X returned from holiday before obtaining a satisfactory response?
3. HQ/Head Office approval process. Do the decisions made and offers of support become amended or withdrawn once approval from the higher authority is sought?
4. Are you happy with the solutions and the response given; is the costing thereof satisfactory and helpful?
5. Do you detect a real willingness to help and a desire to invest time and energy in the relationship?
6. Have they made the effort to understand your business and the personalities therein?
7. Have you received information from them of overseas prospects which you subsequently followed up?

Most insurers are keen to understand their customers' difficulties and frustrations and have a genuine desire to discuss and put forward possible solutions across a wide range of territories. It is vital to gain a good relationship, particularly at this time of considerable change as the early warning of potential difficulties in a particular territory can save considerable marketing resource.

The same applies to the relevant departments of state. The desk officers are keen to understand the type of products – targeted territories, successes and failures – in order to build up a good picture of the capability of the company concerned. Another potential source of information and support can be accessed through the various trade associations. Most associations have specialist committees dedicated to lobbying for improvements in legislation, understanding the existing ground rules and finding the most equitable solution for its members. The Export Finance Manager can obtain useful feedback and support from these committees.

Finally, it is important to be professional in your approach to the exporting fraternity and in being prepared to be guided by those professionals better qualified than yourself.

Appendix 1

List of useful addresses

Banks

ANZ Grindlays
Minerva House
Montague Close
London SE1 9DH

Bank of America
1 Alie Street
London E1 8DE

Banque Bruxelles and Lambert
1 Appold Street
Broadgate
London EC2A 2BY

Banque Paribas
68 Lombard Street
London EC3V 9EH

Barclays Bank PLC
Fleetway House
25 Farringdon Street
London EC4A 4LT

BHF Bank
61 Queen Street
London EC4R 1AE

Chartered West LB
33–36 Gracechurch Street
London EC3V 0AX

Chase Manhattan
Woolgate House
Coleman Street
London EC2P 2HD

Gulf International Bank
2–6 Cannon Street
London EC4M 6XP

Lloyds Bank Plc
Hay's Lane House
1 Hay's Lane
London SE1 2HA

Midland Bank PLC
International Division
110 Cannon Street
London EC4N 6AA

National Westminster Bank
25 Old Broad Street
London EC2N 1HQ

Royal Bank of Scotland
Trade Finance Department
5–10 Great Tower Street
London EC3P 3HX

Brokers

Berry, Palmer and Lyle
24/26 Minories
London EC3N 1BY

The Credit Insurance Association
13 Grosvenor Place
London SW1X 7HH

Consultants, specialists and countertraders

Davies Mehra Ltd
86 Hatton Garden
London EC1N 8QQ

Morgan Grenfell
23 Great Winchester Street
London EC2P 2AX

Philip Brothers
Victoria Plaza
111 Buckingham Palace Road
London SW1W 0S1

Tristar Marketing
Lloyds House
Headley Road
Grayshott
Hinhead
Surrey GU26 6LG

International insurance agencies

Australia

Export Finance and Insurance
Corporation (EFIC)
Export House
9th & 10th Floors
22 Pitt Street
Sydney, NSW
Mailing address
PO Box R 65
Royal Exchange
NSW 2000
Telephone: (61 2) 231 2655
Telex: EFIC AA 21224
Fax: (61 2) 251 3851

Trade Indemnity Australia Ltd
PO Box 577
(367 Collins St. Post Office)
Melbourne
Victoria 3000
Mailing address
4th Floor
31 Queen Street
Melbourne
Telephone: (61 3) 612 1777
Telex: 31341 TICMEL
Fax: (61 3) 614 7245

Belgium

Compagnie Belge d'Assurance-Crédit SA (COBAC)
15 Rue Montoyer
B-1040 Bruxelles
Mailing address
15 Rue Montoyer
Bruxelles
Telephone: (32 2) 506 21 11
Telex: 22337 CREDAS
Fax: (32 2) 506 24 99

Office National du Ducroire (OND)
Square de Meeus 40
B-1040 Bruxelles
Telephone: (32 2) 509 4211
Telex: 21147 OND B
Fax: (32 2) 513 50 59

Canada

Export Development Corporation (EDC)
151 O'Connor Street
Ottawa
Ontario
Mailing address
Box 655
Ottawa, Ontario K1P 5T9
Telephone: (1 613) 598 2500
Telex: EXCREDCORP OTT 0534136
Fax: (1 613) 237 2690 (Xerox 495)

Denmark

Copenhagen Credit Insurance Co. Ltd
PO Box 2168
DK-1016 Kobenhavn K
Mailing address
Vestergade 5
Kobenhavn
Telephone: (4533) 91 19 11
Telex: 27127 GARANT
Fax: (4533) 91 19 17

Dansk Kautionsforsikrings-Aktieselskab
PO Box 2168
DK-1016 Kobenhavn K
Mailing address
GI.Torv 14
Kobenhavn
Telephone: (4533) 91 19 00
Telex: 16414 DANKAU
Fax: (4533) 12 47 30

Finland

Pohjola Insurance Co. Ltd
Lapinmaentie 1
SF-00300 Helsinki 30
Telephone: (3580) 5591
Telex: 124556 PLA
Fax: (3580) 559 3259

France

Caisse Franco-Néerlandaise de Cautionnments
82 Rue Saint-Lazare
F-75009 Paris
Mailing address
82 Rue Saint-Lazare
Paris 9e
Telephone: (33 1) 42 85 46 20 and 48 74 56 40
Telex: 283069 FRANCAU
Fax: (33 1) 42 81 29 19

Compagnie Française d'Assurance pour le Commerce Extérieur (COFACE)
12 Cours Michelet
La Défense 10
92800 Puteaux
Mailing address
Cédex 51
F-92065 Paris La Défense
Telephone: (33 1) 49 02 20 00
Telex: ASEXP F 614884
Fax: (33 1) 49 02 20 49

Société Française d'Assurance Crédit (SFAC)
1 Rue Euler
75008 Paris
Mailing address
19x Cedex 10
F-75460 Paris
Telephone: (33 1) 4070 50 50
Telex: SFAFC F 630850

Germany

Allgemeine Kreditversicherung Aktiengesellschaft
Postfach 1209
D-6500 Mainz 1
Mailing address
Ernst-Ludwig-Strasse 2
Mainz
Telephone: (49 6131) 1431
Telex: 4187676 AKV
Fax: (49 6131) 22 47 11

Gerling-Konzem Speziale Kreditversicherungs-AG
Postfach 10 08 08
D-500 Köln 1
Mailing address
Hohenzollernring 62
Köln
Telephone: (49 221) 1441
Telex: 881132 GK
Fax: (49 221) 144 3970

Hermes Kreditversicherungs-Aktiengesellschaft (Hermes)
Friedensalle 254
Hamburg-Bahrenfeld
Mailing address
Postfach 50 07 40
D-2000 Hamburg 50
Telephone: (49 40) 88 70
Telex: HK D 212631-90
Fax: (49 40) 887 7744

Treuarbeit Aktiengesellschaft
New-York-Ring 13
Hamburg
Mailing address
Postfach 60 27 20
D-2000 Hamburg 60
Telephone: (49 40) 6378 0
Telex: TAHH D 2174118
Fax: (49 40) 6378 103
(Tenofax 31 Group 3)

Italy

Concordato Cauzione Credito 1973
Casella Postale 6317
1-00100 Roma-Prati
Mailing address
c/o UIR
Via del Giuochi Istmici 40
00194 Roma
Telephone: (39 6) 323 931
Telex: 610348, 611529 and 614386 UIR
Fax: (39 6) 327 3398 and 327 3198

Sezione Speciale per l'Assicurazione del Credito all'Esportazione (SACE)
Piazza Poli 37
00100 Roma
Mailing address
CP 253 Roma Centro
Telephone: (39 6) 67361
Telex: 613160 SACE I
Fax: (39 6) 6736225
(ITT 3533 Group 2 & 3)

Società Italiana Assicurazione Crediti SpA (SIAC)
Casella Postale 253
Roma-Montesacro
Mailing address
Via Raffaello Matarazzo 19
00139 Roma
Telephone: (39 6) 81691
Telex: 620616 SIACREDI
Fax: (39 6) 8820424

Società Italiana Assicurazione Crediti SpA (SIAC)
Via Raffaello Matarazzo 19
00139 Roma
Mailing address
Casella Postale 2446 AD
I-00108 Roma
Telephone: (39 6) 81691
Telex: 620616 SIACRE 1
Fax: (39 6) 8820413
8820424
8820512
8820548

Japan

Export-Import Insurance Division
International Trade Administration Bureau
Ministry of International Trade and Industry (EIDMITI)
1-3-1 Kasumigaseki
Chiyoda-ku
Tokyo 100
Telephone: (81 3) 501 1665
Telex: EIDMITI J 22916
28576

Netherlands

Nederlandsche Credietverzekering Maatschappij NV (NCM)
Keizersgracht 271-285
1016 ED Amsterdam
Mailing address
Postbus 473
NL 1000 AL Amsterdam
Telephone: (31 20) 5539111
Telex: 11496 NCM NL
Fax: (31 20) 5532811

Norway

Garanti-Instituttet for Eksportkredit (GIEK)
Dronning Mauds gt 15 IV
0250 Oslo 2
Mailing address
Postboks 1763 Vika
0122 Oslo I
Telephone: (47 2) 20 51 40
Telex: 121153 GIEK

Portugal

Companhia de Seguro de Créditos EP (COSEC)
Avenida da Republica 58
1094 Lisbon Codex
Telephone: (351 1) 760131/766055
Telex: 12885 COSEC P
Fax: (351 1) 734 614

Spain

Compania Espanola de Seguros de Crédito a la Exportacion SA (CESCE)
C/Velaquez 74
E-28001 Madrid
Mailing address
C/Velaquez 74
Madrid
Telephone: (34 1) 577 60 66 and
577 60 77
Telex: 23577 CESCE
Fax: (34 1) 576 51 40

Compania Espanola de Seguros y Reaseguros de Crédito y Caucion SA (CESCC)
Apartado Correos 524
E-28003 Madrid
Mailing address
Raimundo Fernandez-Villaverde 61
28003 Madrid
Telephone: (34 1) 253 6800 and
253 8704
Telex: 43163 SCYC
Fax: (34 1) 535 33 73

Mapíre Caucion y Credito Compania Internacional de Seguros y Reasuguros
Paseo de Recoletos 23
E-28004 Madrid
Mailing address
Paseo de Recoletos 25
Madrid
Telephone: (34 1) 581 13 40
Telex: 43225 SCIC and 42544 MAPFR
Fax: (34 1) 581 13 34

Sweden

Exportkreditnämnden
Norrlandsgatan 15
Stockholm
Mailing address
Box 7334
S-103 90 Stockholm
Telephone: (46 8) 23 58 30
Telex: 17657 EKN S
Fax: (46 8) 11 81 49 (Nefax 3500) (CCITT Group 1 & 2)

Svenska Kreditförsäkringsaktiebolaget
Box 7435
S-103 91 Stockholm
Mailing address
Norrmalmstorg 4
Stockholm
Telephone: (46 8) 22 10 60
Telex: 10124 SVENSKA
Fax: (46 8) 20 16 82

Switzerland

Geschäftsstelle für die Exportrisikogarantie (GERG)
Kirchenweg 8
CH-8032 Zürich
Mailing address
Postfach
CH-8032 Zürich
Telephone: (41 1) 47 66 54
Telex: 816519 VSM CH

The Federal Insurance Company Ltd
(Eidgenössische Versicherungs-Aktiengesellschaft)
Flössergasse 3
CH-8039 Zürich
Mailing address
Postfach
CH-8039 Zürich
Telephone: (41 1) 208 44 22
Telex: 815353 FED CH
Fax: (41 1) 201 28 04 Panafax UF-400 (CCITT Group 2A/3)

United Kingdom

American International Underwriters (UK) Ltd
120 Fenchurch Street
London EC3M 5BP
Telephone: (44 71) 626 7866
Telex: 883381
Fax: (44 71) 929 1453

Credit and Guarantee Insurance Company PLC
Surety House
Lyons Crescent
Tonbridge
Kent TN9 1EN
Telephone: (44 732) 770311
Telex: 957607
Fax: (44 732) 770361

Export Credits Guarantee Department (ECGD)
PO Box 272
Export House
50 Ludgate Hill
London EC4M 7AY
Telephone: (44 71) 382 7000
Telex: ECGDHQ G 883601
Fax: (44 71) 382 7649 (Canon 401H Group 3)

PanFinancial Insurance Co. Ltd
International House
World Trade Centre
1 St Katharine's Way
London E1 9UN
Telephone: (44 71) 481 3122
Telex: 921021 PanFin G
Fax: (44 71) 488 3070

Sun Alliance Insurance Group
Sun Alliance House
50 Fenchurch Street
London EC3M 3JY
Telephone: (44 71) 588 2345
Telex: 888310-G
Fax: (44 71) 826 1135

Trade Indemnity PLC
12–34 Great Eastern Street
London EC2A 3AX
Mailing address
Trade Indemnity House
12–34 Great Eastern Street
London
Telephone: (44 71) 739 4311
Telex: 21227 TICLON
Fax: (44 71) 729 7682 and 739 4397

United States

American Credit Indemnity Company
300 St Paul Place
Baltimore
MD 21202
Telephone: (1 301) 554 0864
554 0714
Telex: 87907 ACI
Fax: (1 301) 554 0882/3

American International Underwriters
Division of American International Group
70 Pine Street
New York NY 10270
Telephone: (1 212) 770 7000
Telex: 125227
Fax: (1 212) 770 7821

Export-Import Bank of the United States (Exim Bank)
811 Vermont Avenue NW
Washington DC 20571
Telephone: (1 202) 566 2117
Telex: EXIBANK 89461
(In-Safe No.): EXIBANK 6710607
Fax: (1 202) 566 7524

Foreign Credit Insurance Association (FCIA)
40 Rector Street
New York NY 10006
Telephone: (1 212) 306 5000
Telex: FCIA NY 428807
428818
Fax: (1 212) 513 4704
(Rapicom 330)

Overseas Private Investment Corporation (OPIC)
1615 M Street NW
Washington DC 20527
Telephone: (1 202) 457 7200
Telex: OPIC UI 440227
Fax: (1 202) 457 7158)

Appendix 2

Information sources on international aid

There is a multitude of information sources on international aid business. The choice of which to use on either an occasional or a continuous basis must be determined by the individual exporter's products or services, and the regional markets and types of funding best suited to their promotion.

A selection of the more important and most frequently accessed information services is given below.

UK government

World Aid Section, Department of Trade and Industry (DTI)

The World Aid Section (WAS) is a unit within the DTI's Project and Export Policy Division (PEP). WAS maintains an information base on over 5,000 current projects in the lending programmes of all the major multinational development agencies. Available data include operational summaries of the various agencies, economic reports, sector analyses, procurement notices, contract award information, project appraisal reports and agency directories. WAS acts as a reference point in that information can be noted within the unit but, whilst some information sheets and reports are distributed free, documentation for the most part cannot be purchased, loaned or copied.

Overseas Development Administration

The Overseas Development Administration (ODA) is the UK government department responsible for the United Kingdom's aid programme for developing countries. Specific information about country programmes can be obtained from geographical desk officers at the ODA headquarters at Eland House, Stag Place, London SW1E 5DH (Tel. 071 272 3000) or through direct contact with the five overseas British development divisions in Barbados (Caribbean), Nairobi (Eastern Africa), Malawi (Southern Africa), Fiji (Pacific) and Bangkok (South East Asia).

The ODA publishes a number of useful basic guides to international aid business. These include the following:

1. *Britain's Aid Programme: Opportunities for exporters.*
2. *Overseas Development and Aid: A guide to sources of information and material.*
3. *ABC of Aid and Development: Some terms and institutions.*

Export Intelligence Service

The Export Intelligence Service (EIS) brings together intelligence received by WAS and gathered from UK Embassies and High Commissions overseas and many other sources. Marketing and delivery of EIS information has now been sub-contracted by the UK government to Export Opportunities Ltd (Export House, 87A Wembley Hill Road, Wembley, Middlesex HA9 8BU).

Development Business

Development Business is published every fortnight by the United Nations Division for Economic and Social Information. It provides information and articles on projects funded by all the major agencies. This information includes the following:

1. The monthly operational summaries of the World Bank (WB), the Inter American Development Bank (IDB) and the quarterly operational summary of the African Development Bank (AfDB).
2. Advance project information, prequalification notices and contract awards.

Development Business is a fundamental priority source of information for all UK exporters who wish to do business on WB, IDB or AfDB projects.

Scan-a-bid

Scan-a-bid provides on-line data link access to all information given in *Development Business* up to two and a half weeks before publication. Updates are fed to subscribers three times a week. It is available only to subscribers to *Development Business.*

On a similar basis, access can also be obtained to information on European Commission projects with *Tenders Electronic Daily* (TED).

World Bank: International Business Opportunities Service

The International Business Opportunities Service (IBOS) is specifically restricted to WB-funded programmes. It provides the following information:

1. General procurement notices on the general nature of goods, works and services which will call for international competitive bidding on individual projects.
2. Specific procurement notices which provide detailed information on components of projects already covered by general procurement notices. This includes details of items to be procured, the executing agency and how bid documents can be obtained.
3. Notices of contract award on all contracts of above $5 million or more on civil works and $500,000 or more on consultancy services.
4. Monthly operational summaries.
5. Technical data sheets.

A restricted IBOS service providing the monthly operational summaries only can be arranged.

Agency publications

A wide range of publications on aid business are available from both the multilateral and bilateral agencies. One of the most wide-ranging, detailed and definitive publications on international aid is the Organisation for Economic Cooperation and Development (OECD) annual report on *Development Cooperation.* If the WB group is taken as an example of the multilateral agencies, the following documents are available ((F) is used to indicate free publications and (P) those which may be purchased):

World Bank Staff Directory (P)
World Bank Annual Report (F)
World Bank Development Report (P)
World Bank Development Atlas (P)
Guide to International Business Opportunities (F)
Guidelines: Procurement under IBRD loans and IDA credits (F)
Guidelines for the Use of Consultants by World Bank Borrowers and by the World Bank as Executing Agency (F)
Procurement and Cofinancing: Methods and procedures (F)
IFC Basic Information (F)
How to Invest in Development with IFC (F)
The Project Cycle (F)
Questions and Answers: Bidding for contracts in World Bank financed projects (F)
Bank Financed Projects (F)

Procurement of Goods: Sample bidding documents (P)
Procurement of Works: Sample bidding documents (P)
Sample Form of Contract for Consultants' Services (P)

The above are a sample only of the more generally requested documents. They represent the tip of an iceberg when compared with the thousands of specialised sectoral and country reports and papers which are currently listed. Internal operational reports, such as staff appraisal reports, are confidential and cannot be obtained from the agencies. They can, however, be viewed in the WAS at the UK DTI.

A similar range of documents can be obtained from the other major multilateral agencies such as the Asian Development Bank, the Inter American Bank and the African Development Bank. In the case of the European Commission funded projects in the developing countries, the free monthly *Courier* magazine is essential reading. It is, however, difficult to get on the mailing list of the *Courier*.

Bilateral agencies

As indicated in Chapter 4 on the DAC member countries bilateral aid programmes, many bilateral agencies may offer significant opportunities to exporters because of the untied status of much of their aid funding. If a particular bilateral agency programme shows a business potential for an exporter, it is, therefore, worthwhile to investigate information material available from that agency. Whereas with the multilateral agencies a great deal of information can be obtained by subscription to such services and publications as *Development Business*, Scan-a-Bid, IBOS and EIS, in the case of the bilateral agencies such information can only really satisfactorily be obtained by visiting the agency headquarters in the country concerned. If this is done, much useful material can be gathered, though necessarily some of this is not in English.

General background

Various publications can, according to the regional bias of the exporter, offer useful background information and, occasionally, specific project leads. Two of these are *Africa Economic Digest* (AED) and the *Middle East Economic Digest* (MEED).

Glossary

This glossary is intended to provide a brief explanation of the terms most frequently used in the world of international trade finance and in the text of the *Handbook*. It is not designed to be encyclopaedic and it should be noted both that important terms are explained in their context in the chapters, and that several of the more complex chapters (e.g. Chapter 12) have their own specialised glossaries.

Acceptance credit A bill of exchange drawn by an exporter on any member of the Accepting Houses Committee for subsequent sale at a discount. The proceeds are credited to the exporter, and when the bill matures, the exporter's account is debited. A device for achieving the best rates in the money market.

Advising bank The bank that sends on the necessary documents required in a letter of credit for collection and payment by the issuing bank of an overseas buyer.

Agent A local representative in the export market, typically trading in the appropriate market sector and of good financial and local standing.

Bill of exchange An unconditional order in writing, addressed by one person to another, signed by the person giving it, requiring the person to whom it is addressed to pay on demand or at a fixed or determinable future time a sum certain in money, to or to the order of, a specified person, or to bearer. An exporter prepares a bill which is drawn on an overseas buyer for the sum agreed as settlement.

Bill of lading A transport document in common use and vital for arranging payment through the banking system which acts as evidence that there is a contract between buyer or seller and the shipper. It is also a receipt for goods shipped. Most importantly it is a document of title – the person named on the bill of lading has the right to possess the goods.

Bonds A written instrument issued to a buyer by a bank or insurance company stating that an exporter will comply with the terms of the contract, or the buyer will receive compensation. There are several different kinds, including bid and performance bonds.

Buyer credit A medium-term financial technique providing medium-term credit (five years and more) where the exporter's lending bank lends directly to the buyer or his/her bank thus enabling the buyer to make payments direct to the exporter.

Cash against documents A system whereby the exporter uses the banking system. Only the shipping documents are sent and the exporter instructs the bank to release them only after payment by the buyer.

Collecting bank When a bill of exchange is passed to the exporter's local bank, that bank forwards it to its overseas branch or correspondent in the buyer's country for presentation to the buyer for payment under the stated terms. This is the collecting bank.

Commercial invoice A claim for payment for the goods under the terms of the commercial contract with the buyer. It should include a detailed description of the goods, together with unit prices, total weight and terms of payment plus shipping marks and packing details.

Comprehensive insurance A form of insurance which covers all, or an identified part of, an exporter's sales against non-receipt of funds due from the overseas buyer.

Comprehensive Short-Term Guarantee An ECGD policy which provides cover for exports up to 180 days or in some circumstances up to two years. Cover is 90 per cent for commercial loss and 95 per cent for political cause of loss.

Confirmed irrevocable letter of credit The most secure form of documentary credit, where a bank in the exporter's country assumes the payment obligation of the issuing bank by adding its confirmation.

Confirming house A financial intermediary which provides payment directly to the exporter and undertakes collection of due funds from the buyer. Frequently used by overseas buyers as a buying agent, or by exporters as a source of non-recourse funds.

Credit insurance Insurance policies sold to exporters to provide different degrees of protection from loss arising from the failure of funds to arrive as contracted. They are provided largely by state bodies, but private insurers are also active. Policies cover periods of credit from a few weeks out to several years.

Documentary credits Documents, correctly completed, are presented to a bank by the expiry date of the credit. If correct, payment is made. This provides the exporter with immediate payment against satisfactory documents.

Export finance house A financial intermediary, usually a bank subsidiary, which provides cash to the exporter on shipment and credit to the buyer. The EFH will administer the contract, insurance, etc, and is well placed to handle larger or more complex transactions.

Factoring The purchase of export or domestic receivables at a discount to provide cash up front. Typically, 80 per cent of face value is available and the factor becomes responsible for sales ledger administration.

Foreign exchange borrowing The practice of raising funds in a currency other than your own either to offer the buyer a purchase in his or her own currency, achieve a more favourable interest rate or speculate for potential exchange profit.

Forward exchange contract A device for protecting against loss in foreign exchange transactions by selling anticipated forex receipts in advance for a fixed sum in domestic currency.

Incoterms A system of trading terms agreed by the international trading community to standardise trading and contract terms and thus make it easier to ascertain what obligations, expenses, risks, etc. in the export contract affect the invoice. The principal terms in common use include:

'Ex-works' – the price for the goods at the factory gate. All additional costs are for the buyer's account.

'Free carrier' (FRC) – the price including all costs to a loading point into a container.

'Free on board' (FOB) – all costs of the goods loaded on board a ship whose destination is stated in the contract.

'Freight carriage paid to' (DCP) – cost of goods, packing and transport by container, excluding insurance, to a named destination.

'Cost, insurance and freight' (CIF) – the cost of all goods loaded aboard the ship plus cost of freight and insurance to an agreed delivery point.

'Cost and freight' (C&F) – as for CIF but insurance costs are for buyer's account.

'Freight carriage and insurance paid to' (CIP) – the cost of goods, packing, insurance and cost of transport by container to a named destination.

'Delivered duty paid' (DDP) – this price is for all costs of delivery including duty paid up to the buyer's address.

Leasing A technique whereby the exporter sells the goods to a leasing company either in his own market or the buyer's. This provides immediate cash to the exporter and permits payments by the overseas customer over a predetermined period. There may also be tax benefits.

Open account The goods and relevant documents are sent direct to the buyer without security against a simple undertaking to pay.

Option A form of forward exchange contract which permits flexibility in the date for ultimate payment of the contract. There are many complex varieties in use.

Performance bond A guarantee to an overseas buyer that an exporter will fulfil the terms of the contract.

Premium The amount paid by the insured to the insurer for covering specified risks.

Pre-shipment risk Any cause of loss arising after contract signature but before shipment.

Promissory note An alternative to a bill of exchange. A simple document issued by a buyer who promises to pay an exporter a specific sum of money within a specified time.

Recourse The situation whereby any interested party to a contract may seek redress and repayment from the exporter for any shortfall in funds paid by the buyer. Interested parties would include credit insurers and financing banks.

Risk The possibility of any event giving rise to loss, but most commonly in international trade:

Commercial – non-payment as a result of default or bankruptcy of the buyer.

Political – non-payment as a result of any political event such as revolution, debt moratorium or suspension of overseas payments.

Sight draft A bill of exchange payable at sight, that is to say on demand.

Short-term Any credit period up to two years.

Spot rate The rate a bank is prepared to pay for foreign currency at any moment of time.

Supplier credit A financing structure in which the exporter receives deferred payments from the buyer and receives funds by selling the relevant documents to a bank. Such arrangements frequently involve credit insurance.

SWIFT The Society for Worldwide Interbank Financial Telecommunications, a computer based system to achieve same-day transfers between participating banks.

Tender bond Also known as a bid bond, issued by a prospective exporter to an overseas buyer to cover the position where the exporter fails to fulfil the contract conditions.

TIR carnet Transport documents for goods carried by road into countries not controlled by the CT (Community Transfer) system, and designed to simplify border formalities.

Index